GRIEF, GRACE
AND GRATITUDE
Transforming through your grief journey

Also by this author:

Heartbreak, Healing and Happiness: Flourishing after a heartbreak

GRIEF,
GRACE AND GRATITUDE

Transforming through your grief journey

Grief, Grace and Gratitude
Author – Lara Casanova

© Lara Casanova 2018

www.lifeinthepink.com.au
lara@lifeinthepink.com.au

This book is sold with the understanding that the author is not offering specific personal advice to the reader. For professional advice, seek the services of a suitable qualified practitioner. The author disclaims any responsibility for liability, loss or risk, personal or otherwise, that happens as a consequence of the use and application of any of the contents of this book.

All rights reserved. This book may not be reproduced in whole or part, stored, posted on the internet, or transmitted in any form or by any means, electronic, mechanical, photocopying, recording, or other, without permission from the author of this book.

Editing and design by: www.authorsupportservices.com
Photography by: www.realmomentsphotography.com.au

ISBN: 978-0-9876158-7-9

 A catalogue record for this book is available from the National Library of Australia

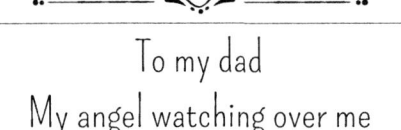

To my dad
My angel watching over me
I love you to the moon and back!

"Sometimes, only one person is missing and the whole world seems depopulated."

—Alphonse de Lamartine

PREFACE

"Grief only exists where love lived first."

—Franchesca Cox

The journey through grief is a story about a great love, and this book will guide you through that story, both yours and mine!

It is a story about how grief irrefutably rises from where a great and profound love first lived. It is a story that will help guide you through the peaks, troughs and stages of Grief, Grace and Gratitude on your grief journey.

You will trek through the 'Forest of Grief', nurture the 'Field of Grace' and finally reap a 'Garden of Gratitude'. This is where the torment of loss subsides and the sadness stays yet the grief journey propels you towards a rich and fulfilling life. Each destination will have you transforming though your grief journey.

A story about the loss of your Loved One and your soul-shattering grief and journey through transformation is not always a happy one. As your guide, I share my grief story and the loss surrounding it when my world fell apart in having to say goodbye to my dad. I have not written this book specifically for the loss of a father, however. It is for *you* and your loss, be it of a family member, a friend or anyone who touched your heart so deeply that you are left feeling bereft and broken.

Grief, Grace and Gratitude

The person who we lost may be different, but we still travel on the same long, hard journey through grief. This same story can ultimately lead to a rich, full and happy life despite the struggles along the way; a life full of love, tears, sadness and sorrow. You can experience a kaleidoscope of colourful emotions and a loving relationship, like mine, which continues to span a lifetime with infinite love, trust and respect shared between my father and me.

It is a story predominately about love. Not just any love, but deep unwavering, unconditional, warm and all-encompassing love. The best kind!

It is a story about taking one day at a time and gently piecing your delicate life back together when you would prefer to stay in numb denial to avoid your painful reality. It is a story about how to transition that love from a physical presence in your life to one that exists and lives on eternally in the heart. Allowing yourself to work through the tumultuous and gruelling journey will ultimately allow your sadness to surface in the form of beauty in honour and remembrance of your Loved One.

Travelling this journey, you often move one step forward only to be flung three steps backwards, flailing and confused like an upside-down turtle. You will be guided, however, to allow this all to happen naturally. Giving permission for these feelings to arise will, in time, allow grief to shine its wisdom deep into the cells of your being. This in turn will bring healing and lessons galore to enable the empty space in your heart to slowly fill up with love once again.

Ultimately, when you can look deeply, see clearly, listen intently and feel fully, underneath the intense grief can be found colossal gratitude for the entire experience. You see, without grief there is no love. This grief experience attests to the enormous love you have for the one you lost.

I am incredibly lucky to have had my relationship with my dad. I am exceedingly grateful for the time he spent, physically, in my

Preface

life. I now accept and integrate into my life his role as a spiritual guide, knowing he resides eternally in my heart. Every ounce of grief and every tear I shed are worth every morsel of love we mutually hold.

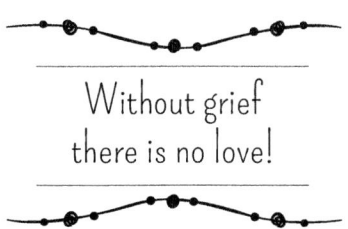

Without grief there is no love!

Many parts of my life have changed; I have changed. I would wish my dad back beside me in a heartbeat, if only for an afternoon tea, one more hug, one more smile, one more energetic connection, one more 'I love you', one more conversation. Knowing this is not possible, I look instead to the gifts grief has given me in my dad's honour. Grief has gifted me the opportunity to truly appreciate love more intensely and to understand and integrate my sadness and vulnerability more internally. The love lives quietly beyond the sadness and grief, for me to tap into and unleash. When you allow yourself to be in the feelings and to progress through the natural grief journey, you will find an abundance of love, despite any reluctance to do so.

I have researched, studied, gained qualifications and personally lived through the experience of loss and grief more than once. Alongside this I have written this book, hugging a deep passion and life purpose to express all of this to you. I hope you can see parts of yourself in my journey, even in a small way, to help you navigate your own personal grief journey.

When you are in a state of loss and confusion, teetering on the cliff edge and hoping not to fall, reading about others who have lived through a similar experience may give you energy and snippets of hope. Such hope can help you believe that you too can walk through your grief journey and arrive at your destination still whole, having pieced your life back together despite how grim it may look in this moment.

These stories and hope become the butterfly wings that carry you through while your own strength is shattered and needing to be rebuilt to begin the road to healing. I ask you to allow me to be your butterfly wings, giving you strength and hope while your own wings heal through the words, stories and exercises in this book.

It is in the deep of the night
My feelings wake me with a fright.
The intensity so strong
I feel it must be wrong.
Not used to my new reality
You are gone, and I'm left with fragility.
I hug myself looking for hope
That appears nowhere in my scope.
I hold our memories deep in my heart
And cherish our love now we are apart.
I crave my sleep and to dream
Only there I feel you like a sunbeam.
So I close my eyes again for the night
Wishing so much I could hug you tight.

Contents

Preface vii
Introduction 1
Your Pink Treasure Box Of Tools 7
My story, My dad 17

PART 1
Forest of Grief: The Grief

Greeting grief 25
Five stages of grief 41
In the pink process 51
Path of goodbye 89
Final contemplation 125

PART 2
Field of Grace: The Sabbatical

Greeting grace 131
Self-love 139
Pink tribute 155
Yearnings 179
Signs 205
Final contemplation 217

PART 3
GARDEN OF GRATITUDE: The Rebirth

Greeting gratitude 225
Final contemplation 283

Epilogue 291
Life in the pink 295
Thank you 301
Extra resources 305

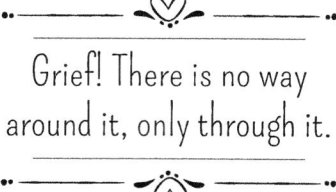

Grief! There is no way
around it, only through it.

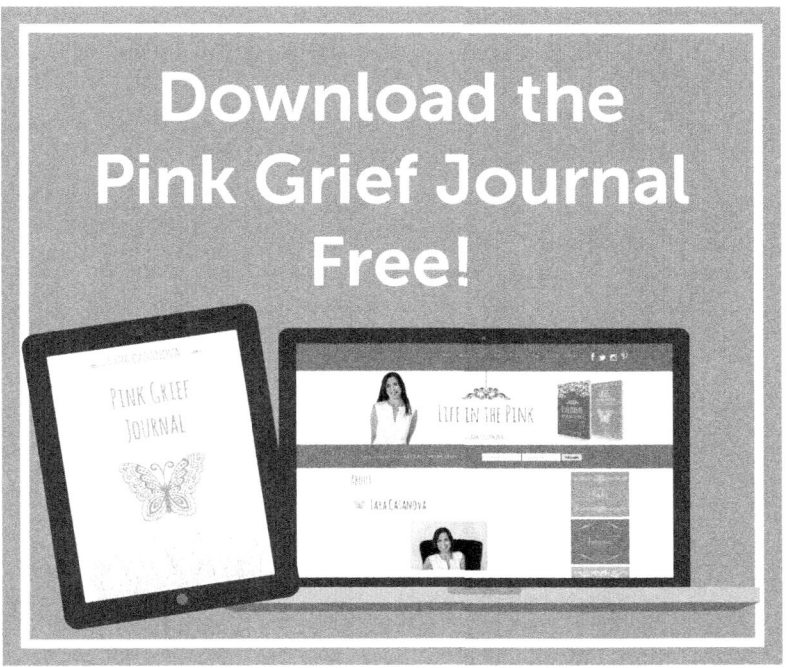

Download the Pink Grief Journal Free!

Read this first.

As a big PINK thank you for investing in my book I would like to gift you the accompanying

PINK GRIEF JOURNAL 100% FREE!

The PINK GRIEF JOURNAL is a sacred space you can connect and record your feelings, emotions, thoughts, hopes, fears, dreams and the special memories of your loved one as you transform through your grief journey.

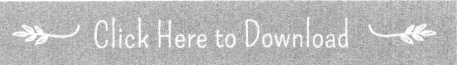

Or go to this link:
https://mailchi.mp/067ba2d5c8e2/pink-grief-journal

Introduction

"Grief is not a disorder, a disease or a sign of weakness. It is an emotional, physical and spiritual necessity, the price you pay for love. The only cure for grief is to grieve."

—Earl Grollman

Grief! There is no way around it, only through it. The goal of this book is simple: to walk you through your grief journey and support you along the way as you find a place where you can remember your Loved One without the pain, living with their love within you. Your relationship with them has not gone; it is merely transforming, as are you.

As you progress through *Grief, Grace and Gratitude* you will explore ideas, philosophies, thoughts, beliefs, emotions and concepts to unlock the gifts, healing and lessons found in your grief. You will survey the hidden parts of yourself that are in pain and stuck in emotional suffering. You will create space in your mind, life and world to process this searing pain, ultimately leading to the small reprises of normalcy and the peace you seek.

What you will learn and discover in *Grief, Grace and Gratitude*:

- ♥ how to understand grief, its journey and the randomness of grief

Grief, Grace and Gratitude

- 💕 how to nurture your sorrow, sadness and vulnerability, and accept that feeling introverted and raw is normal
- 💕 how to appreciate that your vulnerability is part of your beauty and your humanness
- 💕 how to honour yourself and your deceased Loved One more and more, with smiles and joy amidst the tears and sadness
- 💕 how to come out of denial into the hurtful, truthful reality and learn to deal with your scary emotions
- 💕 how to find the gifts that grief leaves behind
- 💕 how to understand and facilitate your healing, accepting grief is a long road but one you will gently integrate into your life
- 💕 how to feel your Loved One walking by your side, being mindful of the signs they are sending you
- 💕 how to implement new skills and tools to survive and thrive
- 💕 how to navigate the five stages of grief
- 💕 how to ask the pertinent questions that will bring you home to your true self
- 💕 how to transform through your grief journey.

Grief is about love. Love is about grief. To allow yourself to love allows grief in. To avoid grief, you would need to avoid love. To be able to love fully and wholly, you need to accept and walk with your grief as it arises.

Each time you are faced with grief and walk the path it asks of you, the more you are able to access your ability to give and receive love. Life is about allowing all this to happen naturally and finding the courage to come out of denial into reality. You face the grief and walk through the middle of it, allowing everything that is thrown at you to be just as it is, knowing you will survive.

Introduction

Grief, Grace and Gratitude takes you on the journey to three special places where you can assimilate your grief. You will trek through the 'Forest of Grief', nurture your 'Field of Grace' and finally reap a 'Garden of Gratitude'. Each destination leaves you transforming through your grief journey and bestows coping abilities and tips, lessons, healing and gifts for you to cherish as you walk towards a future without your Loved One.

The Forest of Grief in Part 1 walks you through the intense, penetrating grief, teaching you how to endure the emotional pain and process the stages of grief, navigating day-to-day survival, sharing your story and saying goodbye to your Loved One. The Field of Grace in Part 2 allows you to take a truth sabbatical while providing a space to nurture yourself. It teaches you about self-love and how to reorganise your wants and needs, noticing the changes while becoming aware of your yearnings and learnings, and compiling a special tribute. The Garden of Gratitude in Part 3 is where a rebirth of self takes place, allowing you to blossom and show gratitude for your Loved One as you reassimilate into your world and live your life's purpose.

One aspect of grief is that everyone has a different journey. However, there will be many similarities and many parts that you can relate to, helping to guide you on your grief path. Notice the parts of the book that pull your heartstrings and make your ears prick up; the parts you can relate to and the parts where you instantly say, "That's me!" To see yourself in others' stories helps you to feel less alone, and insight can be found, providing comfort and healing.

Woven throughout the book are three stories: (1) My personal grief journey when I lost my dad, (2) A fictional story of one character's loss, which may mirror parts of your grief story, and (3) Your own story, which you share safely in the exercises while creating a tribute to your Loved One.

Throughout this book there will be references to the colour pink for two reasons. Firstly, I live and love by the phrase 'In the Pink' that was coined in the sixteenth century to mean being strong, running well and in perfect condition. The colour pink has deep spiritual meaning and in the ancient tradition of yoga is symbolic of the heart chakra. It represents tenderness, caring, compassion and unconditional love, and is associated with giving and receiving while producing a calming effect on our emotional energies. All of which are needed in our healing journey.

Secondly, I love the colour pink! It makes me happy and fills me with joy. It is me! My business 'Life in the Pink', my books, my yoga, my website and my social media platform are all housed around finding ways to live a Life in the Pink.

Colours however are very individual and present different meanings and energies to different people, so in alignment with your truth and to gain the most from your healing journey you may wish to interchange the colour pink with the colour that most resonates with your own soul.

Tools found in your 'Pink Treasure Box of Tools' are placed throughout the book to support your journey. You will be offered time to express your feelings in a special handpicked journal – your 'Pink Grief Journal'. Exercises found in the 'Pink Grief Corner' offer different approaches to help you understand yourself and gently steer you through your grief. 'Pink Ponderings' at the end of each chapter give you an opportunity to contemplate your grief, and 'Pink Butterfly Tips' flutter throughout to help you on the grief journey.

Investing in your grief journey by reading, learning, applying your Pink Treasure Box of Tools, and allowing time for your inner landscape to unveil is your greatest gift to yourself at this heart-wrenching time. Grief is exhausting, stressful and demanding. You learn to adjust your life little by little or all at once according to grief's natural flow. It is not convenient nor pleasant, but necessary.

Grief can take all your control, strength, rationale, sanity and energy, leaving you empty. Feeling your grief and letting it do its

Introduction

work will slowly allow the empty void to fill up again, and in time a love so great can grow in its place.

You may emerge feeling like a different and even improved version of yourself. That's okay. If you truly give permission for grief to walk its path through your inner landscape, it will unearth all the love buried deep within and shine it throughout your body, filling your heart to its brim.

I believe that when your Loved One passes they infuse a piece of their love into your heart, their final legacy to you. Their most precious gift ever! This love fills your being and you carry it around forever, making your life brighter and more loving. It gives you the ability to honour them eternally and allows this love to be showered over the loved ones left behind. Even though you no longer have your Loved One by your side, you can remain connected by the heartstrings, never to be separated.

The only way forward is through the grief, not around it. Be loving to yourself and make a choice to walk through the grief. Yes, there is pain, but there is also beauty as a result that appears as an abundance of 'love, roses and butterflies'.

I refer to 'love, roses and butterflies' regularly as symbols of the beauty of my loss, which enable me to sense daily my dad's loving spirit still surrounding me. To you the objects may be different and may represent something dissimilar to my experience. But it's in seeking the symbolism of the beauty that we bask in the memories and the love of our Loved One, gone but never forgotten.

> Make a choice to walk through the grief.

To run away, avoid or suppress the pain may appear to be better options in the short term. However, these choices will create more intense emotional or physical suffering later and keep hidden the love beneath. Grief waits for you!

Give yourself the gift of time and step back from your busy life to allow this grief journey to be taken. It may be inconvenient and come at the wrong time. But you are given one life and it can be so full of love. Even though you only feel the grief right now, by walking its path in a healthy way, you will find more love than you could ever imagine. This love is the tribute to both you and your Loved One at the end of the grief rainbow.

I invite you to walk through the rainbow of grief emotions with me. Integrate the learnings, ponder at 'Question Time', complete the exercises, share your story and express yourself through journalling. Gift yourself the time and energy to invest in your health and happiness, and through this grief journey you will find a place where healing, acceptance and peace exist. This is my deepest desire for you.

May you live a deeply rich and full life abundant in love, truth and purpose in honour of your Loved One. I am sure that is what they would dearly desire for you.

Come with me and let my butterfly wings guide and lift you through the grief journey and over the grief rainbow to where the world is filled with your version of love, roses and butterflies.

Your Pink Treasure Box Of Tools

> "Grief can be the garden of compassion. If you keep your heart open through everything, your pain can become your greatest ally in your life's search for love and wisdom."
>
> —Rumi

On your grief journey, a treasure box of tools to help you manoeuvre the peaks and troughs is imperative. Embedding these tools deep within will aid in your dark and lonely moments when you feel immobilised by emotional pain and clueless about how to continue.

Following is an overview of these tools and a guide on how to utilise them effectively in the exercises to help you walk forwards. Entrenching these into your current reality will see you walk with more ease through the rough and rugged path of grief.

While I am here to support you through this book, I ask that you are honest and raw with yourself as to whether you need immediate professional help. We all need that sometimes. I did too. This book is not a replacement for medical advice. So please seek professional help immediately if you:

- cannot cope with basic day-to-day tasks
- are involving yourself in something illegal

- ♥ feel triggered by any content in this book
- ♥ feel your grief is not normal grief (There are several types of grief which are not covered in this book)
- ♥ feel like you may harm yourself or someone else.

The Pink Grief Journal

Starting a grief journal is one of the most helpful tools I used throughout my grief journey. As humans, we can easily resist what is difficult and push our feelings down. You may distract yourself with a myriad of activities to run away from yourself.

You may try talking to a therapist or friends, which is an excellent outlet, but they cannot be available all the time. You need a means to sit quietly with yourself and be honest about what you are feeling. Expressing yourself in your Pink Grief Journal will help to shift the energy of grief.

Journalling gives you permission to be open, raw and honest, which helps you get to know yourself during this scary time. It helps you to explore who you are, what you fear and what is hurting you. The more you know about yourself the easier the grief journey becomes.

A grief journal allows you to write about your deceased Loved One and the memories, both sad, happy and in between. If you fear forgetting your memories, penning them to paper will prevent this. This was a huge fear of mine. Trust me; you will not forget the important parts if you put your thoughts down in black and white. This will prevent excess worry too.

Sometimes some of the smaller memories may become hazy, but you never forget how a person made you feel, which is why grief often remains long term albeit in a different form. This is why you need to assimilate grief into your life somehow.

Your Pink Treasure Box Of Tools

You can let the pen dance across the journal pages to express and then release what is inside. Don't think, just write; your feelings will arise and appear on the pages. This is a good form of release. It is amazing what is presented to you on a blank page if you allow yourself to open up and see what resides deep within you.

Write, express, release.

Spend some time searching for a notebook that will be right for you; one that you are drawn to as a place of comfort to house your innermost vulnerable feelings, hurts, grief and fears. Store this diary in a part of your house where it is quiet and soothing. Create an environment that feels safe and comfortable. There will be times you feel so overwhelmingly vulnerable, so being able to retreat to your safe space is important to help you process your grief.

When you spend time in your quiet place, which I call your Pink Grief Corner, you can reach for your Pink Grief Journal and let the words and feelings flow. Admit the truth to yourself and describe how you are feeling.

Here you can write all the memories about your Loved One. You can write down all the words you still want to say to them. Talk to them through the written word. Here you can list your hopes and dreams, your biggest challenges and greatest fears.

This is the open space where you can talk about what led you to take this grief journey, why you are here and what you hope to achieve. Scribble away and purge all the information into your Pink Grief Journal. Don't think about what you are writing; just let the words appear in front of you. Be honest, be open and be willing to unleash self-discovery.

In my first book *Heartbreak, Healing and Happiness*, I introduced your journal as the Little Pink Book of Love. Now you have your Pink Grief Journal. You can feel comforted that these journals hold all your thoughts, feelings and emotions. They are fabulous friends because they are non-judgemental.

They allow you to purge everything onto the pages and help clear and release any negative energy you are carrying around. They can save you from many emotionally destructive evenings. Once you deliver all your feelings onto paper, you can breathe and relax, knowing you have processed more of what has been troubling you.

Your journal will allow you just to be you. When you feel lost, scared and confused, start writing. Before long, your true self will return. Tap into your innermost feelings and thoughts. Tap into your authentic self, buried beneath the raw loss and emotional suffering. For a moment, at least, this gives you a reprieve from the grief, until the next wave.

When you feel you have lost yourself entirely, it is such an enlightening feeling to see snippets reappearing. Journalling is one tool that may help restore optimism in your soul and enable you to carry on to another day, knowing everything in time will be okay.

When you miss your Loved One you can write a letter to them. You can talk about what you would say if they were here. You can write about funny things you did together and how much you love them. It helps you to feel more connected to them.

Yes, it's different, but you can convey what you feel. You can send it out to the world and hope that, somehow, they feel this love and energy coming their way and will respond by sending you loving signs in acknowledgement. I will elaborate further on these signs in Part 2.

You may like to take your Pink Grief Journal outside to a garden or a park, a local church or just your favourite room. Find a place where you feel connected to yourself and your Loved One that brings you peace and helps you find the answers, awareness or epiphanies.

Your Pink Treasure Box Of Tools

Honour and nurture your thoughts and rainbow of emotions written in your Pink Grief Journal. These tender, vulnerable and raw expressions of yourself deserve to be treated with utmost respect, loved beyond measure and kept safe and private.

Pink Grief Corner

The Pink Grief Corner is a place for solitude and healing where you can sit quietly with your Pink Grief Journal and be honest with your feelings through questions, letters or other creative activities. In the Pink Grief Corner, you can safely explore your inner world in relation to your grief. You can give permission for your heart to open and share its innermost thoughts and feelings.

Creating space and time will often highlight feelings and emotions that you otherwise did not know existed. Walking slowly yet directly into the epicentre of the pain through exercises and questions is difficult and can be emotionally draining. They will take you deep into yourself and highlight the most painful and tender parts and expose all the sadness. It will hurt, and you will feel like it will never get better. But, on the flip side, be reassured that the exercises will:

- provide knowledge of your grief journey
- support you when you feel alone
- assist you in getting to know yourself in this new situation
- reconnect you to the love buried below
- facilitate healing, which transforms you and walks you slowly to your new life.

Each time you visit the Pink Grief Corner, please slow down and stop. Take a few deep breaths into your belly, feeling it expand; as you exhale allow your belly to fall.

Grief, Grace and Gratitude

This type of deep belly breathing relaxes the body and mind, brings clarity, releases tensions and toxins, and helps to relieve physical and emotional pain. It activates the parasympathetic nervous system to allow the body to rest and digest rather than fight and flight. The ancient practice of yoga focuses on breath work for this reason.

You may like to:

- create an altar to your Loved One
- pick flowers and place them in a favourite vase
- light a candle
- burn essential oils
- play some soft music.

Practise any ritual you can think of that makes this space special, protected and only yours for personal self-discovery.

When you are in the Pink Grief Corner, answer the questions or try the activities as openly and honestly as you can. In your Pink Grief Journal, write or journal any thoughts, feelings, reactions, epiphanies and healings. Adding any creative touches such as colours, drawings or poems to your journal may also help.

Each time you rest at the Pink Grief Corner to reflect and complete exercises, I leave a gentle reminder that the Pink Grief Corner is a place to honour and love yourself. Be mindful that you may be taken out of your comfort zone, so remain self-loving during this challenging time.

Your reminder is: *Stop and take three deep breaths. Honour yourself with patience, gentleness and a compassionate spirit. Come from a place of love: your love and the love of your Loved One. The whole point is* love!

Record your feelings in your Pink Grief Journal. If you don't feel ready to complete the exercise or answer the questions, simply reading the information is a good start. You can always return to them later when you are ready. Go at your own pace and do what you can when you are ready.

Being aware of where you are at is important for you to discover the way forward and to understand more clearly what is happening below the surface.

Pink Ponderings

During your grief journey, it's imperative to stay connected to your feelings. Not only do you need to understand how grief works, you also need to feel it, moving your energy towards healing. The Pink Ponderings statement below will be placed at the end of each chapter to remind you to tap into your feelings and be open and honest with yourself. You will be asked to identify your particular feeling of grief at that time, where it wants to lead you and what it can teach you. Express your emotions and feelings in your Pink Grief Journal.

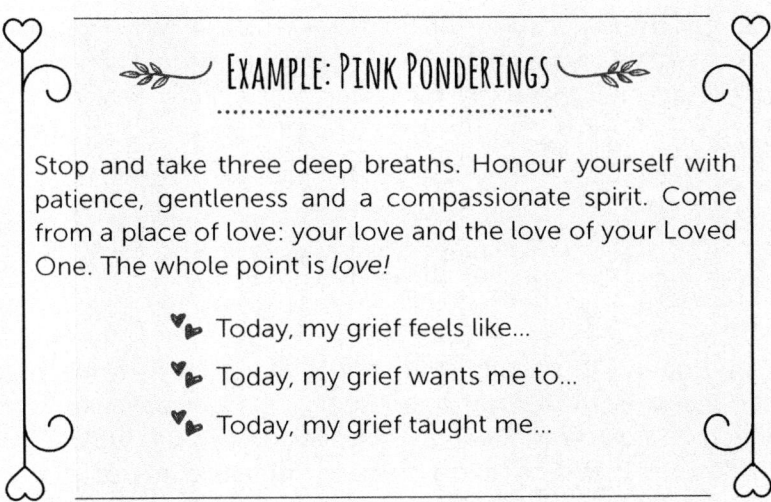

Example: Pink Ponderings

Stop and take three deep breaths. Honour yourself with patience, gentleness and a compassionate spirit. Come from a place of love: your love and the love of your Loved One. The whole point is *love!*

- Today, my grief feels like…
- Today, my grief wants me to…
- Today, my grief taught me…

Your grief will have you feeling a certain way, and it is good to acknowledge what you are feeling. If you listen hard your grief will want you to do certain things such as rest, eat better, go to bed earlier, exercise or not exercise, sit and contemplate, be with friends, be alone and a host of other things. Listen to what it wants and allow yourself to follow its lead. Grief will teach you things about yourself, your emotions, your body, your heart, your Loved One, others and just life in general. Pay attention and notice what you are learning and allow it to swish around inside.

Keep your notes in your Pink Grief Journal. Sometimes doing some of the work and then continuing with your day allows healing to assimilate inside you. Then when you least expect it, an epiphany arrives.

If you feel the rainbow of emotions rising inside, that is good. If you are struggling to deal with them, take some more deep breaths and give yourself time to just sit quietly with the feelings. If the emotions scare you, call someone close you can talk to. Sometimes talking out loud with a friend can help enormously, or, alternatively, journal in your Pink Grief Journal.

Use this space to become more connected with your true self and allow all the hurt inside to arise and present itself for your healing. Give yourself permission to be vulnerable. Don't fear your tender, fragile side; it is the loving and beautiful side that we overshadow for fear of feeling weak. To show your tender side is a huge show of strength, honouring yourself and your Loved One.

Pink Butterfly Tips

Pink Butterfly Tips flutter throughout the book as a means to summarise some of the important points and revelations we touch on as you walk through the grief journey. They are provided as dot points and provide a means of further contemplation on

YOUR PINK TREASURE BOX OF TOOLS

your journey. They can be utilised as another effective tool as you come to terms with your loss and new reality.

Now, as we begin the journey through *Grief, Grace and Gratitude* together, here is my story of my dad, my grief, my love, roses and butterflies, and me!

My Story, My Dad

"How lucky I am to have something that
makes saying goodbye so hard."

—A.A. Milne (The Complete Tales of Winnie-the-Pooh)

My beautiful dad. My rock. I thought he would be here forever!

I had never visualised or contemplated a life where my dad was not there. At least not until the dreaded phone call eighteen months prior to his passing.

As a child his strong family values always guided me. I felt like a princess who was safe and sound. I was blessed with a wonderful childhood, basking in all the family activities and adventures that kept us close and created a deep bond. Most importantly, we talked, we laughed, we loved.

He was a strong role model in my life, portraying goodness, love and values that I continue to live my life by. He let me be me, always. He radiated warmth and love. He taught me a great deal at every stage of my life. He continues to teach me, even now. He may not have been perfect, but he was a perfect father, impeccably picked just for me.

I am not sure that Dad realised the impact he had on me and how special he was, but that was also a part of what made him so special. He stood solid as a person. He was consistent, modest, genuine and a good, decent gentleman. He was always there for his friends, his family and me.

Wandering around Italy with family, digesting his heritage and meeting his relatives was the start of his illness. He tried to keep up with us all, yet we could tell things were becoming more difficult. What followed on our return was the dreaded phone call, the dreaded diagnosis and the dreaded word 'inoperable' that continues to echo through my mind. The term 'terminal illness' suddenly had a brand new and awfully personal meaning.

The shock waves that ran through our family were catastrophic. The day I heard those words my life started to unhinge and fragment. One day I woke up normal yet retired to bed that night shattered. The anticipatory grief entered my life like a bullet to my heart, eighteen months before he even passed away.

Those months were a gift in a bittersweet way if I choose to look at the positives, which I try to most of the time. My dad had a chance to come to terms with what was happening and prepare himself for his next journey to the unknown. It gave my family and I the same opportunity.

We focused on what was most important in life and lived in the beautiful, heartfelt moments. We learnt to better voice our feelings, vulnerabilities and emotions out loud. We talked. We soaked up all his history. We shared in his laughter and love. We cried together over lost time and memories to come. We made new memories to carry us for a lifetime – the lifetime after he was gone.

We laughed amidst the tears and cried amongst the laughter. We all knew what was coming yet lived in the moment, the truth and the love. I wanted every last ounce of him and his loving energy around me, warming me for all the time to come where he would no longer be there. I wanted to hang on to every moment, every word, every smell, every mannerism, all his energy and every memory, ensuring they got all soaked up inside.

My Story, My Dad

In the days leading up to his last breath, Dad became more fragile and less responsive. His pain was under control, fortunately, and he managed to say an abbreviated and partly silent version of 'I love you' one last time, the day before he passed away. They were the last words my father spoke to me. His final conscious goodbye.

The day he died my heart broke into tiny little pieces.

My dad was eighty and I was forty-eight. He had battled his illness for months and his passing was no surprise. Yet I had happily remained in denial for as long as I could. I am the eldest of four girls, known to be sensible, professional, mature and stable, yet I still felt like a child. That was up until the day I lost my dad. Then I suddenly felt like I had to be a grown-up when all I needed was to be a child with my dad comforting me.

My father, my nurturer, my protector, my friend – one of my most favourite people in the world who loved me dearly – was no longer here. He had been preparing to leave for some time.

I thought the anticipatory grief leading up to his death was dreadful, but knowing I was coping fooled me into believing it would be the same after his death. How incredibly naive I was. It was so much worse once he passed – soul-destroying. I'd had no appreciation of what grief would throw at me, how it would unfold or how or if I would cope. My worst nightmare had materialised.

What resulted was the onset of crushing grief, heartbreak, loss, mourning, remembrance and confusion. Numbness, misery and disbelief overwhelmed me. I felt detached. I was utterly lost.

My emotionally mature and stable backdrop converted to one of sadness and vulnerability in a split second. I suffered constant physical pain in the belly. My heart was an open wound, red raw and unbearably sensitive.

I felt privileged to have had my dad for forty-eight years yet ripped off. I considered myself too young to be losing him. I wanted forever. I wanted the invincible, the unfathomable, the indestructible, the miracle, the phenomenon. But, alas, life is no fairy tale. Even though I felt like my dad's princess, my fairy tale did not have my forever ending. Although, in my eyes, I had the fairy tale while he was alive.

Yes, there are scars and life will never be the same. But sometimes the scars are made from beauty carved perfectly from a beautiful pure love, reminding us of our loved ones and special times that are etched into and live on in our hearts. However, it took time to understand and appreciate the truth of this.

I now know that the end of his physical life was a new beginning, a start to a new relationship between Dad and I and a new relationship with my new self. A me that is more grown up. A me that now believes I can cope with anything and everything. A me that found the love buried below.

> People and times live on in our heart.

He left me so many gifts in his departure and he brought me so many in his life. I was, and am, so blessed and honoured to be his daughter.

However long Dad was here would never have been long enough. I will always wish for one more conversation, one more hug, one more day and one more 'I love you'. I couldn't have felt more loved. I hope he felt the same. I hope he left with a heart full of love. I hope he took a piece from my heart for his journey.

He stays in my heart. The piece of love he left with me has helped me get though. I nurture it and hold it tight. I have survived, just. I still cry, I still sob as grief overwhelms me. Then it pauses, and I appreciate the hiatus to gather my energy till the next wave hits. Then the love gets me through again.

I feel him beside me, loving me in a very different way. I am adapting to my new life, incorporating grief into it and living every day with Dad in my heart, always remembered, honoured and most of all loved. So very loved!

My Dad, My Beautiful Dad.

The first day your eyes stared down on me
Was the day my life began to see.

Our life together was especially fun
You always were my number one.

The years passed by so very quick
Enjoyed immensely by this sensitive chick.

Taking your last breath
Learning I must live with death.

My life defined by
The grief inside.

My tears stream like a river
Washing my soul as I quiver.

My fears jump out to haunt
Realising I lost my confidant.

My anger sends signals of pain
Leaving my heart forever stained.

I ponder the loving memories
Wearing them like accessories.

Grief, Grace and Gratitude

I yearn for your smile
Feeling it was always worthwhile.

I think about you a lot
Pretending you're still here, not.

I laugh at the funny things
Holding on tight to everything.

I hope and pray that you are resting
Feeling at peace at your new place of nesting.

From this place I can no longer see you
But in my heart you feel true.

Because no matter how far away you reside
You are always right by my side.

My guiding star, my heavenly angel
I envisage you wearing your halo.

Loving you from afar is full of pain
Journeying through my grief domain.

I wait and pine for that hug
Till we meet again my heart strings will tug.

My dad, my beautiful dad
I loved you before I met you
I love you now that you're gone.

Your darling daughter, Lara

PART 1

FOREST OF GRIEF

The Grief

GREETING GRIEF

> "When you are sorrowful look again in your heart,
> and you shall see that in truth you are weeping
> for that which has been your delight."
>
> —Kahlil Gibran

Yesterday, life was normal and today you find yourself standing at the entrance of a giant, thick, dense forest – the Forest of Grief. You feel numb, foggy and in shock. Everything is surreal, cementing the feelings of bewilderment deep inside your core. You wonder if you are having an out-of-body or even an out-of-life experience.

All you can see in front of you are tall trees stretching to the sky and a mass of lifeless trunks and branches strewn on the ground amongst the thick shrubbery. It's eerie, dark, cold and clammy. There is no greenery, no flowers, no sunlight and seemingly no possible path to get through. 'Why am I here?'

You quickly turn around, ready to run to the clearing behind you. You hope your feet will miraculously take you as far away from this place as possible, preferably back home to where everything is warm, safe, sound and normal. Or is it?

Normal is where your Loved One is alive and well. Family dinners are the same as always with your Loved One seated at the head of the table, laughing and loving, full of vitality and energy that fills the room and your hearts.

Normal is where phone calls together are never-ending, games are played and meals are shared. Life continues like it has always been. Your rock-solid role model and special person is where they are meant to be, at home drinking warm cups of tea.

Sadly, your feet are stuck in the mud, threatening not to move. Going back is not a choice. Suddenly a realisation bursts you out of your numbness for a second: nothing is the same. Home is not the same. Your special person has passed away. You need to repeat it over and over to believe it.

You don't want to go back to a life where they no longer exist. But you don't want to accept that they are not here by your side any longer either.

Going forwards through the trees into the scary, thick growth is surely not possible. You have no idea how to navigate this landscape. You have no warm clothes, trekking shoes or food for the journey. Where will you sleep?

So you stand still. And you stand still. And you stand still a bit longer.

Then finally, with your feet sinking further into the muddy earth, you contemplate your weird state of confusion and realise you must make a choice before you get swallowed up.

Pick one. Forwards or backwards!

Backwards promises denial and safety yet a long-term state of unawareness with no authenticity or sense of reality. Pressure-filled, stressful days of repressed emotions will eat away at you, and your heart will slowly cut off from love.

Going forwards offers promises of growth and love, fond memories, and a rich, full life and heart. To reach that space, however, you must

GREETING GRIEF

first manoeuvre through the challenging dark terrain that lies ahead known as the 'grief journey'.

'I don't think so. I am not going into that forest ... I will not ... I want to go home ... I'm confused ... I don't know what I want.' It must be forwards. It is the only choice. But how will you know you have made the right choice?

Finally, you conclude that surrendering to the unconscionable terrain of the grief journey is the only way. But it's scary, it's daunting, it's unfamiliar, and it's cold and uncomfortable.

Inside, a silent voice guides you to take the path that promises the ultimate outcome of genuine, deep love. Regardless of the tough journey it will escort you to a peaceful state.

Three steps in past the first towering pine tree a path emerges underfoot. It is uneven, wet and muddy, full of stones and ditches. But it beckons you to follow. All you can hear is the hissing of the wind and a rustling in the bushes.

Looking up you glimpse an old wooden sign with an arrow pointing directly into the middle of the forest. On the sign is carved the word 'Love'.

Love

Seeking love and healing, you walk straight into the depths of the Forest of Grief, allowing grief to lead the way. You hope for the best with the little hope you have left.

The daylight suddenly fades, and you are shrouded by trees. Visibility is poor and fear rises. Already you want to give up when suddenly a beautiful white butterfly glides past, taking you out of your sorrow momentarily.

A torch appears at your feet. You pick it up, wrap your scarf tightly around you and on you go!

RAW GRIEF

"It is both a blessing and a curse to feel everything so very deeply."

—David Jones

Wrapped tightly in your favourite scarf, you trudge along the path through the wet clumps of leaves in the direction of another arrowed signpost with 'Love' written on it. You feel alone and scared and have no idea where to go next. The path abruptly turns a corner and a stone slab sits to the left. This is what is carved on it:

The Forest of Grief greets you

Your purpose here is to trek through this intense, all-consuming grief journey slowly and gently. You will learn to relinquish control as you realise you have none. You will learn to surrender willingly with a commitment to honour your grief. You will meet the gut-wrenching grief face to face, endure emotional pain and suffering, deal with high levels of stress, make difficult choices, face adversities, fill a big empty void, navigate day-to-day survival, share your story and say goodbye to your Loved One.

Follow the signposts and the butterflies.

The Forest of Grief for you is a mass of confusion, disorientation, vulnerability, sadness, anger, anxiety, raw gaping wounds and fear. Literally the whole rainbow of grief emotions reside inside. The forest

GREETING GRIEF

is also full of lessons, healing and gifts that you will discover later in the journey.

Pause for a moment and contemplate if you can relate to this journey so far, or aspects of it. This is the journey of so many of us who have gone through grief.

Some days you may scarcely cope, functioning like a robot on autopilot, numbed by your grief and the world that continues to operate while you are falling apart. It seems no one understands that nothing is the same. You don't speak the language and don't know how to exist in this reality. You have lost the most special person, and the upheaval in your life has sent everything into an eerie land of gloomy emptiness.

You may feel you can't connect to anyone and everyone else appears strange yet normal. You however may no longer feel normal, only a new kind of weird. Outwardly the world goes on as normal; inwardly you have no idea where you are or who you are. Your whole world appears to have changed in the blink of an eye or in the moment of a last breath – a disconcerting and peculiar existence.

When I was in the Forest of Grief, I needed time to integrate what had happened and space to process my thoughts and emotions. While life kept plodding along for some, mine stood at a standstill with me hanging on to the edge of the precipice for dear life. Limbo land! I didn't know where I was or who I was anymore in relation to my new altered world. So I fell into an emotional and physical hibernation, bunkering down in the forest and wondering why I did not feel like being around others. My introverted side knocked loudly within, keeping me disconnected from others at a time when I would have benefited from a little more support.

Grief, Grace and Gratitude

I learnt to accept that my normal mildly extroverted personality desired time out, so my more introverted, vulnerable side could come to the surface and seek what it needed to heal. I had to be quieter to allow this side to come out of hiding. She is a lot less demanding and comes from a deep, quiet and beautiful wisdom. I had to stop and listen; she had valuable things to teach me.

I learned that layers of emotional suffering can pile up on top of each other, as what you avoid and deny only gets heavier and sits unprocessed within you. This can create emotional toxins that run through your heart, body and soul. The more suppression tactics you use, the more energy is needed to keep everything beneath the surface. This ultimately can destroy aspects of your life and the lives of those around you.

I understand that life and even daily survival can become too much to cope with. Normal life becomes hard. Depression, stress, anxiety, anger, overwhelm, disconnection, poor coping mechanisms and drama can settle deep within you. This may send you looking for other means to cope like food, alcohol, mind-numbing drugs (prescription or recreational), overworking or other obsessions. Later you may find yourself needing to stop the further pain you have inadvertently placed upon yourself in trying to avoid the initial pain.

Unaddressed pain is a vicious circle. The only way off the cyclic nightmare is to stop, turn around, step out of the circle and walk directly into the middle of the bright red hotspot of pain at the epicentre – surprisingly the only place that offers any resolution. Embrace yourself and hold on tight for the initial onslaught with hope that this brave act will later bring you the peace and calm you are seeking.

As you make the choice to fight for yourself and not take flight from yourself, you decide to walk the bumpy path right now.

GREETING GRIEF

You choose to follow the signposts. Love was a good start. You also remember to watch for the butterflies. Grief will surely lead you to where you need to go on its hazy, frightening journey. That's what the signpost had promised anyway.

Your faith renews slightly as you spy a pair of trekking boots on the path in front of you. Shoe attire is important on this most difficult journey of a lifetime. These are used and a little roughed up but fit perfectly. As you lace up, you feel something brush past your arm. Shooing it away you look up and see two butterflies flittering high up into the trees.

One foot in front of the other in your new trekking boots, following love, feeling cold and alone and hoping for another signpost, you keep moving forwards. You seem guided by the unspoken words of someone who has gone before you. You listen intently.

GRIEF RISING UP

"There is a sacredness in tears. They are not the mark of weakness but of power. ... They are the messengers of overwhelming grief, of deep contrition and of unspeakable love."

—Washington Irving

At this stage in your grief journey, you may feel the grief rising and threatening to spill over. You may feel various scary emotions swilling around. I did. At this stage in my journey, my insides felt like they were bleeding and raw. Tears washed over me and sorrow from grief ran through my veins, threatening to never stop. Nothing made me laugh or feel joy. It was all I could do to endure the basic moments of life.

GRIEF, GRACE AND GRATITUDE

My body was trying desperately to rid itself of the mourning it was heaving around. I would clear a wave of deep sorrow only to be bowled over by another wave shortly afterwards. Fetal position pretended to allow a little protection for an instant. Then it would start again, producing soul-destroying sobs.

Sometimes I would sense a clearing for a split second, like in the morning when I first woke up. Then the thoughts started rolling in thick and fast, and the reality and tears would return. Most of the time I felt physically weak from carrying grief like a heavy backpack.

I rationally understood that this was the grief journey and that I needed to take the grief path despite my uncertainty and disorientation. I had studied and knew what was to come in theory. Yet, in real life I didn't want to take the journey. To accept my dad was no longer here and deal with the suffering of grief would make it all too real. I knew it would nearly destroy me before it turned around to rebuild and transform me.

Emotions, of course, often erased all the rationale and threw me into mayhem. I dug deep to hold on to some sort of faith that I would get through. I was on a seesaw of rationale versus emotion. In a little quiet place within, however, I felt guided to own up to my responsibility to look after myself and dive headlong into the pain, the grief and the unknown.

Deep down I knew that I could do it. I had to; I didn't have a choice. For my dad I could not totally crash and burn. I eventually decided to live a rich, full life in his honour. He would not want me to squander it in misery, depression and 'victim-ville'. He would want the best for me. He would want me to grow through the tears and sadness, using the experience to build a better life and blossom more every day into the beautiful woman he knew I could be. He would want his darling daughter to be happy at all costs; to smile, live, love and enjoy life. How could I disappoint him or myself?

GREETING GRIEF

I gave myself permission to grieve. I allowed grief to reside and flow inside me, trusting it would take me through the journey safely and delicately.

Permission to grieve

"Life is a balance of holding on and letting go."

—Rumi

In giving myself permission to grieve, I sat and felt. I processed and expressed. I wrote and meditated. I spoke to Dad and I spent time with family. I visited the cemetery and made his passing feel real. I sat with him and talked and listened to his favourite music. I hung out where I felt safe and spent time with those who nurtured me. I soaked up the innocence of the dog park. I walked and spent time with my emotions. I invested in my grief journey and my healing.

Life became solely about grief. Grief does that to you when you walk headlong into it. You dive in, literally hit rock bottom and slowly surface. Every now and then you are flung back down again to flounder as grief tries to hold you prisoner. You feel compelled to do as it asks, hoping you will be given a reprieve to return to a normal life, which will eventually happen. Once you start the grief journey, moving forward is the only choice. While the path in the forest is rough and winding, to me it appeared better to be on the path to somewhere than be stuck going nowhere.

Know that wherever you are on your grief journey it is okay. It is normal to feel totally lost and befuddled; that is part of the grief. You will not feel like yourself. That is okay also. Remember, I am here as your butterfly wings and your faith as you journey through the nooks and crannies of grief.

Handling your grief

"What we have once enjoyed deeply we can never lose. All that we love deeply becomes a part of us."

—Helen Keller

One day at a time is how you decide to tackle your survival. And survival it is, dodging tree limbs and crawling over fallen trunks. Sitting on a trunk for a moment, tears roll down your cheeks and turn into powerful sobs. You let them flow.

When the tears abate, you continue to try to stay warm and dry in the wet and clammy surroundings. The forest makes you feel alone, lost and frightened in a kind of isolated grey bubble. Everything in your life has changed. There is no room for laughter and joy.

Turning the next corner on the path, you climb over more shrubbery and see a run-down wooden picnic table with one bench. On the table is a plethora of foods such as antipasto with fruits and sweets. You are still not hungry but know that to continue you need all your energy. Butterflies rise and flutter away as you sit at the table. A bunch of leaves on the table catches your eye.

Wiping them away you discover an engraving that reads: 'To my sister, I love you to the moon and back, 2016.' Someone else has been here before you. They have lived this journey and sat at this same table.

Tears well up and gently roll down your cheeks as you feel their sorrow and pain stabbing at your heart, mimicking your own. You wonder how they traversed the Forest of Grief and whether they found acceptance, peace and the love the signpost promises.

A snippet of hope shines through for a moment as you understand you are not alone. Then it quickly vanishes. You acknowledge your feelings while devouring the delicious food.

GREETING GRIEF

When dealing with grief emotions you can only handle so much at one time. It is normal for grief to fling you around from one emotion to another, sometimes from moment to moment. One minute you may feel immense sadness and then anger, and the next fear and maybe even like laughing. It's hard to keep up. It's emotionally hectic and overpowering. Grief is random and mystifying.

You don't come prepared to handle your grief. There is no grief manual, and often your first loss is your first experience of indescribable grief. The toll it takes on your health and ability to cope can be huge. Your spirit can break. While you need to deal with your emotions, sometimes you need healthy distractions to give your mind, body, heart and soul a rest from the arduous internal work going on inside – if only for a minute! Just like your physical body, your mental and emotional bodies need time to rest, regroup and recover. You could go to the movies, the park or have coffee with a friend.

Be careful how you invest your time and energy. Your emotions are heightened and precious already. Try not to introduce more stress or drama into your life as this will only compound your emotional state. Treat yourself with the ancient practice of yoga and meditation. These can offer such powerful respite to your overall being on all levels that you may notice immediate benefits and possibly profound transformation.

Invest in yourself

Remember, there will be many bad moments and bad days. Accept that's where you are at; that's grief. Don't resist as this will contribute to you getting stuck. I know it feels like life will never change; I have been there. You may wonder: 'What's the point?' There is a point! Be patient as the next section helps you to uncover it.

While searching deep inside for the point that you cannot yet find, you pick up the knife and begin to carve your own inscription on the picnic table. 'To my...'

You want others that follow you on this journey to know you were here. Even though they may feel alone, you want them to realise that reaching out to others lessens the isolation and helps you feel more connected.

You hear a noise and see something furry scuttle away. It's waiting for the food no doubt. Time to go. It's getting dark and you will need somewhere to rest soon. You pack up some food and head onwards.

THE POINT

> "The risk of love is loss, and the price of loss is grief. But the pain of grief is only a shadow when compared with the pain of never risking love."
>
> —Hilary Stanton Zunin

Walking further on into the afternoon, everything is drab and dark. The happiness and joyful colours of life don't exist. Your legs are getting a little sore, but on the next corner you get a reprieve.

You see before you a wooden shelter decorated with a carving of butterflies. It's beautiful and obviously made from a deep love, maybe by the person who created the inscription at the last stop. Are you following their journey? A slab of stone in the shelter is inscribed:

The Forest of Grief – resting place

GREETING GRIEF

You have travelled a reasonable way through the twists and turns of the forest and it is time to rest. Inside a cupboard in the shelter you are thrilled to find some basic necessities such as warm clothes and bedding.

You know the grief journey is not about comfort but about walking through the pain and the uncomfortableness. It is about doing and feeling things that you don't want to. You are here and willing to heal, so camping in the shelter it is. Hopefully, the furry creature has scuttled to his own home and will not want to share yours!

After arranging your space and bedding, you eat some food and lay down to rest. You are grateful for the little bit of comfort being provided by the warm clothes and bedding – a sign that you are supported on this difficult journey. As you say "I love and miss you" to your Loved One, surprisingly, sleep comes quickly.

It's in your waking that an important epiphany arrives. You've heard often that time heals all wounds, only now you realise that without the work, time means nothing. If you trust and love yourself enough to invest time and energy into your healing, delicate little shifts will slowly occur. Small changes will be noticeable and subtle nice emotions will return. You realise that the point is love!

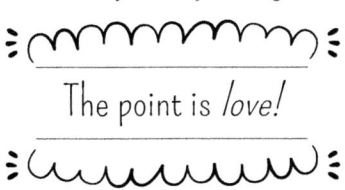

The point is *love!*

You feel a warm, fuzzy and loving feeling inside. You bask in its beauty briefly until suddenly the little furry critter scuttles past again, ruffling the nearby leaves and bringing you out of your beautiful epiphany, back to your horrid reality.

Jumping up, you shake yourself all over, trying to find that loving space inside once again. Sadly, it's gone; you can't. You remember, though, the message: The point is love! *You hold that close and pray for the day it comes to fruition.*

You pack up to keep moving towards the love the signpost promised. While still full of sorrow, you understand the theory. You hope that in time the reality of it will shine through you again, showering you with beauty, just like the beautiful butterfly carving on the shelter.

Looking up, you see another wooden signpost with 'Love' written on it, and once again you follow the direction of the arrow.

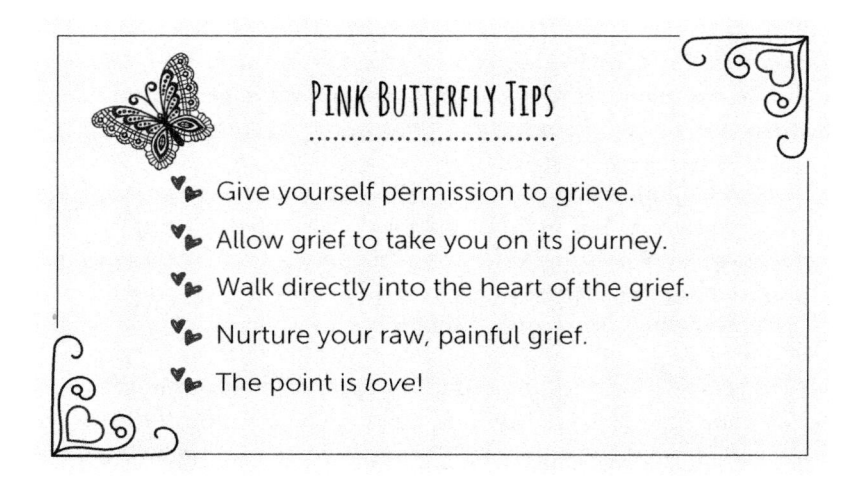

PINK BUTTERFLY TIPS

- Give yourself permission to grieve.
- Allow grief to take you on its journey.
- Walk directly into the heart of the grief.
- Nurture your raw, painful grief.
- The point is *love!*

Yes, you had a cataclysmic earth-shattering loss, and nothing can ever change that. But that love is still available. You may not see this today and only be in the grief. Slowly, however, you will notice a shift; that is the beginning.

Don't give up. Keep going through the process. Even if you haven't seen any light yet, one day it will shine a little. And that glimmer will bring with it hope – just enough for you to know the gift is truly there.

Again, the point is *love!* All the different kinds of beautiful, wondrous, exquisite, tender and soul-moving love. The piece of love that is gifted to you from your Loved One, added to the love you will build for yourself through this journey, will transform you. You are then able to shine this joint love out to the world.

GREETING GRIEF

~ PINK PONDERINGS ~

Stop and take three deep breaths. Honour yourself with patience, gentleness and a compassionate spirit. Come from a place of love: your love and the love of your Loved One. The whole point is *love!*

- ♥ Today, my grief feels like...
- ♥ Today, my grief wants me to...
- ♥ Today, my grief taught me...

FIVE STAGES OF GRIEF

"The best way out is always through."

—Robert Frost

Later in the day, you stumble over a thick branch. Looking down, you are stunned to see a perfect pink rose at your feet. How is this resting here so perfectly? There is no light or rose bush.

You pick it up and gently run your fingertips over the smooth petals; a sense of love arises within you. You become aware of tenderness and vulnerability housed around your soul. You savour the love for a moment and place the flower gently in your hair. As you treat the rose with care and love, you realise you need to treat yourself the same.

At the next twist in the path a wooden staircase appears, winding upwards. Looking up, you see a little treehouse nestled between the trees, tenderly inviting you in. Climbing the rickety stairs, you enter the treehouse, admiring a big butterfly carved above the entrance. You know this is part of the journey; the butterflies are guiding you each step of the way.

As you sit on a bright cushion on the floor, you wrap yourself in beautiful throw rugs to keep warm. In front of you is another wooden sign with a carving that reads:

GRIEF, GRACE AND GRATITUDE

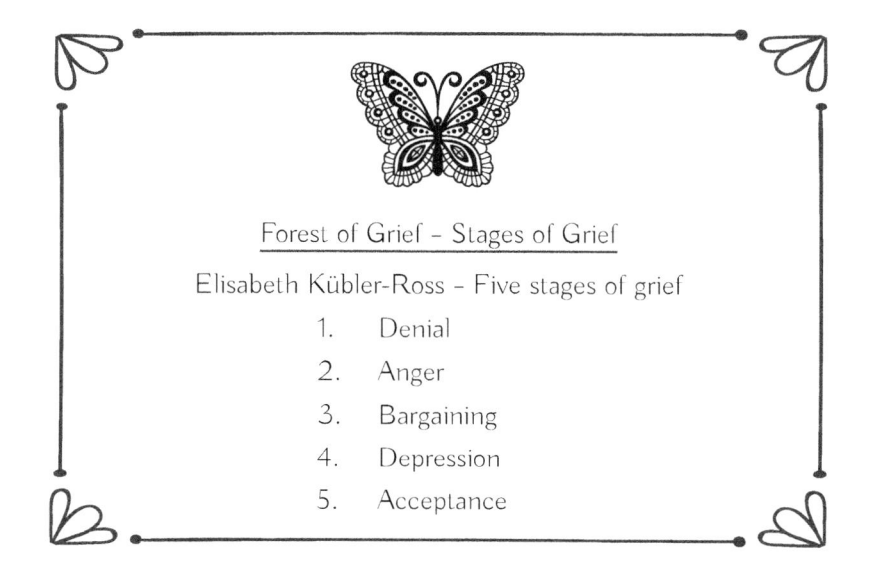

> Forest of Grief – Stages of Grief
> Elisabeth Kübler-Ross – Five stages of grief
> 1. Denial
> 2. Anger
> 3. Bargaining
> 4. Depression
> 5. Acceptance

As you sit and get comfortable, ready to spend the afternoon here, you ponder how the person who was here before you felt and coped. You check that the pink rose, a piece of beauty amongst the sadness, is still in your hair and wait for the next lesson in the grief journey.

To understand a little more about our journey through grief is to understand a little more about grief itself, making the ride gentler or at least a little easier to navigate. There is no map of grief, but there are aspects of grief we can become familiar with, so when they arise we can acknowledge what grief wants from us – instead of it bowling us over.

Swiss-American psychiatrist Elisabeth Kübler-Ross is noted for developing a five-stage model of grief. Initially created for terminally ill patients, it explains the emotions prior and near to death. Later she expanded her model to include any form of loss such as the loss of a loved one, which I explain in this section.

The model describes what is to be expected in response to a loss. You may flow between one stage and another. You may not go through all the stages or you may go through some or all stages many times. You could remain at each stage for different time frames, and some may be more intense and seemingly destructive than others. They all have one shared element, however; each stage allows you to process your grief and move the grief energy through your body, heart and soul.

To feel it is to process it. To process it is to express it. To express it is to start to heal it.

Your experience will be different to others'; we all grieve individually. Be mindful of this and gentle with yourself as you journey through the five stages of grief.

1. Denial

This is not happening to me...

Denial is the first stage of grief, where you experience shock, disbelief and confusion. This stage helps you survive your massive loss. It is a stage where you may refuse to accept your reality and your loss, with a voice inside reciting repetitively, 'This is not happening to me'. You do this to protect yourself from the initial shock and the overwhelming emotions about to arise.

You may feel numb and dazed. 'How will I cope?' This stage allows you to slowly assimilate the loss and move through the initial stages of grief. You will begin to move out of denial and into the onslaught of emotions. This is a normal part of the grief journey.

2. Anger

Why me? Aarrgghh...

As the denial wears off, your ghastly reality will set in. Deep inside you are more vulnerable than ever and hurting so much you may redirect this internal pain and find someone to blame for your pain and loss. You may feel angry at yourself, others, the doctors or the world in general.

Rationally, you may understand that blame is illogical; however, your emotions will override your rational thinking. Your anger needs to be felt to move forward. It is the emotion that covers most of your other emotions and underlying hurt, which in time will surface to be dealt with. The anger often brings you out of your numb denial into a rainbow of emotions. The more you allow yourself to feel the anger the sooner it will begin to dissipate. This is a normal part of the grief journey.

3. Bargaining

If only...

Your loss makes you feel like you have lost control of your control. You feel vulnerable and powerless and are looking to gain some type of inner control of your world. Endless 'What if...' or 'If only...' statements dominate your thoughts. More than ever, you want life to return to what it was, with your Loved One by your side. You may consider what you would do if you had another chance. You can begin to feel guilty for things you didn't do or see sooner and initiate more internal pain through self-loathing. You may even bargain with a higher power to change your reality. It may not seem rational, but that is the randomness of grief. This is a normal part of the grief journey.

4. Depression

What's the point?...

During this stage, you may feel disconnected, sad, afraid, regretful and numb. Common symptoms of depression set in as you feel overwhelmed and weighed down with the loss. You may withdraw and avoid communication with others. As a result, grief enters your life at a deep level. This stage can be where you look to facilitate some sort of internal goodbye. Depression from a loss is an appropriate response at this stage of the grief journey and healing process. This is a normal part of the grief journey.

5. Acceptance

I think I can cope...

At this stage, you feel pulled to re-engage in life and social activities. You begin to move forward, slowly and delicately. It does not necessarily mean you are happy, but you have surfaced from your depression and feel a little lighter. You have accepted that the loss is now part of your new reality. You do not like it but can live with it.

Some people may never reach this stage. They stay locked in anger, sadness and blame. Not feeling and moving through your grief can keep you stuck in earlier stages and never allow you to find the peace and calm of acceptance. This peace is available to everyone upon moving gently through the stages of grief. This is a normal part of the grief journey.

Living through the stages

> "When we meet real tragedy in life, we can react in two ways — either by losing hope and falling into self-destructive habits or by using the challenge to find our inner strength."
>
> —The Dalai Lama

So much information is given on this journey that you find it hard to take it all in at once. Shuffling around restlessly you finally stand up to stretch your legs and stop, realising it's important to rest and regroup. You walk over to take a closer look at the butterfly carving at the entrance and notice its meticulously crafted markings.

You appreciate the thought and emotion that was put into creating it, as you ponder the stages of grief. Running your hands tenderly over the carving you feel the love inside it. This love was created from an understanding of how each stroke creates the bigger picture of beauty. As you follow the strokes with your fingers, you start to realise it symbolises your path, that is, that the bigger picture of beauty will unfold after you invest love and energy into your healing.

The stages of grief are not pleasant and can be overwhelmingly difficult and complex. The grief is resting inside, just below the surface, and until you allow it to surface you cannot start to create healing. Avoidance only worsens the grief. Conversely, honouring yourself by understanding and starting to walk through this delicate part of your life will ultimately bring the peace and calm that is presently elusive.

Become familiar with the stages listed above to recognise where you are residing on any day. This awareness may make it a little

FIVE STAGES OF GRIEF

easier and prevent you from feeling like you are going crazy. Let me reassure you that you are not going crazy; you are grieving a deep, soul-shattering loss.

The stages of grief can run rampant within your fragile soul. The grief journey is like a rollercoaster, and your emotional climate and moods can change instantly, swaying from anger and sadness to snippets of peace. Grief toys with you, and those snippets of peace often only stay for a moment to remind you of the hope of a better state of mind … until the grief comes crashing back in.

I missed my dad. Even saying the words ignited the grief and drew out racking sobs of disbelief and sadness. I was often teetering on the edge of survival, trying not to fall into darker depths of despair. In the absence of my own butterfly wings I looked to Dad's: his life, his values, his beliefs, his humour, our memories and mostly our love. I knew I could cope, and so I did. While I continued to be hurled around in the spin cycle of grief and the rainbow of emotions, I went with the flow. I accepted any moments of respite, hoping that one day it would come to an end or at least be the start of a new beginning.

And it did! However, this was some time later!

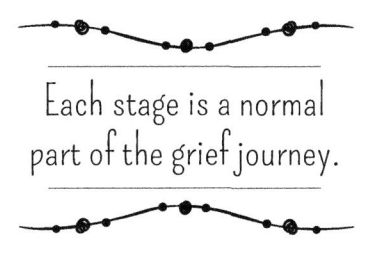

Each stage is a normal part of the grief journey.

Pink Butterfly Tips

- Denial is a normal part of grief.
- Anger is a normal part of grief.
- Bargaining is a normal part of grief.
- Depression is a normal part of grief.
- Acceptance will follow if you walk through the grief journey.

Pink Grief Corner – Question time

By answering the questions below and allowing time and space for self-reflection, you will delve just a little below the surface to gain some initial awareness.

Stop and take three deep breaths. Honour yourself with patience, gentleness and a compassionate spirit. Come from a place of love: your love and the love of your Loved One. The whole point is *love!*

Record your feelings in your Pink Grief Journal:

1. In which stage of grief are you currently sitting?
2. Which stages have you experienced?
3. Can you recognise the different stages?

FIVE STAGES OF GRIEF

4. Does any stage appear to be hiding from you?

This is a tough exercise. Take some time out to integrate what you have read, written and learnt. Try not to take on too much at once in case you feel overloaded. Run a bath, listen to some music or curl up in bed and get all warm and cosy.

If you need to, cry your heart out. Feel your feelings but always remember the love.

Feeling tired at the end of the day, the treehouse has brought many lessons in helping to understand your grief. You walk down the staircase and feel grounded by the earth beneath your feet and the trees all around. A sense of confusion and loss still surrounds you, and you feel exhausted. Yet you try to maintain the hope the butterflies and signs promise.

Leaves crunch nearby and you see something rush out and up the stairs, no doubt another furry critter scrounging around for food. Looking to the tree with the butterfly carving you notice a huge gaping hole and are thrilled to find more supplies inside – and no critters! A place to rest for tonight.

Unfolding your bedding, you build a warm and cosy place to sleep and unpack the food. You eat and drink enough to satisfy your hunger and thirst. It's been a big day and you are exhausted.

Familiar sobs rise from deep within. Allowing them to surface, you appreciate what you have learnt yet wonder how the grief journey will lead you through each stage, and how you will survive. Just in case the critter is hiding in the treehouse, you throw some scraps out on to the ground below. You hope he will chase the food and leave you on your own with your grief.

Snuggled up in your bed, you tell your Loved One that you miss them and love them. You hope to dream of the love, roses and butterflies sent by them, as you allow your body to drift into sleep.

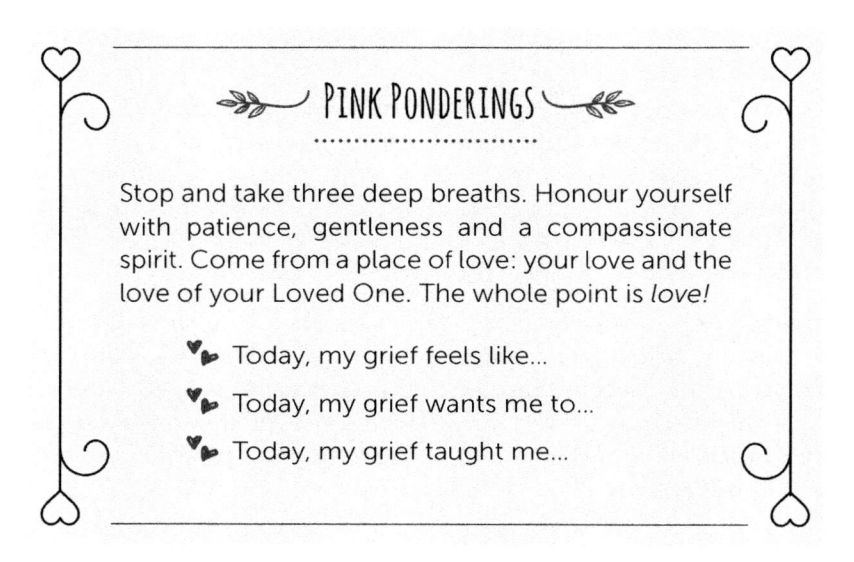

PINK PONDERINGS

Stop and take three deep breaths. Honour yourself with patience, gentleness and a compassionate spirit. Come from a place of love: your love and the love of your Loved One. The whole point is *love!*

- Today, my grief feels like...
- Today, my grief wants me to...
- Today, my grief taught me...

IN THE PINK PROCESS

> "When you are standing in that forest of sorrow,
> ... if someone can assure you that they themselves
> have stood in that same place, and now have
> moved on, sometimes this will bring hope."
>
> —Elizabeth Gilbert (Eat, Pray, Love)

Waking up, you set off early. The Forest of Grief continues to be a dark and lonely place. The road is undulated and rough, the trees poisonous and scratchy, the atmosphere clammy and the insects 'bitey'. Wild emotions in your heart produce a constant stream of sadness.

All you can do for now is put one foot in front of the other. What to do next? What to do, what to say, where to go, what to feel or even how to function? You forget how to BE! This is all normal. Unfortunately, though, it's a dark, scary, cold type of normal. You will need to get comfortable living with the unknown, the uncomfortable and the unpleasant.

You will also need to get comfortable living with a sense of being out of control, at least for a while. Attempting to resist this will only make your journey more difficult. You look for the next sign post with the 'Love' arrow. There it is! On you go!

> **Don't repress or suppress – FEEL!**

Now that you understand the five stages of grief and have recorded your thoughts in your Pink Grief Journal, I would like to introduce another process I developed called 'In the Pink Process' (ITP Process). I first presented this five-stage process in my book *Heartbreak, Healing and Happiness*. The process is beneficial when used in conjunction with Elizabeth Kübler-Ross's five-stage model to create an overall understanding of grief. The more grief information you are equipped with in your emotional 'tool belt' the more in control you will feel and the easier the ride will be.

I used this process during a devastating relationship breakup, and again when I lost my fur child Maxy, a 15-year-old Golden Retriever, and again with the loss of my dad. Three times in three years. Losing Dad was such a colossal loss, and while a different type of grief from my other heartbreaks, I discovered the process was the same.

The ITP Process gave me a place to begin. It didn't lessen the emotional response, but it provided a structure and understanding of what I was going to go through. It helped me move through the treacle-like grief that threatened to keep me stuck at many points.

With the process, I could pre-empt my steps by doing a little work on myself. There were a few little surprises, but no giant surprise parties of grief arrived at my door. I was still crushed, though, and my fragile soul was crying for help. At times I felt the beauty of my flowing tears, believing they watered my soul in honour of my dad. At other times I felt so shattered I wanted to give up. I knew that if I only kept moving forward, one tiny footstep at a time, I would get somewhere eventually. And I did!

These valuable tools will open your heart and eyes to a structure or a path, providing you with a few blocks and butterfly wings to prop you up while you feel yourself hanging on the edge of the cliff. Opening yourself to an understanding of grief will open your heart to heal. Opening your heart to heal ultimately opens your heart to love again.

I understand your butterfly wings are still stilted and lie in hibernation, and with these tools I hope you can be buffered by mine. My wings are here, hoping to help you through your grief journey a little at a time.

Introduction to In The Pink Process

> "Give sorrow words; the grief that does not speak whispers the o'er-fraught heart and bids it break."
>
> —William Shakespeare

Coming around a corner and another twist in the path, you approach a small opening and step straight into some shallow running water. Turning to the right you see you are standing in a creek that runs for some distance and is bordered by thick shrubbery on either side.

Near the edge of the creek where you are standing, there are two tall trees. Hanging from one of the branches is a wind chime with five small butterflies flittering around. As the gentle breeze passes through the dangling butterflies, you are surrounded by beautiful tinkling chimes.

Taking a few steps further, before the thick shrubbery threatens to encapsulate you, a bench appears. A nice space to rest! You sit and hear the water running, the breeze hissing and the butterflies chiming. As you close your eyes for a moment, you inspect your inner landscape to see if it is as restful as this special place on the bench. Unfortunately not!

Your eyes are roused open and you look closer to the wind chime, noticing that each of the five butterflies has an inscription. Just below the wind chime is a big stone, and etched into it are these words:

Forest of Grief – ITP Process

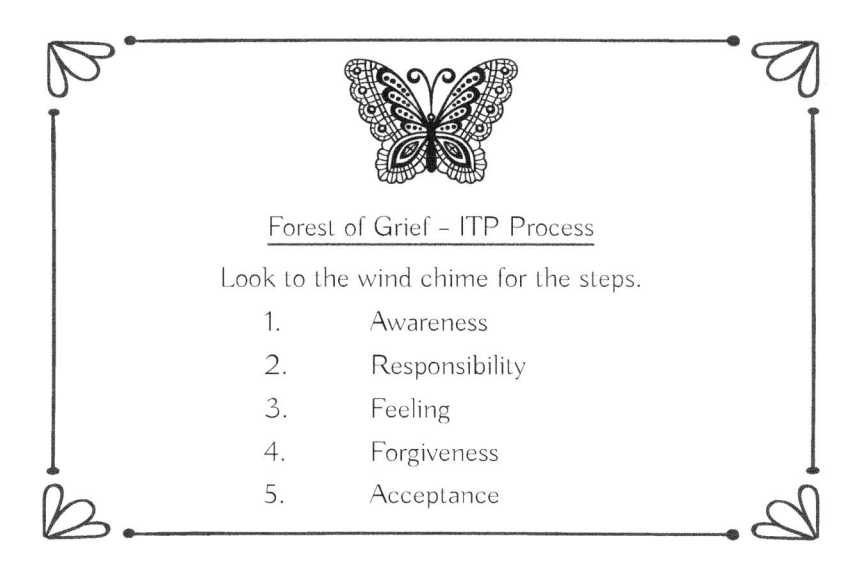

Look to the wind chime for the steps.
1. Awareness
2. Responsibility
3. Feeling
4. Forgiveness
5. Acceptance

You settle in for the day, knowing the five lessons to come will be big ones. The bench seems comfortable, and behind you is a wooden box, which you think is used to house firewood. But upon opening it, it reveals more supplies, lunch, rugs and a bag of seeds. You read the wind chimes, and the lessons reveal themselves, one by one...

You can use the ITP Process tools during your grief and in other times of heartbreak and loss. They will help you develop emotionally and heighten your emotional intelligence, staying with you forever like the memories of your Loved One. They are the backbone and foundations to rebuild yourself through your grief journey.

Like the stages of grief, you may not necessarily go through these five steps in the order I present them. The response to the loss of your Loved One, your own grief, is your individual story. So just allow it to unfold the way it presents itself. Use this process as a guide and another learning experience only, to become more connected to yourself, remain connected to your Loved One and begin the healing grief journey.

To honour myself, my grief and my emotions, I found that I first needed to create *awareness* for where I was and what I was feeling. This is the first step in the ITP Process. Awareness allowed me to reveal my thoughts, feelings and truths to myself. So out came my Pink Grief Journal and I began to write furiously, seeking what lay within.

These revelations gave me an opportunity to take ownership of my thoughts, feelings, choices, grief and behaviours, and moved me on from victimhood and a blaming mentality. I took a small amount of control back and realised I had started the healing journey. I had to take *responsibility* to take this journey — the second ITP step. I didn't want to travel it but knew that, despite everything, it was best for me to do so.

The third ITP step was to allow myself to feel my *feelings*. This released internal pressure and continued the healing. I began to understand my feelings, put names to any new scary feelings, and learnt why they were there and what they were telling me. I had never experienced so many different emotions. I survived. Just!

Forgiving myself and others was the fourth ITP step. I began to forgive myself for any acts that were not in line with self-love. I was also able to inspect internally if I had laid any inappropriate blame. Finding forgiveness during my anger stage was particularly difficult. Just to accept that anger was part of the grief was difficult enough! The depth of anger you can experience at your loss, and how it covers so many more emotions, was quite new to me.

Forgiveness led me to a higher appreciation of my heart and soul and finally to an *acceptance* of my new reality — the fifth and final ITP step. I was still grieving but had acceptance. I had survived the worst of it and was able to accept my new life. I could find the gratitude for my dad, our lives together, and the whole experience of life with its twists and turns. Once I had gained acceptance, I was injected with an intense, deep-seated yearning to live as rich and full a life as possible in honour of my dad. And this again took me on a new soul path.

Let me now guide you through the five steps of the ITP Process in more depth while I stay beside you at every step.

ITP Step 1: Awareness

Awareness is your first step to profound internal change, especially in your grief journey. It is the key to being truthful with yourself.

Awareness opens your eyes, ears, heart and mind to what is happening within, be it good or not-so-good. This awareness of your inner landscape allows your experience to shine through. You begin to see your truth and understand it is beneficial for the suffering to surface rather than bury it in avoidance and ignorance.

Being at the start of your grief, you are likely not to know exactly what you are feeling. You may be experiencing new and unwanted thoughts and emotions and feeling like you are being held prisoner by them. This is normal. Developing awareness and being mindful of your thoughts, emotions, feelings, behaviours, choices and all other areas of your life will assist you to make more informed decisions about your grieving and environment. You can then start taking back some power, gain some control and align yourself closer to your authenticity.

Be aware of what you are thinking: Thoughts dictate how you feel and feelings dictate how you behave. Notice when thoughts pop into your head and write down any concerning thoughts you may want to revisit later. Just let the thoughts swirl around in your head but be mindful of them. Try not to attach to them and be taken on a downward spiral. Become the observer. Take notice. Be aware.

IN THE PINK PROCESS

Be aware of what you are feeling: Sit with the feelings and allow them to flow through you naturally. Cry, vent, roar, wail; do whatever your grief asks you to do. Express it. Journal about your feelings to help ease the confusion. Become the observer. Take notice. Be aware.

Be aware of your behaviours: Notice what you are doing, what you are not doing, what you are saying, how you are treating others and how you are treating yourself. Again, become the observer. Take notice. Be aware.

Awareness brings with it honesty, authenticity and truth. This can result in tough decisions being made that bring consequences. Being aware of your grief and being truthful with yourself is a big responsibility. Yet when you follow its lead through your grief, you can live an authentic grief journey and ultimately an authentic life.

You will need courage to face your awareness through your grief. Grief taps into your vulnerabilities and can add to any feelings of powerlessness. So rest on my butterfly wings, granting you that courage while you wait to regain yours. Know that the strength you had before the loss is still available to you. It is just lying dormant, overshadowed by the intense grief emotions.

I initially found awareness difficult. I lived with awareness and denial in the same bed. Before Dad passed away, I knew he was ill and that we would not have him for much longer. Yet I lived in denial, trying to pretend nothing was going to change. After he passed I was aware of my feelings but still tried to dodge them, hoping I could just bask in the ignorance of unawareness a little longer before the emotions came crashing in. Which they did soon after! Awareness at this stage helped me acknowledge the severity and enormity of my situation and the depth of my hurt.

To heal and continue your journey through life, it is necessary to go through the season of grief. To do this you need to develop awareness, not just in grief but in life. You can go on to honour those you have lost and any you lose in the future. It is a deep mark of respect for your Loved One and yourself to grant yourself entry into the gruelling grief journey, which starts with awareness.

Give yourself permission to start here. One day, today, and one piece of awareness at a time.

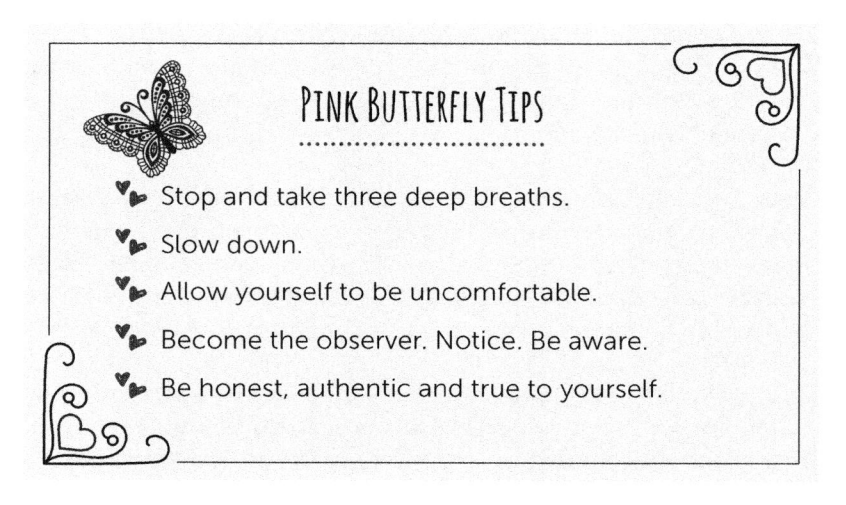

Pink Butterfly Tips

- Stop and take three deep breaths.
- Slow down.
- Allow yourself to be uncomfortable.
- Become the observer. Notice. Be aware.
- Be honest, authentic and true to yourself.

Pink Grief Corner – Question Time

Below are more questions around finding awareness for you to ponder.

Stop and take three deep breaths. Honour yourself with patience, gentleness and a compassionate spirit. Come from a place of love: your love and the love of your Loved One. The whole point is *love!*

Record your feelings in your Pink Grief Journal:

1. Are you aware of your thoughts, feelings and behaviours?

2. If not, are you willing to create awareness of your thoughts, feelings and behaviours?
3. What can you do today to increase your awareness?
4. Are you able to stop and listen to what your grief is asking of you?
5. Do you give permission for your grief journey to access your awareness?

Review the words and feelings you have expressed and take some time out.

Delving into your soul to answer these questions while dealing with your grief can be arduous. Take one day and one exercise at a time, refraining from doing too much at once. You need to allow the information that rises to the surface to sit and integrate within you before moving to the next step.

Be proud of yourself for taking the grief journey; you are on a tough road. Just by being on the road you are brave, courageous and self-honouring. Admitting that you feel proud of yourself may make you teary. Remember, you are now most likely overly sensitive and vulnerable, so it doesn't take much to start the tears rolling. Even a mini-moment of pride, which is self-love in disguise, can create a stream of tears. Allow them to flow; this is a healthy, normal part of grief.

For me, everything good and not-so-good made me cry for an awfully long time. Eventually, those tears of grief became tears of beauty. Sometimes I swung between both. Allow the free flow of sadness and love to rain from your eyes, water your soul and start to wash the grief away.

Once you are developing awareness, you can move on to the next step of the ITP Process becoming the author of your life: Responsibility.

ITP Step 2: Responsibility

Taking responsibility is tough! Some days it just seems more fitting to stay wrapped in ignorance, surrounded by denial and in a bubble of unawareness. However, this means you do not take responsibility for your healing and instead hinder it.

You are not responsible for the loss of your Loved One. You are, however, responsible for what happens now, that is, how you respond or react to your loss and how you continue to live your life. It is your decision now to either take responsibility or not that will determine whether your heart opens or remains closed to your future, shaping the rest of your life.

The life purpose of your heart is to give and receive true, pure love. Right now, your heart is shrouded in grief, which is normal. Be reassured that even though your heart may feel permanently closed, if you keep moving forward, the love of your Loved One in your heart will slowly surface again and one day shine brightly — when the time is right.

> The life purpose of your heart is to give and receive pure love.

It is this shining of their love that fills your heart to the brim and creates a softness and tenderness inside. The grief process can allow your heart to feel more love than ever before, which is ultimately passed on to others and returned to yourself.

To access and give away this love housed in your heart, your heart needs to be open and functioning well. To achieve this heart purpose as part of this process, you need to take responsibility. Although you can gain support from others to move towards healing, they cannot do it for you. You need to do that for yourself. This simply means saying to yourself, "I am responsible for my feelings, pain, suffering and healing" – a simple statement but difficult to invoke.

You may be angry and blame others, which is a convenient avoidance of the grief journey and looking within. Staying in blame mode makes you a victim and removes self-responsibility in not allowing yourself to feel the hard feelings and walk towards healing.

If you are in this victim mode, your feelings depend on another person. This can send you on a dangerous downward spiral to a more helpless state or even a deep depression. When you are not being authentic and not taking ownership of your feelings, you will sway back and forth in the grief breeze with even less control.

There may be blame apportioned correctly to someone else. To heal, however, you need to look at your thoughts, feelings, emotions and behaviours, and take ownership of them and your healing while walking to forgiveness. Taking responsibility for your feelings removes you from victim mode and places you on the correct path to healing your grief.

You only get one life, and it's tragic that you have to deal with this loss, I know. It will put your life on hold for a period, maybe a long time. It will break you wide open and change you. Nothing will be the same again. Hang in there! Taking responsibility will mean you are taking ownership of your life, how you walk to your future, and how you will allow your heart to give and receive love in the years to come. It is your choice. The secret is that wise choices will lead you to the healing peace you so desperately seek.

Learn to say, "I own this grief journey" even if you don't like it. Learn to say, "I take responsibility for my grief" even if you don't like it.

Taking ownership and responsibility will strengthen you as you walk through the grief journey and keep you feeling connected to your true nature, to shine out love and gratitude.

Give yourself permission to be the creator and author of yourself, your life and your grief journey. Take the path to healing that works best for you, allowing the love that is buried to slowly surface and shine.

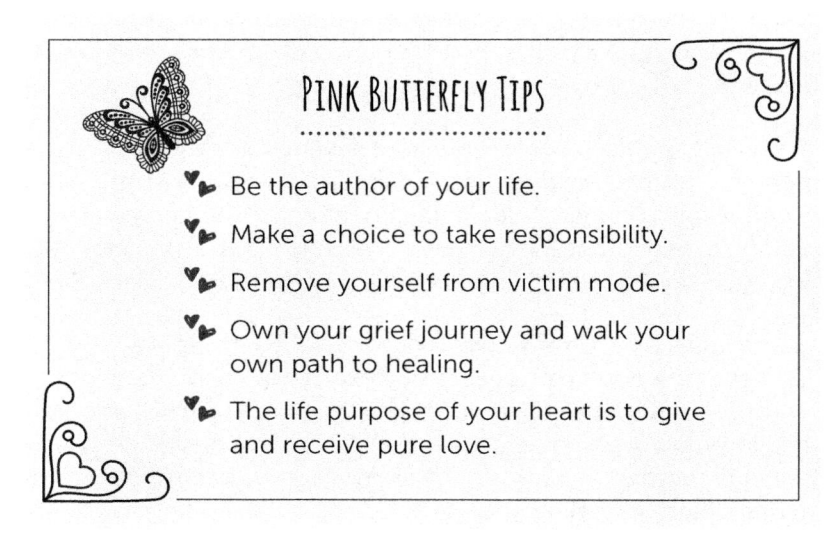

Pink Butterfly Tips

- Be the author of your life.
- Make a choice to take responsibility.
- Remove yourself from victim mode.
- Own your grief journey and walk your own path to healing.
- The life purpose of your heart is to give and receive pure love.

Pink Grief Corner – Question time

The questions below are the starting point for you to move towards taking ownership and responsibility.

Stop and take three deep breaths. Honour yourself with patience, gentleness and a compassionate spirit. Come from a place of love: your love and the love of your Loved One. The whole point is *love!*

Record your feelings in your Pink Grief Journal:

1. Are you taking responsibility for your grief journey?

IN THE PINK PROCESS

2. Are you deflecting responsibility by blaming others?
3. What payoff do you receive in your life right now by not taking responsibility?
4. What are you avoiding by not taking responsibility?
5. If you took responsibility what would be difficult for you?
6. What would you need to do differently if you took responsibility?
7. Are you willing to begin taking responsibility for yourself and your healing?

Review the words and feelings you have expressed and take some time out.

I commend you for walking this path while inwardly dealing with the tremendous pain and suffering of your loss. Continue to feel your grief while allowing self-love to flow.

Give consent to your vulnerabilities and gentle side to lead you. This is the side of you that knows what it needs. It is the quiet voice inside directing you. To hear her you need to remain still and quiet and be patient with yourself.

Having learnt more about taking responsibility for your grief journey, you can now move on to the next step of the ITP Process and the key to shifting some of the intense grief energy: Feeling.

ITP Step 3: Feeling

Feeling our feelings sometimes verges on the threshold of impossible. But not quite!

Let me tell you a secret. No matter what you are feeling and how far you have fallen, it is always possible to stand up, brush yourself off and climb back up that cliff face to continue the journey. It is possible to feel your feelings and not be forever ruined. In fact, it is the opposite.

Each moment you repress your feelings you allow negative, anxious energy to be stored within you. Each feeling you bottle up creates more internal tension, and eventually you will need to release your pressure valve. If you don't know how to do this in a healthy way, you may automatically start developing negative behaviours and issues.

Once you acknowledge your feelings and allow yourself to fully experience them, you can release them. In doing so, your interlinked body, mind, emotions and soul will thank you enormously, creating more spaciousness and light. This release enables you to breathe freely once again, often removing the knot or pressure in your chest.

I promise you, you will feel lighter, more connected to yourself and more loving towards yourself. And this is when the magical moments of peace, joy and happiness start to appear through the cracks of despair. You can then access some more free space to remember your Loved One fondly.

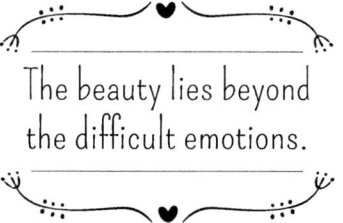

> The beauty lies beyond the difficult emotions.

Feeling your feelings may well be the one part of the entire process that is the most challenging, and rightly so. It is, however, the master key to moving forward. The beauty lies beyond the difficult and hurtful emotions. The love that has been gifted to you is there under all the pain. Working through the pain will give a chance for the love to emerge, in time.

Some feelings and emotions can be frightening and constantly command your attention. You could run and hide, but they will chase you down till they are heard, creating all sorts of disharmony until you stop and listen. Once you have experienced their intensity a few times, it becomes easier to accept them. And it is easier if you know how to deal with them, or at least just permit them to send their grieving energy through your body without resistance.

It was not till I lost my dad that I understood the depth and intensity of losing someone you love so much. At times, my mourning had me huddled in a ball, hugging my knees to try to reduce its intensity, willing it to go away. It begged me to let it out, and so I did. The intensity shocked me. I had never experienced such a forceful and penetrating feeling before. I felt I was losing control. But I eventually handed the reins over and surrendered to experiencing the feelings as part of my grief journey. This enabled the deep grief and emotional pain to slowly clear. I had to learn to do this with a whole rainbow of emotions such as anger, frustration and sadness that surfaced over time, begging me to feel them.

Anxiety also surfaced amongst a plethora of fears. I feared I wouldn't be able to cope and that I would forget my dad or aspects of my dad. I feared life would never be the same and I would be unbalanced and grieving forever. I now know that anxiety is a normal human emotion, particularly during a stressful situation. It is your thoughts creating havoc in your mind, throwing all kinds of 'What if...' questions your way that bring up deep worries. The symptoms of anxiety are agonising and torment you, which is why most people try to run and hide from them. Anxious thoughts at their worst can be ludicrous. They are like a big scary monster, but once you face them head on, like a school bully in the playground, they normally back down.

GRIEF, GRACE AND GRATITUDE

Anxiety demands authenticity when you are being inauthentic. Feeling highly stressed, people pleasing and not listening to your needs will see anxiety heighten even further. The more you ignore and repress the anxiety, the more it will increase. In heightened anxiety, your body will scream at you to listen. It wants you to slow down and acknowledge what you are feeling. It will continue till you choose to hear its message.

When you choose to listen, anxiety can teach you many things. It turned out to be my guiding star, leading me to turn inward and look after myself. Until I had this epiphany I needed to deal with the anxiety and grief attacks as best I could. And there were many.

The anger and frustration surfaced, and it was hard for me to wrap my head around them, and even harder to just let them be. Each moment I felt either angry, cranky or irritable. It was an extremely uncomfortable consequence of grief. I learnt to be in the moment of the feeling, whatever that happened to be. I learnt to accept and surrender to it. When I did, things inside gradually shifted and improved.

Burying your anger will keep toxic energy running through you and possibly complicate your grief. It will eat you up inside and make it impossible to access the love and other emotions housed within you. Accepting that anger is a part of the grief journey can allow your anger to move through you. Yell, vent and scream; do whatever you need to clear the anger energy. When you move the anger, it will start to fade. You may notice things are a little better and that you feel a little lighter. This will enable you to access and harness the emotions that lay beneath the anger, like sadness.

The sadness I experienced was the gift I relished beyond the anger and the anxiety. It enabled me to get in touch with my vulnerability and my hurt. The hurt was so deep and heartbreaking, but I was finally ready to acknowledge this and cried endless streams of tears over what I had lost: Dad! I sat with my tears, allowing them to purify my soul with the love I had for Dad.

IN THE PINK PROCESS

I savoured the sadness and allowed myself to immerse in the warm haven it provided. I allowed my sadness to spill into a chasm of tears. I treasured their message and purpose. I realised that my sadness represented all the love I had lost, and for that I valued it. It was all my love for Dad rising to be felt. A softness and gentleness appeared within, allowing me to feel closer to my soul.

I was waking up to the love. My love!

I finally realised what was so important: *love!* I truly realised it, not just in theory but as a deep, heartfelt love running through me. And that love included the piece of love my dad had infused into my heart when he left. I cherish this piece beyond measure.

Like me, you may experience so many emotions waiting to surface to allow healing to start. They will come with pain, suffering, insights, lessons and finally, much later, love. That I can assure you! My emotional rainbow included many more difficult feelings and emotions than I ever imagined until that loss. Unleashing these, however, gave rise to a new range of loving and spectacular emotions.

By feeling the full spectre of your negative emotions, you get to experience the entire rainbow of emotions. Feel the anxiety, anger, sadness, and all the emotions in between and around, then the loving emotions follow soon afterwards.

Use this ITP step of feeling the feelings to tap into the beautiful, loving and miraculous emotions buried below. To process grief there is no way around this; it is the master key to your healing and happiness. If you can only learn one lesson let this be it.

Allowing yourself to feel your emotions is the biggest gift you can give yourself. It will bring healing, connection to your Loved One, a deeper connection to yourself and ultimately a richer life. It brings you closer to your true essence – the self that is shining brightly below the suffering. The beautiful true you!

To integrate grief fully into your being, each feeling that arises needs to be given space and respect to move through you. To process your feelings, firstly stop. Be aware of what is swilling around inside; feel the emotions as you immerse yourself in them. As they arise naturally, express them: cry, yell, scream, laugh. Repeat as needed. Healing will take place each time.

Process = STOP, Be aware, Feel, Express, Heal.

Most importantly, remember to be gentle with yourself. One step at a time. Don't push yourself. You are in a learning phase, and when we learn new lessons we are sometimes clunky. Let yourself make mistakes, and in time and with practice, living life in your new way will become easier, more familiar and more natural.

Pink Butterfly Tips

- Feeling emotions is the key to healing.
- Repression and suppression heighten anxiety.
- Anger hides other emotions.
- A beautiful love is buried below the grief rainbow of emotions.
- Process = STOP, Be aware, Feel, Express, Heal.

Pink Grief Corner – Question time

The questions below will take you directly into your feelings.

Stop and take three deep breaths. Honour yourself with patience, gentleness and a compassionate spirit. Come from a place of love: your love and the love of your Loved One. The whole point is *love!*

Record your feelings in your Pink Grief Journal:

Remember, just do what you can.

1. Do you feel like you are in shock or denial? If so, what are you in denial about?
2. Do you feel angry? If so, what do you feel angry about?
3. Do you feel you are bargaining? If... I will...
4. Do you feel depressed? If so, what depresses you?
5. Do you feel scared? If so, what scares you the most?
6. Do you feel sad? If so, what creates the most sadness?
7. Do you feel alone? If so, how can you feel more connected?
8. What is the feeling that is most prominent right now?
9. List any other feelings that you are experiencing.
10. Are you allowing your emotions to surface?
11. Are you using avoidance tactics? If so, what are they?

12. Are you scared to feel your emotions? If so, what are you afraid of?
13. Where is your grief rising from; what part of the body? Notice what it is doing.

Review the words and feelings you have expressed and take some time out.

Having gained an understanding of your feelings, you can move on to the next step of the ITP Process that creates freedom: Forgiveness.

In the Pink

By honouring your anger, you can learn to love.
By facing your anxieties, you can flourish and thrive.
By feeling your sadness, you can feel your happiness.
By acting responsibly for your grief,
you will start to move past it.
By expressing your emotions, you will become unstuck.
By walking through the darkness, you will head
towards calm, peace and acceptance.
At the end of the grief rainbow is a beautiful, pure *love!*

ITP Step 4: Forgiveness

Forgiveness is tricky! During your grief, you may be angry and blame a myriad of people: doctors, nurses, family, friends, God, the family dog, yourself and even your Loved One. Yet for true healing, it is necessary to understand how forgiveness is the kindest and most compassionate gift to yourself. Forgiveness puts your heart at peace and allows you to find small openings for the warmth and love to flow in.

Some of the blame may be absurdly irrational and just a response to the depth of your hurt. You may need to find someone to blame and you could lash out at others – anyone – to dispel your anger and to find a reason for this disaster.

Some of the blame may be totally just and apportioned exactly where it should have been. People may have done the wrong thing, acted against their values or your values, said the wrong thing, made a mistake, and hurt you or your Loved One. That is now in the past.

Some of the blame may be attributed to the Loved One you lost. How could they die and leave you behind and cause all the hurt or maybe a mess to clean up? This style of thinking starts the rollercoaster of guilt or regret, bringing with it more complex emotions. All the emotions start piling up like a giant Jenga waiting to topple over.

Grief can make you feel like you are going crazy. Your mind is not your own. Grief hijacks most of your common sense, and for a while you are on grief autopilot. Being angry with your Loved One can create anger towards yourself for being angry at them. It can be a vicious circle and cycle of grief. Self-forgiveness will be your salvation.

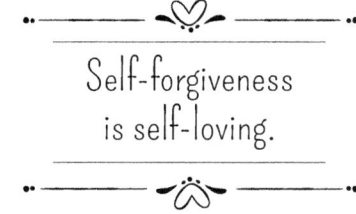

Self-forgiveness is self-loving.

GRIEF, GRACE AND GRATITUDE

Whoever you blame, keeping the anger and blame tucked inside will only cause more damage to your already fragile soul. Forgiveness changes this!

With Dad, I was lucky that I didn't have anyone to forgive in the wake of his passing. I had time with him to say what I needed and wanted. The doctors and nurses were excellent and did everything they could to make him comfortable. As far as losing someone goes, in the respect of blame I was free. I was angry at the world, which is normal, but there was no one to whom I apportioned blame and anger and needed to forgive.

I did seek self-forgiveness later, though, for running myself into the ground. My ignorance in trying to survive affected my health. My Type A personality traits (being a doing junkie, a perfectionist and a list ticker) all came to the surface during my grief, despite working on this a lot over the past decade. I wanted everything, including my grief, sorted quickly and took on a lot of the responsibilities myself. Pushing myself so hard while grieving took its toll on me and was categorically not self-loving. I had to learn again how to be self-loving and nurse my grief; it took a while.

Forgiveness had always been one of my most difficult issues to deal with. I struggled with it, so I understood its complexity. I would stubbornly stand my ground; it was my way or no way. A completely irrational and unjust perspective that I learnt to overcome the hard way. Eventually I learned that it is not always about being right or apportioning blame. It is about living your life with a peaceful inner self free from burdens and suffering. Forgiveness provides this!

Forgiveness is a beautiful gift with a colourful bow allowing you to acknowledge what has happened and to let it go. Forgiveness enables you to untie the bonds and attachments to a person, a decision, thoughts or a situation that keep you stuck in blaming mode.

IN THE PINK PROCESS

If you can untie the attachments, it will in turn remove the resentment, bitterness and toxic energy that it has been generating, allowing the inner wounds to heal. Following true forgiveness brings lightness and spaciousness inside that feels white, pure, tender and loving.

It is a choice to forgive but not an easy one! Some people find it is easier to remain in blame towards others because blame is a precursor for not accepting responsibility or knowing how to heal healthily. Not wanting to move forward, you remain locked in limbo land where you have the convenience of something to focus on other than yourself.

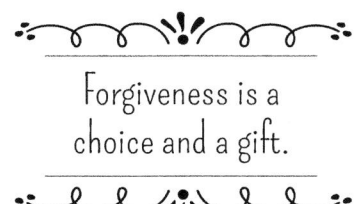

> Forgiveness is a choice and a gift.

Residing in blame mode and refusing to contemplate forgiveness is another guise for not moving forward. You willingly give control to others to manage your life and your feelings. You can remain stuck in blame where you are angry and miserable rather than planning strategies or ideas to step you forward in your grief journey. You may not know how to move forward, so staying there in blame mode may be what you know and are comfortable with.

Your comfort zones can be uncomfortable, but they are familiar and feel safer than stepping out into foreign territory – even if it dangles a chance of a better life and a better state of feeling. As humans we like what we know regardless of its uneasiness.

An uncomfortable comfortableness eats away at your spirit slowly and destroys your energy, passion and light, keeping your spirit broken and fragmented. Down this path you end up staying in the blame and the pain. Inner love and peace remain elusive and you become miserable and negative. It may likely be the easiest way out but far from the loving and responsible way out. Your life is out of your control and at mercy of your anger and irrationality.

On the other side is forgiveness and a heart that recognises it wants to heal. It accepts that things happen and over time finds space for forgiveness. The empty void that appears once the blame and anger are removed by forgiveness is filled with warm, tender emotions, love and a sense of peace. This allows you to spend time remembering and honouring your Loved One; it's a gift you will carry for a lifetime.

Forgiveness, and more so self-forgiveness, is such a courageous and loving thing to give yourself. It is a brave person that commits to their healing journey and seeks a resolution through the gift of forgiveness. Can you choose to be that person?

Pink Grief Corner – True or False?

Read and contemplate the statements below. Next to each one tick if you think it is true or false for you. There are no right or wrong answers. This exercise simply creates more awareness of what is happening inside you and gives you a chance to re-evaluate where you are at in your journey to forgiveness.

Stop and take three deep breaths. Honour yourself with patience, gentleness and a compassionate spirit. Come from a place of love: your love and the love of your Loved One. The whole point is *love!*

Record your feelings in your Pink Grief Journal:

Statement	True	False
Everyone needs forgiveness.		
I can forgive others.		
I can forgive myself.		
Forgiveness is a gift.		
I am willing to seek forgiveness.		

Statement con't	True	False
Forgiveness will accelerate my healing and erase bitterness.		
Forgiveness will release some internal pressure and create space.		
Forgiveness will raise my energy levels.		
I find forgiveness hard.		
Others deserve forgiveness.		
I deserve forgiveness.		
People generally do not intentionally mean to hurt me.		
It takes courage to find forgiveness.		
If I forgive, I can move forward in my healing.		
If I choose not to forgive, I will remain stuck in toxic emotions.		
I have genuinely forgiven others before and can do it again.		
Finding forgiveness is worth it to release the negativity.		
I want to find forgiveness.		
My life would improve if I could forgive.		

HOW TO FIND FORGIVENESS

How much we can forgive others aligns with how much we love ourselves. When we truly love ourselves, we won't live with bitterness and resentment running rampant within. Learning to love yourself more will guide you to forgive naturally and to remove the negative toxins of anger and non-forgiveness.

Yes, it is tricky to forgive but not impossible. Pondering these thoughts and the following strategies may help you change your perception and move you towards forgiveness and a calmer, more peaceful existence. Forgiving makes space for a life filled with more love.

Think about the good qualities the person who you wish to forgive possesses. You may feel like only focusing on the negatives, but this does not help to soothe your sorrowful soul. Showing compassion and gentleness for their human misgivings can. Using affirmations such as 'They did the best they could at the time with what they knew' may help shift your perception and bring you to a more understanding place.

Think back to a time when you made a mistake or sought forgiveness. How did you feel? How did you approach the person you needed forgiveness from? How did you feel when you received their forgiveness? Putting yourself in the shoes of the person needing forgiveness helps you to understand that we all make mistakes and are all human.

Try to remember the last time you forgave someone and how this was possible. What did you do to come to this forgiveness? Is there something you did on that occasion that can help you in this situation?

Thinking about the person who you need to forgive, are you expecting too much from them? Are you placing them in a position that sets them up to fail? Maybe you know they do not have the capacity to live to your expectations. Each person has a different level of emotional maturity. Accepting this and accepting people for who they are, and their limited or not limited capacities, helps us to remove judgement and introduce compassion.

You may think someone's actions are a direct result of them wanting to hurt you. But most likely it has nothing to do with you and everything to do with what they are capable of. They may just be trying to get through their day as best they can.

Check to see if your anger is not misdirected. Sometimes we fire our anger at others to protect us from looking at our anger towards ourselves or the sadness buried below that anger. It is easier to be angry at someone else than ourselves. Be honest for your heart's sake.

In a nutshell, we all make mistakes; we are only human. We do get to choose to eradicate the bitterness and toxins running inside us by forgiving and creating space for love and peace. Remember, this does not mean you have to have this person in your life, but it allows you to take control and release the attachment from the other person.

Empower your heart by integrating this information to find a way to forgive, learn more about yourself, move out of your comfort zone, find forgiveness in your heart and take another step towards healing your grief.

PINK BUTTERFLY TIPS

- Forgiveness is a gift.
- Forgiveness is part of the healing process.
- Forgiveness creates freedom.
- Forgiveness brings light and space.
- Forgiveness allows you to find love.

Pink Grief Corner – Letter writing

The forgiveness letter is another well-known technique to help release anger and blame and find forgiveness. Find a quiet space and remove any distractions. Light a candle or put on some soulful music that will help you tap into your emotions. Give yourself time and aloneness to complete this exercise. You need to be connected to your heart and your truth to receive the most benefit from your letter.

Remember, your letter is private. You do not need to give it to anyone unless you want to. It is purely for your own benefit and healing.

Think about the person who you need to forgive and what harm they caused you. Tell your story even if it appears irrational. Describe what has happened since the event, what you have learnt and how you will continue after the letter is written.

This letter works well also if you need to forgive yourself.

Stop and take three deep breaths. Honour yourself with patience, gentleness and a compassionate spirit. Come from a place of love: your love and the love of your Loved One. The whole point is *love!*

Record your feelings in your Pink Grief Journal:

Consider the questions below as pointers to get started.

1. Who is the person you wish to forgive?
2. What harm did they cause you?
3. How is your heart hurting?

IN THE PINK PROCESS

4. What have they cost you in your life?
5. What emotions do they trigger in you?
6. Why do you want to forgive them?
7. What steps will you take to forgive?
8. How will you benefit from forgiving them?
9. Will forgiving them remove the negativity and pain from your heart?
10. What steps will you take after you have forgiven?

At the end of your letter write a forgiveness summary statement; for example, 'Dear Chris, ... I forgive you for... because...'

Seal the letter and file it away or destroy it.

Now it is important to go and do something nice for yourself. Bask in a moment of purity and light, and allow the forgiveness to wash over you, removing the toxins inside. Watch for the spaciousness to appear, which it will if you have truly forgiven.

Do not be surprised if the gift of forgiveness brings with it healing tears. It is a monumental gift of love to yourself. Be proud of yourself for receiving it. Well done! As you allow forgiveness to wash over you, you can move on to the last step of the ITP Process, which walks you to your new life: Acceptance.

ITP Step 5: Acceptance

Acceptance brings a loving kind of inner light. At this stage, when you arrive at acceptance, you are likely to have moved through the nasty grief attacks and emotions and have settled into a space where you understand what has happened. You accept this is now your new reality.

This does not mean you will stop crying streams of tears. It does not mean you are happy about life as you now know it. It does not mean you don't want things as they were, and it does not mean everything is rosy. What it means is that you have accepted your reality and things feel real again, even though it isn't necessarily a nice real. You will have awareness of and understand your feelings, thoughts and behaviours and how to look after yourself as you continue through your grief journey.

You have had time to allow the grief to wash over your soul, bringing both love and devastation. You have allowed yourself to think about and feel your grief. You have found awareness, taken responsibility, felt your feelings and found forgiveness. You have honoured and thought much about your Loved One. You will have gained some clarity around their death and any ponderings about life and mortality, maybe your own or just in general, that have arisen because of your loss.

Acceptance brings clarity.

Your acceptance can bring clarity around your situation and with it an inner calm, helping you to stop resisting and fighting your grief. You may still swing back to the other stages, but life is starting to get a little easier and you recognise your world once again.

In taking time to think about acceptance and your journey, you can make good use of the lessons about yourself and the grief journey as you move on without your Loved One. You now have an

IN THE PINK PROCESS

opportunity to review, redesign and redecorate your life. Anything is possible when you have acceptance. You are nearing the latter part of the grief journey and can walk forward with more ease.

It is living in the present moment and fully acknowledging your loss that you can find acceptance. You no longer live in denial; you are present in the acceptance phase of grief despite still mourning your Loved One. You have taken responsibility for your life, your loss and your actions. Once responsibility is found acceptance is not far behind.

At the acceptance stage you will feel healthier. You will have more energy and your mind will feel freer to think and do other things besides living with grief. Slowly you will start to assimilate back into your world, albeit a different one.

It took me a long time to reach the acceptance stage, but I knew when I had because life became a little lighter. My extroverted side started to reappear, and my introverted side was happy to nestle back quietly inwards.

A little part of me felt warm and glowing, and my heart and soul were tiptoeing lightly through my body rather than trudging. I became a little excited about going places and doing things. At first this seemed foreign as I had not looked forward to anything for a long time. It was a sign that my internal landscape was turning a big corner.

I felt more confident again and that I had dropped the veil of protection that was keeping me safe. I was opening up to others and didn't feel everything was a sad event. I focused again on the positives before the negatives and the good before the bad. I stopped anticipating the worst at every corner.

I stopped worrying about getting hurt again. Realistically I knew I would be hurt again, but I had learnt I can cope with anything. This made me want to give and receive more love than ever before. Because that is the point!

Grief, Grace and Gratitude

Love is the point!

I had changed. I was becoming a more compassionate and gentle person with a balance of self-confidence and poise, knowing that now I could live through anything. Anything was possible. I could go, be, see and feel everything and anything. This excited me.

I learnt that regardless of how much it had hurt to lose Dad, the hurt was worth all the love. Without the hurt there would have been no love. I was going to open myself up again for as much love as I could muster without fearing the losses. They would come again, but when they did I would be better equipped to deal with them, and I would be more self-loving to allow the grief journey to take place whenever it needed to.

For me, this all just materialised slowly until one day I noticed all these changes. It was a lovely feeling. I felt my dad with me as I made the internal transformation, and I felt he was pleased I had chosen to live my life fully, authentically, lovingly and peacefully once again. He would have wanted that so much.

I still broke down into tears regularly. Things that before did not upset me now brought instant tears – things like beauty. All things of beauty still have me welling up. Memories of Dad bring tears of joy and sadness that leave a sweet, beautiful aftertaste.

My heart has become more tender and sensitive to its surroundings in a good way. This tender side is full of wonderment. I have become more loving and connected to myself, and I continue to feel connected to my dad. He lives in me. The love he gave me when he left has been added to the love I already had for him, and this has amplified our love and connection. I know this connection will remain with me throughout my lifetime and beyond.

IN THE PINK PROCESS

Pink Butterfly Tips

- Acceptance takes time and work.
- Acceptance brings you to your new reality.
- Acceptance still brings tears.
- Acceptance lets you live your life again.
- Acceptance brings love and light.

Pink Grief Corner – Question Time

Reviewing and pondering the questions below will help you to move towards acceptance.

Stop and take three deep breaths. Honour yourself with patience, gentleness and a compassionate spirit. Come from a place of love: your love and the love of your Loved One. The whole point is *love!*

Record your feelings in your Pink Grief Journal:

1. Do you accept your new reality?
2. Are you willing to feel the acceptance of your new reality?
3. What five things can you do to help you find acceptance of your new reality?

4. Will you accept your new reality when the time is right?

Ponder your answers and explore how you feel about your new reality. Are you nearing acceptance? Acceptance is not an easy step and will most likely happen further along your grief journey.

Once you do have acceptance your life will begin to change. If you have flushed out the grief and followed your journey authentically, you will feel light and uplifted. You will begin to expand and test your butterfly wings, feeling the wind beneath them and getting them ready to fly you into your new future.

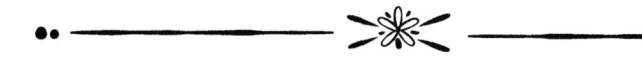

I am learning

I am learning to have awareness of my feelings, my thoughts, my behaviours, my grief and my experience.
I am learning to take responsibility and ownership for myself and my life.
I am learning to feel, process and express all my feelings.
I am learning to forgive, stop blaming and remove negative emotions with compassion.
I am learning to find acceptance and clarity.
I am learning to honour myself and have self-love;
I am learning how to be on my grief journey.

In the Pink Process reflection

"Tears are the silent language of grief."

—Voltaire

Rising from the bench, you stretch your arms skywards, knowing you have come to the end of the ITP Process and its many steps to help you through your grief journey. You feel totally drained yet hopeful. There is so much to do and to feel on this grief journey.

Listening to the water flow down the creek, you allow the learnings and ponderings to come together and assimilate within you, just like the water flowing to a new destination, surrendering to its path.

The different stops in the Forest of Grief help you understand that the grief journey and the rainbow of emotions are not grasped or processed overnight. Grief takes its time – lots of time.

Tapping the wind chimes together so the butterflies can create their harmonious melody, you remember the five steps: Awareness, Responsibility, Feeling, Forgiveness and Acceptance. You get up to leave and notice it's getting dark and you need somewhere to sleep. You gather your things, leave some seeds on the bench for your friendly critter companion and on you go, following the next 'Love' arrow signpost.

Just when you think you have had enough for one day, at the end of the creek you step over the water and back onto the path. The next twist on the path brings you to a small opening that surprises you with a pretty cabin surrounded by empty planter boxes.

A worn bench sits near the front door next to an old raggedy doormat. You are happy there is somewhere to rest for a moment, with proper shelter and maybe electricity and a warm shower.

You can see this cabin has been meticulously hand built by someone special. It is so cute for this dark, eerie part of the forest. Although aspects are run down, an element of love and care radiates from its walls.

It's a little piece of beauty in the desolate, dreary place you have been travelling through. You walk to the front door and knock gently, quietly hoping someone will answer; you are craving company and a break from your isolation.

No answer!

You turn the handle and slowly open the door. The cabin is old and a bit run down inside but warm and inviting. Stepping over the doormat tentatively in case you are intruding, you still can't work out yet if anyone lives there. It has a kitchen with appliances, a couch with some old throw rugs and a fireplace stocked with wood.

A few black-and-white pictures adorn the walls and a bookcase houses an abundance of reading material beckoning you to inspect all on offer. Next you see the first bit of colour in the centre of the room: the hugest vase bursting with fresh pink and white roses in full bloom. The cabin invites you in; you just feel this is all for you.

On the rug in front of you is an embroidery of a big, beautiful white butterfly and some words:

The Forest of Grief welcomes
you to the Cabin of Love

You sit on the couch, relieved, but not before you select a herbal tea and turn the kettle on. You have never been so happy to see a kettle.

IN THE PINK PROCESS

You feel relieved that the signs and grief journey have brought you exactly to where you are meant to be, starting with the first signpost with the arrow pointing towards love. You sense deeply that the next lesson is even bigger, and you obviously need a better and more comfortable space to absorb its wisdom and gifts.

You light the fire and sip on your tea. Shortly after you head to bed, expecting tomorrow will be a big day as you move closer towards healing.

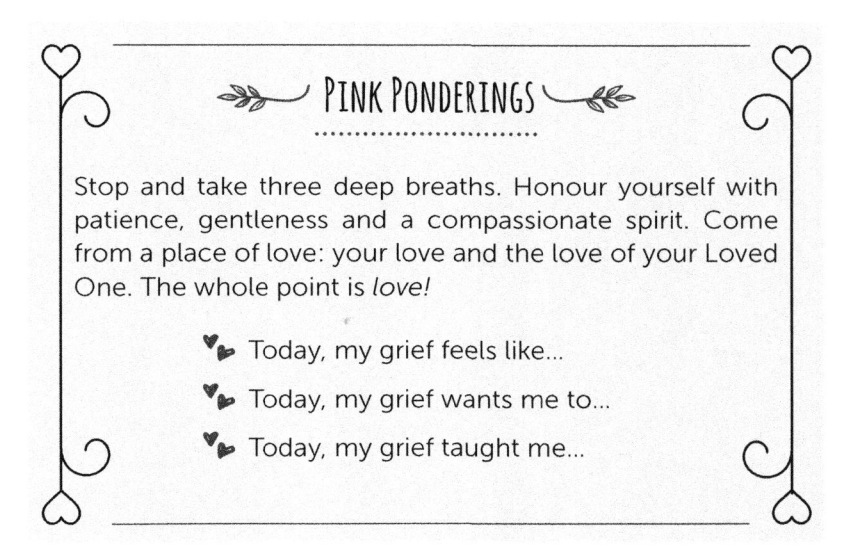

> ## Pink Ponderings
>
> Stop and take three deep breaths. Honour yourself with patience, gentleness and a compassionate spirit. Come from a place of love: your love and the love of your Loved One. The whole point is *love!*
>
> - Today, my grief feels like...
> - Today, my grief wants me to...
> - Today, my grief taught me...

PATH OF GOODBYE

"The best and most beautiful things in the world cannot be seen nor even touched, but just felt in the heart."

—Helen Keller

Waking up slightly more refreshed than of late, you look forward to today's lessons and get out of bed to shower and eat. It's cold inside. The fire is smouldering but nearly out, so you rug up to stay warm.

In the kitchen there is a note asking you to stoke the fire, brew a pot of tea, get two cups, relax and wait! So that's what you do. Not long afterwards you are startled by a knock on the door. Finding your legs, you walk past the pink and white roses and inhale their beautiful aroma, eager to see who is out here in this forest with you. It has been lonely aside from your critter friend.

At the door is an elegant, pretty lady, all rugged up in her winter clothes. She stands with poise and radiates love and wisdom. Her warm, glowing smile envelops you, yet you sense a hint of sadness – a mirror of what you are feeling.

She doesn't need to say anything as you welcome her in. She just wraps her arms around you and pulls you in, hugging you tenderly. You know she has come as the next part of your grief journey and *feel she is carrying the next lesson close to her heart. Confidently and gracefully she walks over to the couch as if she has been here before.*

As you hand her a cup of tea she smiles sweetly and quietly utters, "Hello gorgeous, welcome to the Cabin of Love. I hope you like the flowers I specially choose for you. Please be comfortable as the next lesson is about to begin. I am here to listen and support you while you share your grief love story. Through sharing and recounting your story you may be better able to process your grief".

The 'Path of Goodbye' following the loss of your Loved One is a long, winding and bumpy trek with stops, turns and detours. There is no grief map. Each time you go from the moment of a last breath to the first snippets of hope and acceptance, the road is unique to you and your particular loss. Even for the same person each incidence of grief will be different to their last.

Grief leaves you in the dark, trying to muddle through its randomness. A grief mud map would be nice and handy so that you knew exactly what you would encounter. You could predict and plan the sideswipes thrown at you and prepare meticulously to walk your way through the forest of never-ending sorrow.

Unfortunately, the reality is that you are thrown onto a path that is elusive till you take the first step. Then it remains mysterious until each new step is taken. There is a guide, some reference notes from previous journeys and a beautiful set of butterfly wings. But you are still left aching for more.

Feeling crushed you are left to deal with your grief, emotions, broken spirit and heartbreak. Alongside the emotional maze you may also need to arrange your Loved One's funeral and affairs. This involves having to put on another grief hat. You must utilise your organisational and decision-making abilities when your stress levels are at their highest, your self-esteem has plummeted, your heart screams for peace and your energy levels are seriously obliterated.

You are compelled to contemplate the logistics of the funeral and the million and one things that are entwined with arranging that, like belongings and the memories each piece brings. The estate and the lawyer speak to finalise their affairs. For me, all these big decisions needed to be made without the one person who would normally help me by my side. Adding all these elements of a massive to-do list to the grief mix can send the most logical and rational person headlong into stress, anxiety and depression.

The emotions are still raging around your body while you try and keep them controlled under the surface, if only for a moment to, say, make a phone call to arrange something on your checklist. Sometimes the call may end with you in tears at just mentioning the passing, and other times it only ends in frustration from keeping the tears at bay.

My head felt so full of pressure I was scared I couldn't cope and that one more minor detail or shred of information would ruin me. I was terrified of the phone ringing or someone asking me to do one more little thing. I was overstimulated and on high alert to anything that could add to this internal pressure and send me over the edge.

Whenever my stress levels had seriously surpassed their threshold, however, I was granted right at that moment some added inner strength that prevented me from completely losing myself and my mind, and I miraculously got through it. This deep inner fortitude arose from a constant core belief that I would be able to cope no matter what. I was guided forward to the next moment while balancing my high stress levels. I believe we are built to cope with these difficult times. I see an element of truth in the statement: 'Maybe you are never sent more than you can deal with.'

The grief journey didn't totally ruin me in the long run; however, there was a time when I did feel completely ruined. That's grief! At those tricky times, I used my dad's butterfly wings to lift me up and steer me through. Just!

As you visit the different stops on the Path of Goodbye that are to follow, I will share my story and you will have an opportunity to share your grief story in your Pink Grief Corner. At those times I encourage you to imagine you are in the cabin with the pretty lady. Imagine she is your fairy godmother, if you wish, or your favourite aunt.

You will be asked to sit quietly, remember, and reflect on your story and your Loved One at these stops relevant to your journey, for example, 'anticipatory grief', 'lead-up', 'final day', 'final breath', funeral preparations', 'the funeral day', 'after the funeral' and so on. Remember what happened, how you felt and your memories. As you retell your story you are giving yourself a beautiful gift by honouring yourself and your grief, allowing it to surface. It can then be felt, processed, expressed and assimilated, walking you closer towards healing.

Sharing stories helps us to feel less alone and to acknowledge that others are travelling or have travelled a similar journey – and have made it through. Sharing stories is one of the purposes of my butterfly wings that I give to you, to allow you to share, to listen, and to help lift and carry you through this difficult time.

Sharing all the parts of your story will be a hard exercise. In recalling memories and the tough times, you may feel sorrow deep within your heart. That is where you can begin to find the love and ability to heal.

If you are not ready to share in the exercises to follow, honour yourself and revisit them later when you feel more able. At any destination on the Path of Goodbye, if you have not yet reached the mentioned point in your grief journey, you may also like to leave the section till later. Only do what you feel is right for you at any time through your grief journey. Listen to what your quiet voice inside is telling you.

Remember, honour yourself with patience, gentleness and a compassionate spirit. Come from a place of love: your love and the love of your Loved One. The whole point is *love!* Record your feelings in your Pink Grief Journal as you reach each stop.

Anticipatory grief

Anticipatory grief is the grief that appears as soon as you know a death is imminent. The emotions can be the same as grief after a death but are coupled with grief at the loss of the person's abilities, cognition, hope and functioning as well as the loss of your current reality, future events, hopes and dreams.

Added stress may be placed upon you if you are a carer for your Loved One. Being surrounded by the reality of the impending loss and living it every moment is highly traumatic. Let me share my anticipatory grief experience…

♡♡♡♡♡♡♡♡♡♡

"Hi Dad, what happened?" was all I asked when Dad called me after a visit to his doctor.

He had not been himself on our Italy trip a month prior. On our return home, tests revealed something potentially suspicious. We were patiently waiting on results. I expected the doctor would find some innocent ailment and send Dad on his way with a prescription and an exorbitant consultation bill.

Living in naive denial while waiting on these results helped me continue to live my normal life. Surely, I had nothing to worry about, not yet anyway. Dad was invincible after all. Little did I know the difference one phone call could make!

After an extended pause, the words "It's inoperable" came through the phone in a shaky voice so unlike my dad's. These were not the words I expected nor the words my dad was ever meant to say. I could tell he was confused. As I was breaking down each piece of information and absorbing his words, trying to realise their enormity, he cut the call off. "I'll speak to you later, Lara."

I was stunned. Lost for words. I am sure he was too.

I felt like my life, my mind, my heart and my spirit changed. Everything felt foggy. I couldn't concentrate and things didn't feel real. I didn't know what this meant for him, for me or for our family.

Speaking later, Dad had regained some control and sounded like his normal self, probably to try to lift the mood and quell my fears – forever the protector. He even tried injecting a little laughter into the conversation where possible, which only alleviated the dread for a moment. The underlying energy on the phone was fear and love – his and mine.

The moment I realised we were on a time frame to say goodbye to my father, the grief started. To be more technical, anticipatory grief lodged inside me. I had to accept this new reality. According to the professionals, he had anywhere from six months to two years to live.

To deal with the truth (or not deal with it) I convinced myself we had up to five years. I was playing God and creating my own version of his illness and his time left with our family. I was in the bargaining stage. My dad always taught me to bargain. He was very thrifty – a bartering extraordinaire. Maybe it was just hereditary to ask for a better deal.

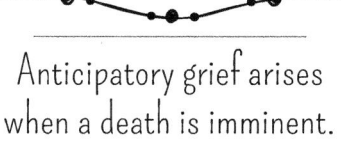

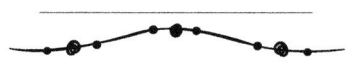

Anticipatory grief arises when a death is imminent.

Disappointedly, I was wrong. We ended up with eighteen months together. We made the most of every minute despite the grief hanging over our heads.

PATH OF GOODBYE

It became mentally and physically exhausting being on heightened alert to every phone call, preparing for the worst, jumping to help when needed, planning things, preparing affairs and visiting once or twice a day in some instances.

My family enjoyed all the moments with Dad, even the moments that were filled with joint tears as we bonded over words that had never been spoken before, beliefs that had never been shared, memories that we would treasure, and emotions that rose to surprise and awaken us. We learnt a lot about Dad and ourselves in these special yet devastating months.

Each family member was walking through the anticipatory grief on slightly different paths. But we would all reach the same patch where Dad would no longer be. There we would remain standing together but alone, without him.

We were there to support each other and be each other's butterfly wings as each of ours weakened at different times. We lifted each up other as best we could and attempted to keep the pieces of ourselves and our family unit glued together.

The time fled by as Dad went through medications and treatment regimes. It was beautiful yet harrowing. It was bonding at its best, and it was distressing and stressful. It was loving and traumatic. It was grief!

It was our close-knit family trying to come to terms with the reality, living through a poignant time as best we could and striving to enjoy all the precious moments knowing they would soon be memories.

We felt so much love. We had so much fun. We felt so much grief. It was exhausting yet lovingly memorable. This is what anticipatory grief is like.

> ## Pink Grief Corner – Share your story
>
> You may or may not have dealt with anticipatory grief in your grief journey as everyone's journey is different. If you did suffer anticipatory grief, it is important to recognise it as an integral part of the grief journey. Being aware of how you felt at this time and how it impacted your experience is a beneficial part of the healing journey.
>
> Stop and take three deep breaths. Honour yourself with patience, gentleness and a compassionate spirit. Come from a place of love: your love and the love of your Loved One. The whole point is *love!*
>
> Share your story!
>
> Write your story of anticipatory grief
> in your Pink Grief Journal.

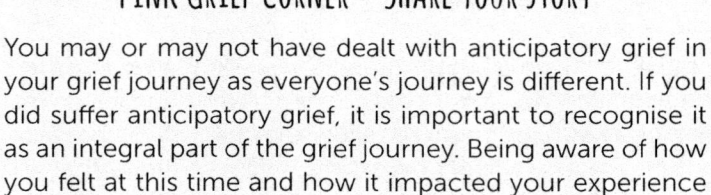

Lead-up

Some people have a lead-up to their loss and have time to prepare and get things in order. For some their experience of loss comes with no warning. Let me share what happened in the lead-up to my father's passing...

♥♥♥♥♥♥♥♥♥♥

Nearing the end of the eighteen months, Dad was hospitalised on three separate occasions. The first two times we were told he may not make it. As a family we prepared for the worst as best we could.

After the hospital managed his pain, his fighting spirit saw him orchestrate his return home. The third time he was frailer and his fighting spirit was flailing. Sadly, he did not go home again. The day before he passed away, he was not very responsive but managed to get out most of the I-love-you statement before I went home for the evening. His final words to me were "I love you". All that mattered was that his last words to me were ones of love.

The whole point is *love!*

The lead-up to his death had its benefits and gifts. The biggest gift was the ability to really talk as a family. Dad's heart burst open with love even more when he knew he only had a little time left. 'I love you' became part of his everyday vocabulary, echoing straight from the hub of his heart to ours every time we spoke. Invisible family bonds of love became stronger every day.

With grace and poise, he spent precious energy sharing stories from his younger years, reminiscing excitedly about his life, and finding the purpose, gratitude and value in his time here. It had its ups and downs, but most of all it was encased with the unwavering love surrounding him.

As he spoke with gusto about his life, his face lit up and warmed our hearts. His life purpose had been fulfilled. He had lived his passions, his hobbies and his business but mostly his family. A family man to his core, he was the most grateful and passionate about his family. He was happiest when he was with us, his joy just flowing out.

Over the months, he became more prepared. He was coming closer to accepting that he was near the end of his life. He did not want to leave but did not want to live in the pain. It was no longer the life he knew and loved.

Grief, Grace and Gratitude

Struggling with your own mortality brings contemplation as you look to the future, unsure of where you go and what happens to you next. Questions arise to ensure you have lived the life you wanted to, taken all the opportunities, felt the love, said all the words, laughed all the laughs, seen everything, been a good person, lived up to your expectations, given to others, lived your purpose, been authentic, felt all the emotions and just lived it to the full.

Life is full of reflection and contemplation. The reflection helps you to know that your life is important, but the contemplation can bring fear and anticipation of the next step after the last breath. My contemplation since Dad's passing has shown me that a death can throw you into being overly inquisitorial. One minute you are here and the next you are gone. Where does your life go? What does it amount to? What does it all mean? What remains? Will I have lived it well? What is my legacy? What can I change today to make it better in the long run? What's the point? What's my purpose?

It's a contemplation that could last a lifetime. You just can't rationally find all the answers for some things and life is a kind of poetic mystery. My conclusion? To live in the moment with love, truth and purpose.

Our lead-up also had its drawbacks such as the emotional and physical toll it took on the family. Maintaining our lives, our health and our emotional states was tiring and difficult. I would not have had it any other way though. The anticipatory grief was worth all the moments we spent together and the love we shared despite the toll it took on us.

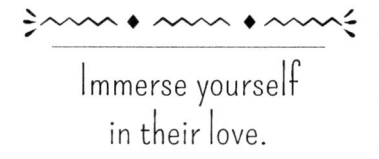

> Immerse yourself in their love.

The eighteen-month lead-up gave us the most beautiful gifts and opportunities to prepare, accept and bond, and mostly to feel and appreciate the love.

Because the whole point is *love!*

Pink Grief Corner – Share your story

If you had a lead-up, you will understand the diversity of emotions and the contradiction you feel between the benefits and the drawbacks. If you had no lead-up, you can use this exercise to write about what you would have liked to have happened if you did have one.

Stop and take three deep breaths. Honour yourself with patience, gentleness and a compassionate spirit. Come from a place of love: your love and the love of your Loved One. The whole point is *love!*

Share your story!

Write your story of the grief lead-up in your Pink Grief Journal.

Your lady friend, who has been listening to you share your story, stops at this point and looks nostalgically at the floor. Maybe she is thinking of times long gone, fond memories, loving conversations and affectionate hugs with her own lost Loved One.

She looks up and you can see her tears threaten to spill over. As they finally roll down her cheeks, she smiles softly, saying in dulcet tones, "Excuse me, but the dichotomy of grief is such a mystery and a beauty. I often find myself smiling sweetly amidst the tears especially when I hold the hand of the love that is deeply embedded within me. Please continue".

Final day

The final day can take us by surprise and is filled with many mixed, powerful and deep emotions. It can be traumatic and may leave you in a sense of denial and a feeling that the whole world has turned upside down. It is another part of the grief journey that unfortunately we can never prepare ourselves for. It is the day we need to allow the grief journey to begin its course and trust that our heart and soul can cope with the long journey to follow. Here is what happened for me...

♡♡♡♡♡♡♡♡♡♡

For me, the sun came up as normal on Dad's final day. I had no idea that that day was going to be the last day my dad would shower his loving energy and magnetism upon our lives. Sensing something, I felt compelled to leave home quite early in the morning to spend some precious solo time with Dad and speak my final words. He was non-responsive and breathing softly and peacefully.

I started by thanking him for all that he was and all that he gave to me. I reassured him of his influence on my life and of the love and values he had given me. I soaked up his energy while I watched and listened to him breathe softly and quietly as I continued to recall our life together.

I talked about old times and loving memories. I laughed out loud and teared up silently. I reminded him of times he may have forgotten. I believe he heard what I was saying. I knew how much he loved me; I didn't need reassurance of that. I simply wanted to ensure he knew how much I loved him in case he needed this comfort to take with him on the daunting solo journey he was about to take, to where I did not know.

I felt so filled up with love as I shared our lives together. He looked more peaceful and calm than he had in days, with no signs of agitation. This led me to believe he was settling into his own inner acceptance and preparing for his journey onwards to the next realm.

My heart was breaking at the tenderness of these shared moments and the fragility of his body and loving soul. He looked so vulnerable, which was hard to comprehend after him always being my solid rock.

Looking at him lying in peace, preparing to leave us, I wanted to wrap him up tightly, hug and protect him, and remove him from any harm he may meet along the way. I wanted to soothe his heart and soul and tell him everything would be okay. All the love I held for him was joined by an intense desire to care for him like he had always cared for me.

The rest of the family arrived soon after and he had all his loved ones surrounding him. We sprinkled our love and energy over him as we felt him slipping away. It was a memorable day filled with love.

Pink Grief Corner – Share your story

The final day is an exceedingly difficult stop on the Path of Goodbye yet another valuable part of your grief journey. Sharing your grief story will allow you to process and express it a little more. Go slowly as you share these precious and fragile parts of your story. Allow your raw and vulnerable heart to go at its own pace.

Stop and take three deep breaths. Honour yourself with patience, gentleness and a compassionate spirit. Come from a place of love: your love and the love of your Loved One. The whole point is *love!*

> Share your story!
> Write your story about your last day with your Loved One in your Pink Grief Journal.

Your beautiful friend draws in a rug to hug and keep her warm as she listens intently to your story. She has obviously walked this grief journey before you and shares how the grief rainbow of emotions no longer frighten her. She shares with you how to allow the emotions to flow in, swish around, create tears and flow out, naturally. She asks you to stop to rest and breathe deeply while she reassures you, imparting confidence for you to continue.

Final breath

The last moments you spend with your Loved One can bring comfort and a sense of peace or it can bring guilt, regret and uneasiness. Both experiences will end in grief. It is one of the hardest days you will ever endure. I know how tough it is. Be extra gentle with yourself. Let me continue my story with Dad…

♡♡♡♡♡♡♡♡♡♡

Later that day, I said, "I love you" to Dad before we all departed. Driving home I was called by a client at the veterinary clinic where I worked. The client was desperate and needed to put their 18-year-old Labrador, Spencer, to sleep. Spencer lived on my street with his owner who had Alzheimer's. I called in weekly to check on Spencer. He was on a lot of medication, overweight and nearing the end of his life also.

PATH OF GOODBYE

It was bad timing, but I quickly arranged to collect Spencer and meet the vet at the clinic. There I cried as I comforted Spencer, telling him he was a good dog and feeding him liver treats as we put him peacefully to sleep. Back in the car the phone rang and I was told to come to the hospital quickly. While we were gone Dad had taken his last breath. I was told it was a peaceful, quiet and soft last breath. His time had arrived to embark on his solo journey with the sprinklings of our love scattered all over his soul.

I find it strangely coincidental that I was not able to be with my dad while he was taking his last breath but was called on to help a beautiful old dog pass over, possibly at the exact same time. Two beautiful souls leaving this world together.

I didn't know Dad would pick that time to pass; only he knew that. Both Spencer and Dad were now free of pain. I hope they both found their peace and maybe even travelled together to their next home.

I believe people choose who will be present at their moment of passing. Maybe Dad thought his daughters would be too sensitive and too devastated to experience his last breath. I dearly wish I had been there with him and for him, holding his hand and feeling his soul saying his grand goodbye as it left his body. But that was not how the universe planned it.

Nothing could have prepared me for the moment of pure anguish knowing he was no longer with us, no matter how much we all expected it. We were propelled into the unknown of shock denial and a forever altered existence. He had passed but I was not ready to say goodbye.

He looked peaceful. We sat with him, trying to piece together the final goodbye to him — an impossible task.

What do you say to a person who has been there for you through thick and thin your entire life? I had to compose my last words and make sure they counted. Feeling in a total state of bewilderment and shock made this undertaking even more hopeless.

The time came to leave the hospital room. 'Should I go?' I knew once I left the room that would be it. While he was still lying in the hospital bed where he had been for a few days, feeling warm and looking peaceful, I could almost pretend nothing had changed. The moment I left it would be a different story.

Finally, I walked out of the room. Leaving him alone, motionless and in the funeral home's care was by far the most heartbreaking ten steps I have ever walked. This preceded the next long path I needed to walk with a lifetime of steps and deep potholes to manoeuvre without my father.

Was he still there in his body? Had his spirit already left? Where did his spirit go? I still contemplate my beliefs. My mind was thrown into chaos, deliberating my new world and my grief. What I do know and feel explicitly is that his presence is around me to this day, and a big piece of his love is lodged in my heart.

The date of my beautiful dad's death will now forever mark my calendar, giving me new anniversaries to mourn or celebrate, depending on how I move through my grief. This one moment in time has altered my life forever.

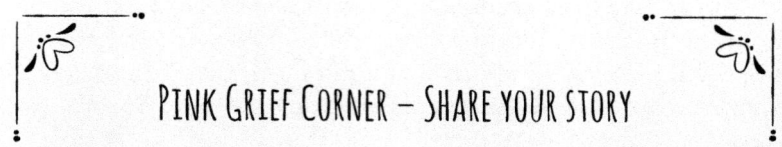

Pink Grief Corner – Share your story

While pondering your last day, reflect on these three sentences to help you tell your story:

1. What was the hardest thing about your last day?
2. What was special about the last day?

3. What do you wish you had done differently on the last day?
4. How are you feeling about your last day?
5. Are you at peace with your last day?

Hold your Pink Grief Journal close and let your love comfort your vulnerabilities and fragile heart. This is quite a hard exercise and you may feel raw and wounded all over again. It is the tending and nurturing of these wounds that will help to soothe and heal them. If it brings tears or sorrow, let the tears fall. It is healthy to release the feelings as they arise. If you feel angry or fearful, write about your emotions and feel the energy move out of you.

When the emotions have subsided, stop and take a break. Reflecting on your last day with your Loved One is a big undertaking. It takes bravery and courage to live this day over again, to seek the healing and goodness in the moments and the emotions.

Stop and take three deep breaths. Honour yourself with patience, gentleness and a compassionate spirit. Come from a place of love: your love and the love of your Loved One. The whole point is *love!*

Share your story!

Write your story about your final moments with your Loved One in your Pink Grief Journal.

Funeral preparations

After the goodbye, the funeral preparations start to swill around your mind. There are countless things to arrange to have this day continue smoothly, paying tribute and honouring the life of your Loved One.

The funeral brings an intense, chaotic and emotional week as you carry all your raw emotions close to your heart, struggling to process their effects. Even though the to-do list can be a welcome distraction from your grief, at such an early stage the resultant stress can make you feel like you will tip over the edge. That was my experience…

♡♡♡♡♡♡♡♡♡♡

The funeral directors arrived the day after Dad's passing with their gentle condolences, their assistance, to-do lists and outstanding professionalism. They walked us through the heart-wrenching time and arranged the church, casket, priest, music, prayers, flowers, cards, invitees, speakers, clothes, burial, headstone, wake and many, many more details.

So many important decisions needing to be made in a split second saw our stress levels rise. This was the final goodbye to our dad and it needed to be beautiful, perfect, special and terrific.

We had one week to write our eulogies and put on paper everything we wanted to say about our father. This mammoth and precious task was highly challenging and emotionally charged. To have the strength to deliver it at the church while maintaining some dignity and coherence came next.

I also wanted to send Dad off with a letter from me, a letter that was difficult yet beautiful to write. I dedicated time alone to write deep from my heart, expressing my thank yous, messages of love, my promises to him and my goodbye to him. I wrote till I had exhausted myself of words. Later that week, I placed the letter in his top pocket near his heart to be buried with him. (I will guide you on how to write your own letter in *The Pink Tribute*.)

The week flew by yet dragged on inside my soul. Retiring to bed every night, once the busyness of the arrangements halted, I realised this was now my reality. My feelings lay waiting for some space to be heard. There was no escape from the harrowing sadness of grief that loomed and settled in each night.

When I woke up every morning, the grief returned with a vengeance, only resting momentarily while my mind was busy ticking things off the mammoth to-do list. In these moments the grief fooled me into thinking I was coping. Sadly, I was not; I was only wading deeply in denial.

Pink Grief Corner – Share your story

Preparations for the funeral may have been made while feeling like you are living in a big blur. You may have been in the denial stage of grief where your body and mind protected you from the enormous amount of hurt waiting to be processed. You may have felt numb and overwhelmed. How will I cope? This stage allows you to slowly assimilate the loss a little and helps you move through the initial stages of grief. You begin to move out of denial and into the onslaught of emotions. This is a normal part of the grief journey.

Reflect on your feelings and how you approached the funeral day.

Stop and take three deep breaths. Honour yourself with patience, gentleness and a compassionate spirit. Come

> from a place of love: your love and the love of your Loved One. The whole point is *love!*
>
> Share your story!
>
> Write your story about the funeral preparation in your Pink Grief Journal.

THE FUNERAL DAY

The funeral day, which can include a memorial service, burial or cremation and wake, is an incredibly special day where you get to honour your Loved One. You can celebrate and reflect on your Loved One's life and share this with all your friends and family. Sharing their story through a eulogy at the memorial service or funeral offers a way to remember and reflect. As difficult as it is, there is an element of deep beauty. This is all for them. Their final farewell is a giant honour that you can hold close to your heart.

Getting through the funeral day takes an enormous amount of strength and courage. Not all funerals run smoothly. Family tensions can rise, grief can be excessive and emotions can be complex, and while you are dealing with other people's needs, you may barely make it through the day. A funeral is a traumatic event and living each moment as it arises can take all your strength. Each experience is different. Here is my story of the funeral day...

♡♡♡♡♡♡♡♡♡♡

The day arrived. I showered and put on my new special dress, a special piece of jewellery Dad had bought me and a pink hat. Even for that day I infused a little bit of pink; I had to be authentic for me and for Dad. My stomach churned while I waited for the others to arrive.

The limousine and hearse collected my sisters and I from my house and took us via Dad's house collecting more of the family and proceeded to the church. It felt special that he came to pick us up on this day albeit in his hearse. The final time.

At the church it took all the energy I had to step out of the limo and the safety of our small, close-knit family into the group of loving well-wishers there to share his final farewell. I beelined to some close friends to seek solace in their open arms. I was hoping some of their strength and courage would rub off on me before entering the church. I needed their butterfly wings to help me through this day.

Walking into the beautiful, welcoming church right behind Dad, with my bottom lip quivering, my legs shaking and my heart pounding, we took our seats in the front row and let the atmosphere wash over us. I felt like I was carrying my tender, raw emotions wrapped in a soft rug close to my heart.

I wanted to make sure I didn't miss anything. I was terrified I would forget the details, the feelings and the day. I needed to remember each moment. The love shining out from every pew from so many familiar faces felt like a gift to Dad and our family and cemented the memories in my heart forever. It was so tender and powerful, wrapping me momentarily in a feeling of loving peace.

> Love shone out from every pew.

Following the funeral, we went to the cemetery for the burial rites — a poignant and beautiful element of his farewell. Listening to the music we had painstakingly selected, each family member placed a long-stemmed white rose on Dad's coffin.

Finally, it was my turn. I placed the white rose symbolising to me our beautiful and pure father-daughter relationship. I kissed my hand and slowly lowered it to the coffin where I held my palm, striving to sense him and send him my love. I said my last silent words. Knowing he was inside, so close yet so far, was excruciating. Yet I felt our hearts connected through time and space.

We had been with him all day, walking through his final farewell together, side by side. Now we had to leave him behind, deep in the earth, as we headed to his farewell wake. The weather looked gloomy during the limo ride there, but the moment we stepped safely indoors the skies turned dark grey and opened up, showering down torrential rain. Perhaps a sign! To me the rain symbolised buckets of tears from heaven. The tears of our grief shed on that day and all the tears for the months to come.

The wake was special and we shared memories of Dad's life with extended family and many of his friends. The tears alongside the laughter reminded me of how loved he was and how much joy he brought to many other people's lives.

Exhaustion set in later that night. I mouthed "I love you" as I finally floated off to sleep, hoping to dream of my beautiful dad.

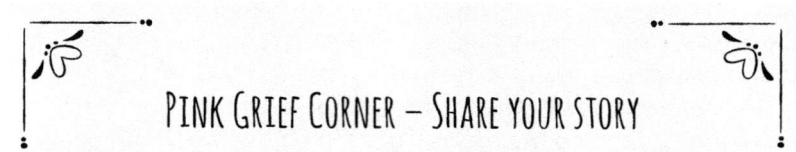

Pink Grief Corner – Share your story

The funeral service, burial and wake are challenging. Hearing about your Loved One at the service and perhaps seeing their body in a casket or photos of them can be gut-wrenching. You may laugh along at stories of them while your heart is breaking. Just as you are striving to remember and hold on to your Loved One even more, you must leave them at the burial or their ashes at the crematorium. Proceeding to the wake without them can seem incomprehensible. Delving deep into your feelings and allowing them to surface will help to process your grief from these experiences.

Stop and take three deep breaths. Honour yourself with patience, gentleness and a compassionate spirit. Come from a place of love: your love and the love of your Loved One. The whole point is *love!*

Share your story!

Write your story about what happened on the funeral day in your Pink Grief Journal.

At this point, your friend gets up and walks over to the pink and white roses. She stands for a minute before gently running her fingers over the petals and places her other hand on her heart. A petal falls into her hand. She holds it tightly in her palm, as if she were holding on to a lifetime of love and memories. She returns to her chair and asks if you are ready to continue.

After the Funeral

Your biggest lesson in the first year might be, like me, to let grief do what it needs to do. Allow yourself to walk into the unknown; let it settle into you. If you allow yourself to honour your feelings and be true to them, you will be taken to the places you need to go. Be mindful that these places may be new to you, and you will change. This experience will alter who you are at the core. This is not always bad! Here is what happened to me...

Grief, Grace and Gratitude

In the first few months after my father's funeral, the grief that had invaded my body seemed to cement itself deeply. A grey cloudiness covered my body, mind and soul, which pulled me further into myself each day and further from reality.

Each night before I would go to sleep, the grief would literally rise from deep within and pour out as a strong physical mourning and pain. Night after night I allowed myself to feel this pain and allow it to surface. Much later I would be comforted by appreciating some of the good and fun things about Dad. I would be still immersed in tears, but at least I could face it without the gut-wrenching pain of sadness.

For months, I looked daily at his funeral card with teary eyes. I could not come to terms with the fact that it was my dad in the photo. Not my dad. I visited the cemetery, taking time out from my chaotic world, where I sat and reflected on his and my life.

I remember the first family dinner. The emptiness of Dad's chair at the end of the table reflected the emptiness in me. Tears bubbled up as it hit me that the familiar chair would never again be filled by him. I accepted I would never again watch him get animated as he talked about his life passions, trips and family stories or feel his warm laughter. I would never again hear him say, "I love you".

> Let grief do what it needs to do.

The grief had me fearing that I would forget him or the feeling of him being around. This feeling intensified for quite a while until it started to slowly diminish. I thought that if I let go of the sadness, I would be letting go of the memories and our connection, and I would be deserting him. Eventually I came to realise I was holding on to the grief unnecessarily and that I could process it yet keep him close. I now know I will never forget him, how he made me feel, his favourite things, his energy, his laugh. He is and has always been a part of me. That doesn't change now that he is no longer physically present; it just changes form.

PATH OF GOODBYE

My photo albums and my grief had me pondering a lot on his life as a young child, so full of life, hopes and dreams, and then seeing him age and pass. Trying to come to terms with the human life cycle and the purpose and meaning of it all sent me into deep contemplation.

A year full of peaks of epiphanies and troughs of grief kept me on an emotional rollercoaster. I had to keep putting one foot in front of the other while honouring my grief and raw aching soul. I wanted to move into the future but felt continually pulled into the past. As time progressed, the intense daily feelings abated slightly. The grief assimilated as part of me. I learnt to live with it, and in doing so some of the joy and smiles gradually returned to my life.

I now see him in my mind and I smile. I visualise him doing his dance or singing his favourite songs and I laugh. I feel him and his mannerisms and the love he radiated, and I tear up. I am grateful for him. For all the good times. For everything he did for me.

PINK BUTTERFLY TIPS

To help you cope in the early stages of the grief journey, be mindful of the following:

- Allow yourself the time to process the grief; remove the time limits.
- Cry bucketloads of tears and let your body release the sadness.
- Know that tears represent all the love you have for your Loved One. It is not weakness but love.
- Yell obscenities at the world and get the negative energy out (without hurting anyone).
- Feel the fears and know they will pass.

- ♥ Don't get busy being busy; walk into the grief.
- ♥ Write, sing, meditate, paint; allow your soul a creative release.
- ♥ Give yourself time each day to honour your Loved One's life. You can create your own memorial or other traditions that honour them (e.g. toasting them at family dinners).
- ♥ Pay tribute to special anniversaries.
- ♥ Spend time at places that remind you of them.
- ♥ Notice how you are changing because of your loss.
- ♥ Remove any unnecessary stress and be in the present moment.
- ♥ Find people you can talk to and share your feelings with.
- ♥ Look for signs that your Loved One is nearby.
- ♥ Know that the point is *love!*

Pink Grief Corner – Share your story

The day after the funeral is when the busyness abates, and you may find yourself feeling more alone to deal with your grief. Sharing this part of your journey and continuing to journal will help you process your feelings.

Stop and take three deep breaths. Honour yourself with patience, gentleness and a compassionate spirit. Come from a place of love: your love and the love of your Loved One. The whole point is *love!*

Share your story!

Write your story about what happened following the funeral in your Pink Grief Journal.

Belongings

Going through your Loved One's belongings can be heart-wrenching. As you find yourself sorting through pieces that they lived with and loved, many memories may surface. It's important to prepare yourself for what could be an emotionally vulnerable experience.

Try and include all your family members and have a plan or structure such as clearing one room at a time. It is normal to want to keep everything, but you may not have the space to store all the items. Try placing items into categories for selling, donating, throwing out, recycling, keeping or storing for a later decision. Taking photos of all items is an effective way to keep the memories when you don't have the space for the actual item.

Taking breaks, pacing yourself, rallying support from others, getting objective opinions from others where needed and being gentle on yourself is imperative as you walk through this process. I had to do all the above when the time arrived for my sisters and I to go to Dad's house and sort through his belongings. Here is a little more on how I handled my experience...

It was our family home. My sanctuary. The one place on earth that was my stable, safe place. Thirty years of safety and love needed to be sorted to prepare for the pending sale. Being surrounded by all of Dad's things brought with it feelings of warmth and tenderness. As we scoured through items, we laughed and cried in surprise at things he had kept, and we stopped to reminisce over tonnes of memories. It took courage, strength and love to complete this task.

Soon after the house went on the market the SOLD sticker went up. The day before settlement, we visited to say goodbye. Absorbing the fact that the house where we had spent many loving times in would no longer be a place of comfort and safety for us was agonising. Giving myself permission to seek the full extent of my feelings, I sensed a gigantic sense of loss welling up, rocking my body. The tears came hard and fast and abated slowly.

The depth of sorrow that arose leaving the house for the last time shocked me. Soon after, tears of gratitude and love flowed. I felt a radiant, pure light and sensed a warm and loving sensation – Dad's love. I felt how much I was loved and how much love I had to give.

As my lovely sister once said, and I echo her statement, "I will not always remember everything that he did or said, but I will always remember how he made me feel". And he always made me feel so unbelievably loved.

I know there will always be more tears, but I have learnt to bask in the aftermath of feeling my feelings and shedding my tears as the milestones pass. Allowing myself to walk straight through the middle of the pain took me to what was waiting on the other side: gratitude, joy and love. For that, all the tears in the world were worth it.

> ### Pink Grief Corner – Share your story
>
> Sorting through your Loved One's belongings may bring laughter, stories and tears. You may find it pleasing to keep some of their belongings with you or you may find you want to donate or throw away a lot of things. It is important to only approach this task when you feel completely ready. Unless it is necessary to deal with it urgently, give yourself some time before you begin this mammoth task.
>
> Stop and take three deep breaths. Honour yourself with patience, gentleness and a compassionate spirit. Come from a place of love: your love and the love of your Loved One. The whole point is *love!*
>
> Share your story!
>
> Write about what happened when you packed up their belongings in your Pink Grief Journal.

ANNIVERSARIES

On special occasions and anniversaries my heart itself felt like it was sobbing. Savouring the past, you realise how many special days you celebrated happily for so many years. You remember fondly the innocence and simplicity of life when you had your Loved One by your side. Back then you didn't think, you just did. Life was sweet.

Abruptly you can be propelled back in the moment, realising with melancholy that these occasions will now be celebrated without them. As well you will have to survive the anniversaries of their passing, knowing each will bring more grief.

Encroaching on you will be the one-month anniversary and each month after that until the first- year anniversary and so on. On top of that there will be the birthdays, Christmases and all the other special occasions individual to your family.

The anniversaries of their death can be especially gruelling, particularly the first. You can feel like you are reliving the traumatic event and having to find a way to get through the day all over again. If you are fortunate you may also sense glimpses of healing and recognise this as a chance to honour and pay tribute to your Loved One.

You may create memorials and rituals that you follow from year to year. Finding a way to lovingly remember and honour your Loved One on the special occasions and anniversaries helps to keep them alive in your heart. It also helps to soothe your broken heart.

As time moves on, the special days in your calendar become a little easier to handle and can induce a cocktail of tears and sadness mixed with laughter and joy. Remembering your Loved One can be so loving and make you feel a warm sense of comfort and peace, yet suddenly you remember they are no longer here. You yearn deeply for their energy and presence. It is part of the grief. Here is a little about my experience...

♡♡♡♡♡♡♡♡♡♡

The date of my dad's passing is forever marked as a significant date in my world. The one-year anniversary was a loving yet difficult day. I had been standing amidst my continual grief haze yet feeling like I was moving forward slowly. On this particular day, however, my emotions played havoc with me and threatened to overwhelm me. I felt like I had taken three steps backwards despite having a beautiful day.

PATH OF GOODBYE

I spent the day with my family honouring Dad. We laughed, we reminisced, we cried. We connected lovingly, fusing the pieces of love that he left in each of our hearts together to produce so much more love. A sweet sadness followed me to bed that night.

I live my life now with one less loved person by my physical side. I have felt raw and scarred in living with my grief, and sometimes I struggle to integrate grief into my new life. I live with an altered view of the world and the life I desire. Some days I feel more vulnerable, see less innocence in the world and feel more adult-like. Other days it may be the opposite. I continue, however, to move forward and heal finding more gratitude and love.

The day after the one-year anniversary of his death, I realised I had survived the first year of grief. I was still standing. I still housed my grief yet was able to sit in acceptance. Around this time I vowed to live my life fully and experience all of its richness. I had always wanted a great life, but it was not till I lost my dad that I became so much more passionate to create this reality in honour of him.

> Vow to live a rich and full life.

That day, I left for my first solo holiday to a beachside resort. I was ready to discover the world and more of myself while reminiscing all the wonderful times Dad and I had together. Life was continuing. I still felt my grief and at times it cut deep, but I was determined to live my life as rich and full as possible. This is the healing journey and grief's dichotomy.

Pink Grief Corner – Share your story

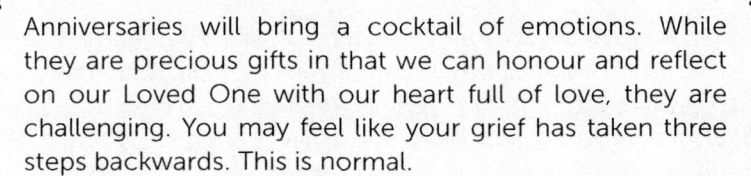

Anniversaries will bring a cocktail of emotions. While they are precious gifts in that we can honour and reflect on our Loved One with our heart full of love, they are challenging. You may feel like your grief has taken three steps backwards. This is normal.

Stop and take three deep breaths. Honour yourself with patience, gentleness and a compassionate spirit. Come from a place of love: your love and the love of your Loved One. The whole point is *love!*

Share your story!

Write your story about the special occasions and anniversaries in your Pink Grief Journal.

Love

The Path of Goodbye is like an out-of-control vine. It clutches, squeezes and envelops you. You may feel stuck and unsure how to untwist the knots surrounding you or how to find some freedom and space. Every part of your mind, body and soul could feel shattered, but putting the first two pieces back together is the start.

You simply need to take the first step and surrender to the grief journey and its purpose, and the rest will evolve. The journey home to healing starts with awareness and willingness. One puzzle piece gently leads to the next until one day there is a beautiful, colourful image in front of you. It is filled with cracks and lines resembling your scars; yet you still see beauty and appreciate your efforts in getting to your new reality.

You see, over time grief changes form as it changes you. You learn to assimilate it into who you are and into your daily life. It takes an abundance of patience and strength, but over time you find yourself altered at your core.

The consequences of grief are bittersweet. What you are left with can be frightening as you continue to feel sad and fragile. However, raw pain may be followed by raw love as you learn to feel all your emotions and move through the journey.

Resisting the pain of grief, on the other hand, may cause your heart to close in fear of being hurt all over again. In the short term, this may feel like the better option. But if you close your heart to pain you also close it to love.

> Grief will expose you to raw pain followed by raw love.

The good thing is that grief waits for you. When you confront your grief, you can reclaim the pure love that is buried within. The longer you leave it the harder it may be. So place your feet solidly on the earth beneath you, ground yourself in the most honest and authentic way, and walk with your tears, scars and sadness to where you need to go. Your destination may not yet be clear, but just keep walking one step at a time.

You will know when you arrive; it will be plainly obvious. You will have found the love!

> **PINK BUTTERFLY TIPS**
>
> 💕 Sharing your story is a big step towards healing.
> 💕 Walk through your grief journey at your own pace.
> 💕 Be extra loving to yourself through your grief journey.
> 💕 Feel the pain but also feel the love that surrounds you.
> 💕 Vow to live a rich, full life in honour of you and your Loved One.

"Thank you for sharing your story," your friend says as she walks over and wraps you in another one of her warm, loving hugs. You find it hard to let go; it almost brings you to your knees as the rainbow of emotions swirl around inside you, taking up all your inner space. You feel tired. You feel thankful. You feel sad. But you feel the love.

She continues. "Thank you for inviting me in, and I hope it has helped you. The pink and white roses I chose for you are a symbol of the colour that the Field of Grace will bring back slowly to your life in the next phase of your grief journey, if you allow it to. This has been my home for some time and has been a place to rest and nurture myself while I needed to feel all my feelings and live my soul-shattering grief journey. It has also delivered all kinds of beautiful lessons and gifts. I have lovingly prepared the Cabin of Love to be your home for a while. I truly hope you are as blessed as I was during my stay here. Please look after my critter friend that I sent to walk you through your journey. It's been nice meeting you."

PATH OF GOODBYE

❧ PINK PONDERINGS ❧

Stop and take three deep breaths. Honour yourself with patience, gentleness and a compassionate spirit. Come from a place of love: your love and the love of your Loved One. The whole point is *love!*

- ❤ Today, my grief feels like…
- ❤ Today, my grief wants me to…
- ❤ Today, my grief taught me…

FINAL CONTEMPLATION

"There's a place where beauty and sadness meet ... It's the place where sadness is no longer ugly, where grief begins feeling like soap in a wound, painful but purgative ..."

—Mark Matousek

WOW. What a day and what a lesson. You wonder what the Field of Grace is she spoke of. You still only see a forest full of trees outside the window and a heart full of sorrow and loss inside. It is nice, though, having a space and a bed to call your own for a while.

Wandering around the cabin you realise, with a small snippet of pride, that you made it through the trek in the forest. You stood at the opening of the forest a long time ago feeling lost, disillusioned and broken. You had no idea where to start, what shoes to wear and how to handle the terrain. But, with a backpack full of grief emotions, you put one foot in front of the other and you made it to a different place and a new phase in your journey.

There comes a point when you may feel big shifts inside that move you from one part of the grief journey to the next. You acknowledge this and stop to deliberate. This helps you realise you have progressed forward in your grief even though you still feel heartbroken.

Looking around the Cabin of Love it looks a little desolate besides the pretty pink and white roses on the table. Where did your friend find them in this grey and gloomy forest? Digging deeper, you notice you feel a little lonely again since the soft, loving energy walked out the door when your friend left. It's just you and your grief emotions once again. You feel scared yet sense some confidence in your ability to handle them.

Trust and faith

It's time for you to allow your sense of trust and faith to take over.

During your trek, you have learnt about the stages of grief: denial, anger, bargaining, depression and acceptance. You have learnt about the ITP Process of awareness, responsibility, feelings, forgiveness and acceptance. You have shared your Path of Goodbye story. You have embedded tools within to help you manoeuvre through this journey.

You have come so far even though you feel you are still at day one. You search inside for the hope that things will continue to improve. You remember the five questions left from your mysterious friend. You only just realise you didn't even get her name!

Before she left she had asked you to answer them before you went to sleep. Feeling drained and tired, you just want to go to bed. But since you had promised to complete them, your good nature leads you to your Pink Grief Journal.

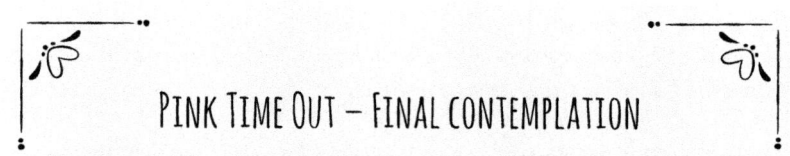

PINK TIME OUT – FINAL CONTEMPLATION

Stop and take three deep breaths. Honour yourself with patience, gentleness and a compassionate spirit. Come from a place of love: your love and the love of your Loved One. The whole point is *love!*

Record your feelings in your Pink Grief Journal:

FINAL CONTEMPLATION

1. What is the most helpful lesson you learnt in the Forest of Grief?
2. What would you share with others about the Forest of Grief and its lessons?
3. What did you struggle with most in the Forest of Grief?
4. Do you take responsibility for your grief journey?
5. Can you acknowledge how far you have come in your journey?

Curling up on the couch after finishing your contemplation, you feel like dozing. You hope for the beautiful dreams of your Loved One to arrive full of love, roses and butterflies. Gazing at the butterfly on the rug and the flowers in the vase, and feeling the love of your recent visitor friend, you finally understand: The point is love!

Trust and faith follow you to sleep, allowing you to welcome the next part of the grief journey and your stay at the Cabin of Love. Your last thoughts are of you pondering what the Field of Grace will bring next.

Love – Truth – Purpose

> "Sometimes you will never know the value of a moment until it becomes a memory."
>
> —Dr Seuss

Grief, Grace and Gratitude

Don't cry for me

Don't cry for me now I have died, for I'm still here by your side.
My body's gone but my soul's here; please don't shed another tear.
I am still here all around; only my body lies in the ground.
I am the snowflake that kisses your nose;
I am the frost that nips your toes.
I am the sun bringing you light;
I am the star shining so bright.
I am the rain refreshing the earth;
I am the laughter; I am the mirth.
I am the bird up in the sky;
I am the cloud that's drifting by.
I am the thoughts inside your head;
While I'm still there I can't be dead.

—Author unknown

PART 2

FIELD OF GRACE

The Sabbatical

GREETING GRACE

"He who learns must suffer. And even in our sleep, pain that cannot forget falls drop by drop upon the heart, and in our own despair, against our will, comes wisdom to us."

—Aeschylus

Sitting up you stretch, allowing your body to rise slowly. Yesterday seems so long ago and so surreal. You snap out of it, waking up fully to your reality. You sense the remnants of a strange dream but can't recall the details. You feel surprisingly lighter yet are still assimilating all the information from the last few days.

You decide today is going to be all about you – sitting, relaxing, looking after yourself and being kind to yourself. It's been an emotionally rough path to arrive at this space. The trudge through the Forest of Grief has taken a lot of your energy and you realise that it is time to focus on loving yourself before the pieces that you have neglected start faltering.

Your grief remains lodged in your heart and the sorrow still rises to meet you, but there is now some extra inner space. A shift, a change, has taken place that helps you to move towards assimilating this grief into your current existence.

The worst part is moving past you. Acceptance is dawning, leaving you with questions on how to proceed. What next? Where? How? Oodles of whys and hows are being fired at your heart.

You can't shift the sense of something being different. You walk past the beautiful pink and white roses to the window. 'What is it?' Looking out you are happily surprised; it is not as dark and gloomy. You continue to gaze out, to let it all sink in.

It's amazing! The clusters of trees surrounding the cabin are no longer there; hence the lightness. It is a cloudy day, but sunlight is beaming down through a clearing between the clouds, exposing an empty field surrounding the Cabin of Love.

You can see the forest in the distance. 'Was that my dream?... How did this happen?' You place your analytical thoughts on pause and befriend your faith. You intuitively know that it's there for a reason, surrendering to let grief guide you.

Opening the door to smell the fresh air you feel the light breeze on your skin and decide to sit on the bench near the front door. Hugging your knees to your chest to ward off the chill you feel a blank space within waiting to be filled up with love and light.

With a sudden shot of enthusiasm, you hop up and walk to the back of the cabin to discover a little garden shed painted in a calming grey. Opening the door an immaculately organised room reveals itself with shelves galore full of everything you need to build a garden of flowery delights.

Your first thought is 'Oh dear! I despise gardening!'

Looking to the side of the shed there is a plaque on the wall. The text, watermarked by a butterfly, says:

GREETING GRACE

The Field Of Grace Greets You

Your purpose here is to allow yourself a truth sabbatical. Your grief journey continues, but your grief is more manageable. It allows you to take time out to reorganise your wants and needs. It is a stage to nurture yourself and allow your life to settle into its new habitat. It is a time to discover your yearnings and learnings from your Loved One's passing, noticing the shifts and transformation. It is about honouring the new version of you and compiling a special tribute to your Loved One in their honour.

Hmmm. A sabbatical! That sounds delightful. But you have work and responsibilities to deal with. 'I don't think so,' you say to yourself. Maybe this is reality and you don't have the time to put your life on hold. Or maybe this thought process is a little self-justification to prevent you from continuing the grief journey. Avoidance!

The term 'sabbatical' originated from the biblical Sabbath and serves an ancient human need to build periods of rest and rejuvenation into our lives. A sabbatical is generally known as a time to take extended leave and travel. Not all of us, however, can afford the luxury of the travel part and need to instead focus on the rest and rejuvenation. The key aspects of the modern sabbatical in my eyes include time to renew, refresh, restore, replenish, revamp, rejuvenate, redesign and redecorate. All the big fancy Rs!

Grief, Grace and Gratitude

A truth sabbatical is a term I created. Its sole purpose is to build this period of rest and rejuvenation into your life while going inward and becoming candidly truthful with yourself. This will ensure you are living with authenticity from your heart and soul.

Investing in yourself now opens you up to yourself, life, love and others. Choosing to avoid this can prove a detriment later. You may not have the ability to quit work and be a devotee to your soul like a monk on a mountain, but you can choose to devote some time each day purely to yourself, away from responsibilities. To your soul's delight you can create your own mountain top at home and be a devotee to your heart without even exiting your front door. It could be one hour, two hours or even five minutes. A commitment to yourself is what matters.

Like the caterpillar in his cocoon before it metamorphoses into a beautiful butterfly, this period of growth is essential for your wellbeing and for growing into your true nature. It is essential to build your own butterfly wings, so you can fly away to find your own love, roses and butterflies.

This is the phase of grief where you get to find and flourish your wings. They are battered and bruised from being dragged around the forest floor behind you. But with a recipe of tender, loving care they will rise from the ground and slowly float their beauty all the way to your new life, however that may look for you.

Your grief journey has taken a shift and you now can redesign and redecorate your inner and outer world around your loss. You have an empty canvas of field and an empty space inside. Both can do with a spruce up.

Grace means elegance or beauty of form, manner, motion or action. It means favour, kindness, love or goodwill to self or others. In the yoga philosophy it implies presence, surrender and mindfulness. Grace is a state of being that is earned through discipline and commitment. Here at the Field of Grace, this and even more than you can imagine are all possible.

GREETING GRACE

It is normal to reach a stage where your grief settles and you feel different. You want to rebuild, so some things will need to change. Over time, you will make changes that will likely see you grow into a more evolved version of yourself through all the beauty, vulnerabilities and love that grief is offering and teaching you. Where will you start?

Redesign and redecorate

Here at the Field of Grace, of course!

PINK GRIEF CORNER – PROMISE AND QUESTIONS

For one moment, pause your yesterdays and your grief and loss. Be in this moment only. Take in what you have read to this point. Acknowledge how you feel about things in this moment.

It's time to make a promise to invest in yourself. A promise is a declaration, a hand-on-heart sacred agreement where you commit to fulfilling its prescribed action and goal. It is a pledge to yourself.

Stop and take three deep breaths. Honour yourself with patience, gentleness and a compassionate spirit. Come from a place of love: your love and the love of your Loved One. The whole point is *love!*

Now call yourself to action and promise to invest in yourself in this phase of your grief journey. Commit to continue on your path, to take time out for yourself and to practise self-love to help change all of your tomorrows.

Craft your promise and commitment in your own words and write it in your Pink Grief Journal. 'I promise…'

Now place your hand on your heart, close your eyes and repeat out loud your promise to yourself, slowly and succinctly. Allow it to soak in deeply. Keep repeating the promise until you can feel it holding a place in your heart, ready to be fulfilled. Honour the promise and yourself. Bring it alive and allow it to guide you deeper into your grief journey and yourself.

Now you have made a promise to yourself there are two questions for you to answer.

1. Are you willing to make a commitment to your truth sabbatical and in turn yourself?
2. How willing are you? Rate this willingness from 0–10, 10 being the most willing.

Record your promise and the answers to the questions in your Pink Grief Journal.

Having spent some time creating your promise and being honest with yourself about your commitment to your truth sabbatical, you are now ready to move forward. Be proud of how far you have come; it's a long and tough road. But you are walking it and you are surviving.

Life sucks! At times this is so true. You will travel up and down peaks and troughs as your life's terrain is forever changing. But it's how you walk the terrain — how you handle yourself — that matters.

Presently you are in the valley, possibly right at the bottom, and the sides of the hill you must climb may look completely vertical. To claw your way up looks impossible. The only thing you need to do is to keep moving, one foot (and one hand) in front of the other; the rest will take care of itself.

Onwards and upwards you go!

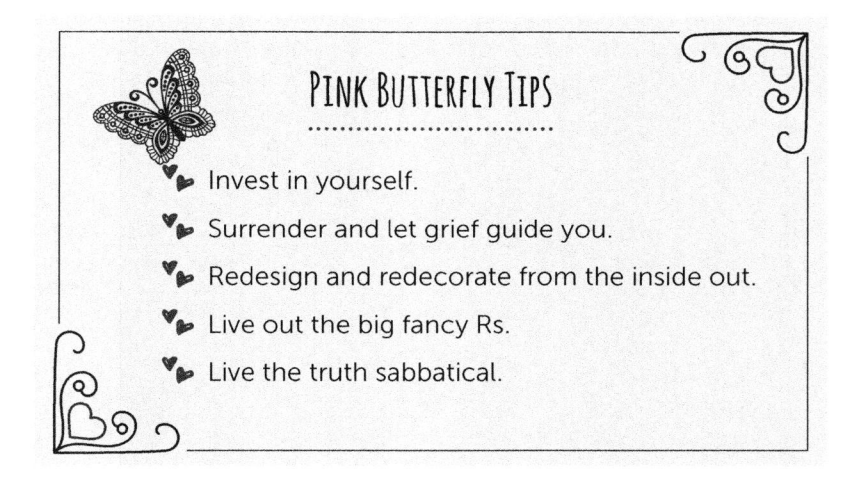

> ### PINK BUTTERFLY TIPS
> - Invest in yourself.
> - Surrender and let grief guide you.
> - Redesign and redecorate from the inside out.
> - Live out the big fancy Rs.
> - Live the truth sabbatical.

At the side of the garden shed you spot a wooden box with a round entrance hole in it sitting under the eve. It has been painted in the same lovely calming grey as the shed, camouflaging itself except for the pink and white roses that have been handpainted around the entrance. A furry head pops out and quickly pops back in again. Aha! So this is where your friendly furry critter lives.

You leave some seeds for him and head back inside for a day of self-love and savouring in the big fancy Rs that the modern-day truth sabbatical bestows on you.

~ Pink Ponderings ~

Stop and take three deep breaths. Honour yourself with patience, gentleness and a compassionate spirit. Come from a place of love: your love and the love of your Loved One. The whole point is *love!*

- Today, my grief feels like…
- Today, my grief wants me to…
- Today, my grief taught me…

SELF-LOVE

"You yourself, as much as anybody in the entire universe, deserve your love and affection."

—Buddha

Yesterday was exactly what you needed with plenty of the big fancy Rs. You familiarised yourself with your surroundings and did nothing except nurture your heart and soul. You did this well with herbal teas, nourishing food, meditation and restful sleep. You enjoyed the fresh air, the daylight and simply being alive.

Today you know it is back to the grief journey's lessons. Taking your breakfast outside to the bench, you wonder how your lesson for today will materialise. As your first mouthful creates a delicious delight in your mouth you wait patiently.

There is no directional signpost showing you where to go. You decide that maybe this is a sign in itself that it is time to make some of your own decisions. Suddenly you feel stronger and able. You have been immersed in your grief for a while now, avoiding big decisions and just being led along. Now it's time to rise to your life and once again be the author and creator.

Sitting there a little longer, you feel a deep, intense desire to be helpful, useful and purposeful. What to do? You observe the empty field surrounding you and consider the garden shed with its plethora of garden tools. The answer materialises, bringing with it a promise of hope and joy: You are going to devote your time and creative energy to build this empty space into a graceful garden and to spruce up the cabin. Alongside this you will be transforming your inner world to house a happy, open and loving heart.

Where to start?

You walk to the garden shed to gather tools to start pottering around in the empty field. On your way you ponder how to build this graceful garden. You need to start from nothing and transform it into the exquisite picture you hold in your mind's eye. It's the same question that appears regularly when you deliberate how you will tend to your internal garden.

Two butterflies float past gracefully, landing on top of the critter's house. They look so pretty surrounded by the handpainted roses. The first lesson then appears and seems to be speaking directly to your heart.

What is self-love?

Self-love is:

- 💖 the ability to be gentle and compassionate with yourself in the face of all odds.

- 💖 the courage to make decisions that are right for you, trusting your heart and following its lead in your journey of grief and life.

- 💖 the willingness to deal with the toughest parts of your journey in life with space to nurture and look after yourself. The grief journey is a challenging time but with self-love comes the desire to look after and rebuild yourself.

SELF-LOVE

- ♥ holding a strong, unwavering sense of self-trust and self-belief, being able to stand proud and protect yourself in a calm and mature way.

- ♥ the capacity to accept, love, respect, honour and value the beautiful, individual person you are. It is about being able to pull yourself out of destructive situations and believe you deserve better, saying no to toxic people, places and situations, and sending clear messages that maintain your self-respect.

- ♥ about forgiveness; having the longing to forgive yourself and others with compassion. Forgiveness means you let go of all the anger and resentment within and return your inner being to a peaceful, calm state.

- ♥ learning to remove all the unnecessary childish drama from your life that you may use to create distraction or self-importance, or even fun and excitement (whether self-created or imposed upon you).

- ♥ stopping when you feel overwhelmed or need to take time out to care for your physical and emotional wellbeing. It is understanding that you are not invincible, knowing you need to care for your body to prevent it breaking down.

- ♥ having a mammoth to-do list and getting halfway through and saying to yourself, 'Enough for today. I am tired and need to rest'. It is believing that you are worthy of that rest. Looking outwardly busy and important is a sign of worthiness for many of us. However, it is not impressive to work so hard that you crash and burn. Self-love is understanding that by continuing to push yourself beyond your limits, you risk burnout or physical injury. It is knowing when you are near those limits and need to pull back.

- possessing laser sharp self-awareness so that you can understand what is happening internally and what you need in that moment to move forward in a healthy fashion.

- allowing fun into your life and having heartfelt tears running down your face from laughter. It is being able to let go of the stresses and struggles of life, be in the moment and just enjoy. When you love yourself, you know exactly what gives you pleasure and fun and will seek it daily.

- being self-expressive and appreciating expression's positive impact. It may be yoga, writing, art, dancing, singing, Pilates, mothering, running, church or whatever your personal outlet is. Express yourself in whichever way you feel most comfortable and natural, being true to you.

- looking after your physical body, your mind and your spiritual self, only taking in things that will nourish you and see you flourish.

- learning to love the parts of yourself that you would prefer to disown. Loving the younger, more naive less truthful parts of yourself that may have housed a false bravado to the outer world to feel worthy and important. The parts that did crazy, self-loathing things that you now look back on and cringe, things that you wouldn't dream of doing or saying now. You were less emotionally and spiritually cultivated back then; you knew no different. You know better now so you do better, but don't forget to love the little girl that was doing the best she could. Until you can show her your true love, you are never capable of fully loving and accepting yourself.

- accepting your old self that may pop up at times when you least expect it and behaving in its old childish, negative and emotionally immature ways. Love the part

SELF-LOVE

of yourself that you want to yell at and put back in its box. It's about loving all the parts of you; this is when true inner growth will occur.

♥ being able to stand solid in yourself, not needing to impress others. You can sit quietly with an internal love that requires only your own acceptance. The anxiety and constant energy required to impress others is released.

♥ acquiring the ability to say 'I love me' and feel the warm, tingly feelings inside that come from true gratitude and self-acceptance.

♥ being thoughtful, considerate, compassionate and caring as you walk alongside Mother Nature to help heal and nurture our planet for the generations to follow.

♥ seeing all sentient beings, big and small, as an extension of your own consciousness and treating them with kindness, love and respect. Being kind to others translates into being kind to ourselves and vice versa.

♥ caring and nurturing yourself through the grief journey, knowing it will have positive consequences on your health and happiness when all the strenuous work is completed and you are gently placed out at the other end.

That is all self-love!

I love me.

My self-love

During the last two decades while I have been walking my spiritual journey, I have learnt all about self-love. I have read about it, studied it, practised it, written about it, built a business around it and built it into my life wherever possible. It is a never-ending journey and often a big struggle, yet one that brings self-knowledge, wisdom, joy and a deep sense of pure happiness.

When you lose a Loved One, it can put a halt on self-love and cause your self-esteem and the desire to care for yourself to plummet. Caring for a relationship, children and everyday responsibilities on top of your grief makes the challenge of self-love even more demanding. This can increase stress levels tremendously while you are trying to keep everyone, including yourself, happy.

Grief can place you right at the bottom of the valley and overtake your life. You may barely be coping with the grief let alone making sure you are being self-loving. Tuning into yourself and allowing self-love to flow in, day by day, will help you survive the tough times.

Love yourself!

As for me, I wasn't looking after myself well. I was cocooned in my dark grief in a space deprived of light, laughter and fun. Alongside this I had to maintain all my responsibilities; self-love came last for a long while.

Soon after the first anniversary of Dad's death, I stood still and looked closely at the wreckage grief had wrought on me. To my sadness I discovered it was slowly decimating my health. I felt lousy, had high stress levels, and was stripped of my precious energy and aliveness. My body was screaming out for me to slow down and listen to it. So I did!

SELF-LOVE

Firstly, I made a solid commitment to be self-lovingly healthy, and secondly, I booked a holiday. I adopted a healthier diet, mostly eating whole foods with less processed foods, dairy, gluten, soy, alcohol, caffeine and sugars. I committed wholeheartedly to a daily yoga and meditation practice. My health, skin and energy levels slowly improved, my body began to repair itself and my stress levels were reducing. I set the atmosphere to allow my body to eliminate discord and move towards balance and harmony naturally.

Often the ailments we suffer are due to a specific root cause that, with problem solving and commitment, we can find and eliminate. Instead, we are often unprepared to go to that effort and are not willing to give up the food and toxins that rain destruction on our bodies. So we turn to prescription drugs to remove the pain and mask the illness instead of healing the root cause.

Sometimes it's not until you hit rock bottom or decide to love yourself more that you become willing to uncover and remove the food or toxin culprit from your diet. You begin to unite with your physical body and have a desire to protect and nurture your health like you would a small child.

The physical body wishes deeply to connect and work with the mind and the soul to bring integration, healing and harmony. Nurturing the body, quietening the mind and soothing the soul is the magic equation.

The body is an amazing cellular vessel and if you give it love, space and time, it knows perfectly how to heal itself. It is our teacher and speaks to us loudly, sending us messages galore about its state of being. We just need to sit up and listen!

Eating well translates to feeling fabulous. Chips and chocolate will always wave their manipulative tastes in front of us and sometimes we weaken. That's life! With self-love, however, it is possible to learn to treat your body with more respect. After all, it is the vessel that will carry you through to old age. No doubt you want it to last the longest distance possible and in the healthiest manner.

I am convinced stress and the resultant cortisol running through our bodies can tip us over the edge into disease or poor health. Reducing that stress and adopting a healthy lifestyle is what walks you back to a healthier and happier body and mind.

To spare further damage, pushing yourself up the priority list is crucial. Despite the grief, sometimes poor health is a wake-up call to look after yourself. The minute you stop resisting and draw the focus back on yourself, your body will take over. It knows what to do, and this is when the physical healing begins.

It is crucial to look after your health. It can quickly become damaging and problematic if you neglect yourself. It can take a lot of time, energy and money to work towards healing once your health fails. But no matter where you are in your grief journey, it's never too late to pause and run a body scan to see how you feel and what is working and what is not.

Stress is literally a killer. Diseases manifest under the surface for years before they come out to create havoc in your world. These days keeping healthy is even more difficult as we are faced with a huge array of yummy unhealthy foods, stress, unhappy environments, toxins and busy lives. To avoid being old, sore, cranky and broken it is vital to make a commitment to look after yourself and practise self-love.

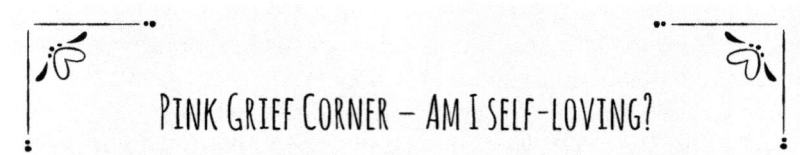

Pink Grief Corner – Am I self-loving?

Despite trying hard to look after yourself on the grief journey, most of the time you most likely fall far short of your good intentions. To nurture yourself while

SELF-LOVE

precariously balancing your grief is a near impossible task. We can constantly let ourselves down and beat ourselves up, and nowhere more so than on a grief journey. It is during the truth sabbatical that you can allow yourself the luxury of being kind to you. Start by rebuilding all the parts of yourself that have become neglected.

You need to STOP STILL long enough to take stock of how you are feeling!

The statements below give you an opportunity to honestly assess how self-loving you are. Indicate whether each statement is true or false for yourself. There are no right or wrong answers. This is solely an awareness exercise in self-love that provides opportunities for growth and development.

Stop and take three deep breaths. Honour yourself with patience, gentleness and a compassionate spirit. Come from a place of love: your love and the love of your Loved One. The whole point is *love!*

Record your feelings in your Pink Grief Journal:

- I am gentle and compassionate with myself.
- I accept, love, respect, honour and value myself.
- I can remain calm and mature amidst my grief.
- I can remove myself from toxic situations.
- I nurture my body, mind and soul.
- I trust and accept myself.
- I have good self-esteem.
- I can give forgiveness.
- I can say no.

- 💕 I can avoid people pleasing.
- 💕 I can stop before I feel overwhelmed.
- 💕 I have laser sharp self-awareness.
- 💕 I can feel my feelings.
- 💕 I can express myself.
- 💕 I can care for myself.
- 💕 I have a sense of belonging.
- 💕 I can accept my flaws and imperfections.
- 💕 I can have fun.
- 💕 I love me.

Well done on completing this exercise and for your courage to go deeper. Celebrate the trues and use the falses to point you in the right direction to further healing.

Having been on the grief journey for so long, you may find your self-love has been neglected and you rated lower than you had hoped. This is normal. Remember that you are here learning new skills and tools to take you through your grief journey. You are not expected to know all these things right now. Allow yourself to be in the learning phase, remove any judgement and use this sabbatical to build your butterfly wings.

Now, please answer the following questions to create further awareness on how self-loving you currently are.

1. On a scale from 0–10, 10 being the best, how self-loving are you being right now?
2. On a scale from 0–10, 10 being the best, how willing are you to be more self-loving?

SELF-LOVE

Pink Grief Corner – Self-loving actions

Self-love is unconditional love and respect directed towards you. Self-loving actions are activities you can take to love yourself during this grief journey. The list below is a selection of self-loving actions you could invite into your life to encourage more self-love. This list is purely a starting point; feel free to add your own ideas and interests.

- Sit and feel your feelings.
- Sit in meditation or contemplation.
- Sit and take long, deep breaths.
- Attend a yoga class.
- Spend time in nature.
- Read for pleasure.
- Watch an uplifting movie.
- Take your dogs for a walk to the park.
- Have coffee with a friend.
- Spend time with your family.
- Listen to the music you love.
- Take an afternoon nap or sleep in.
- Change to a healthy diet.
- Go to bed earlier.
- Discover the varieties of herbal tea.
- Volunteer.
- Cook nourishing meals.
- Create some beautiful artwork.
- Write a soulful poem.

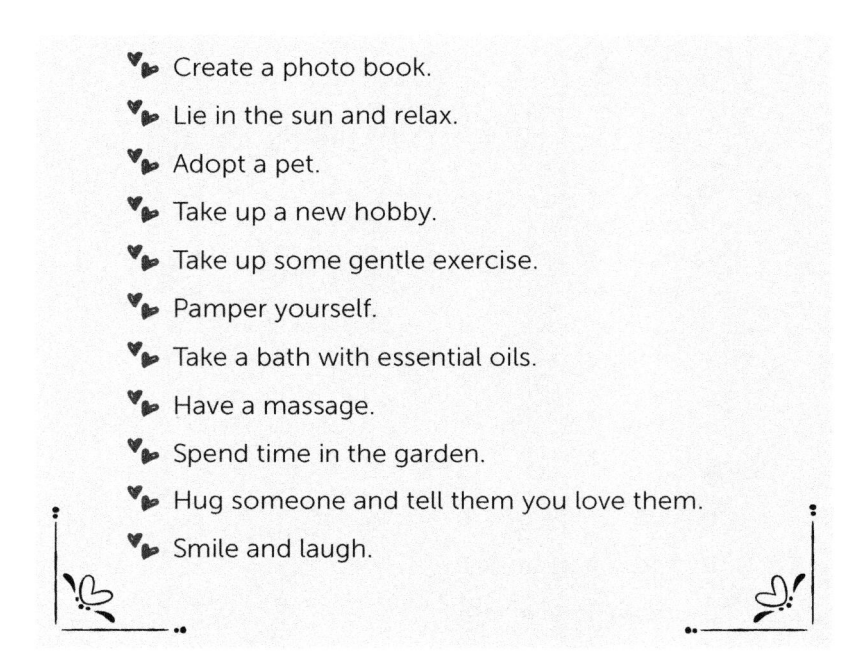

- ♥ Create a photo book.
- ♥ Lie in the sun and relax.
- ♥ Adopt a pet.
- ♥ Take up a new hobby.
- ♥ Take up some gentle exercise.
- ♥ Pamper yourself.
- ♥ Take a bath with essential oils.
- ♥ Have a massage.
- ♥ Spend time in the garden.
- ♥ Hug someone and tell them you love them.
- ♥ Smile and laugh.

It is hard to step outside our grief as it is so consuming. Learning to take some time in self-loving activities will free your mind for a moment to help find some space. This space accelerates the healing and can help you find some of the loving feelings hidden under the challenging ones.

Each day is beyond difficult when you lose a Loved One. However, it is possible to notice the difference between grieving and suffering. Allow yourself to grieve, but don't create added suffering by being unkind to yourself.

Diarising your self-loving actions is another idea to ensure that you allow time for yourself. In our busyness and grief, it is so easy for our days to get filled with never-ending tasks while we forget to look after ourselves. Practise self-love even at this challenging time to help yourself and those who surround you.

SELF-LOVE

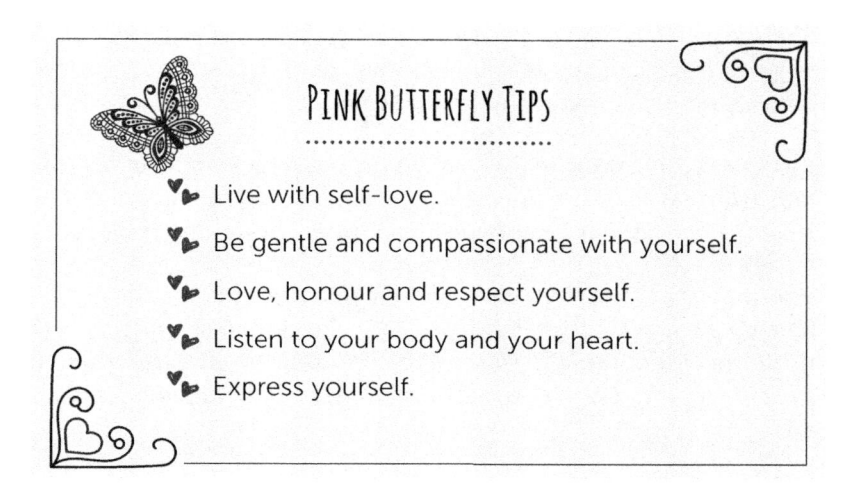

> ### Pink Butterfly Tips
> - Live with self-love.
> - Be gentle and compassionate with yourself.
> - Love, honour and respect yourself.
> - Listen to your body and your heart.
> - Express yourself.

Bloom and Grow

"And the day came when the risk to remain tight in a bud was more painful than the risk it took to blossom."

—Anaïs Nin

Sitting down on the bench again where you started the day, you reflect on your efforts. Your hands are dirty and sore, but you can see change. Areas have been cleared, weeds have been removed, bulbs have been planted, seeds have been laid and the planter boxes have been filled.

You have nurtured the garden with care and love all day. It still looks bare, but with a little water and love it will blossom into a beautiful array of gardenly delights that will take your breath away. You have laid the foundations, and from that it will bloom and grow, just like the 'Blossom of Snow' white Edelweiss flower.

Lay your foundations and they will grow.

Shifting your focus to within, you gauge how you have integrated these self-love lessons. You feel you can now care for yourself confidently with self-love and a desire to protect yourself.

Starting to take your weary body inside, you stop in front of the pink and white flowers to inhale their fragrance, immersing yourself in their beauty. For a moment you exist only in their magnificence.

The next thing, your Loved One appears in your mind surrounded by magical white butterflies. You can see every inch of their face and sense their presence. Through their eyes you can see deep inside to their heart and their love washes over you, bringing tears to your eyes.

You miss them profusely yet you can feel their love filling you and driving you to this new place. Here you give yourself consent to self-nurture and believe that you can cope with your grief.

You feel your butterfly wings have risen just a little from the forest floor, and you have found some of your internal resilience that for so long has been unattainable. You allow your wings to take you to the shower to wash off your day of gardening and you then start cooking dinner. You are eager to fill the empty space in your tummy that is calling out for a nourishing meal.

Your truth sabbatical is nurturing you with self-love. It is going to carry you into tomorrow, all fresh and clean, when you will create a beautiful tribute to your Loved One.

SELF-LOVE

~ Pink Ponderings ~

Stop and take three deep breaths. Honour yourself with patience, gentleness and a compassionate spirit. Come from a place of love: your love and the love of your Loved One. The whole point is *love!*

- ♥ Today, my grief feels like...
- ♥ Today, my grief wants me to...
- ♥ Today, my grief taught me...

PINK TRIBUTE

> "And when great souls die, after a period peace blooms, slowly and always irregularly. Spaces fill with a kind of soothing electric vibration. Our senses, restored, never to be the same, whisper to us. They existed ...
> We can be ... better. For they existed."
>
> —Maya Angelou

After emptying your breakfast scraps onto the ground near the front door, you see out of the corner of your eye your critter friend making an appearance. Once he sees you are turning to walk inside, he scurries to see what delights have been left. He moves fast, but you catch a better look at your friend, who you realise is cute as anything. A little furry soul on a journey of its own, walking beside you and adding some aliveness and energy into your day.

Just as you are nurturing and caring for your garden and your furry friend, they likewise are silently nurturing your soul. It's in the looking after others and watching them grow that we see ourselves grow also. It's in the calamities that we receive beautiful gifts and learning opportunities. We are all in this together and need the love and support of others to aid in our healing and growth.

Gathering pens, coloured pencils, paper and craft tools from a cupboard in the hallway, you lug them all to the table near the window, looking out over the garden. The garden still looks bare, but you trust that with your watering and nurturing, it will bloom and grow. You see a ray of sunshine and know it will bring the garden the love and light it needs.

Pouring a cup of tea, you sit, immersed in paper, pens and memories. You feel ready to look deep inside to extract all the love from your heart to compile a special, loving Pink Tribute.

During the Pink Tribute process, you will be prompted to answer questions, ponder the past and consider relevant information to create different sections of your tribute. The tribute can ultimately be bound together as a book or just kept in your Pink Grief Journal. The process gives you an opportunity to think about your Loved One and put together your memories to compile a special gift for yourself. It will help alleviate your fears about forgetting your Loved One as it will document everything for your future remembrance, to hold close to your heart always.

Creating a tribute is another tool to help you walk through your grief. As you compile each section you will have memories and love appearing close to your heart. Tears of sadness may arise to help your healing process. When you are connected to yourself, you can access the love buried below, which allows you to remain connected to your Loved One.

The sections I suggest are totally flexible and you can create your Pink Tribute however you like. I am simply offering a blueprint for you to get started. Once you begin, you may find you want to be more creative.

On your grief journey, feelings change quickly from day to day, so allow your feelings to be expressed. As the feelings occur walk with them to where they need to go. Be gentle with yourself as you put your tribute together, live in the moments and feel the love that arises. Take a rest if you need. Appreciate your Loved One and what they brought to your life during their physical life and what they continue to bring in their passing. At this stage, in the wake of their death, you can live amidst the memories and cherish the love that lives on in your heart.

Step 1: Timeline

Recording everything you can remember from your lives together is an effective way of remembering the events you lived through with your Loved One. These memories build the invisible strings that maintain the bonds of love that still exist today. For some, like me, your Loved One has been in your life for many years, maybe all your years. For others, your relationship may be shorter or only more recent. This doesn't matter for it is the love and the depth of feeling that makes the relationship special, and that does not always equal decades.

To get started in this section it helps to hunt for old photos, scour through diaries, and pour over old movies and videos. Arrange to meet for coffee with relatives and ask them to respond to a list of pre-written questions to glean all the information you can to fill in the gaps.

I have all my diaries from when I was ten and all the invitations I have ever received in prettily decorated scrapbooks. (I am a bit of an emotional hoarder.) I also have an A4 notebook with a page for every year where I list all the highlights of that year for quick reflection, a practice I picked up from a family member.

Pink Grief Corner – Question Time

Read all the points below and allow time and space for self-reflection. Allow the memories to surface slowly and gently. When you lose a Loved One you may want to recall everything you can. The more the better. Giving yourself permission to recall and feel your memories may be all that you need to draw them to the surface. Try to stop resisting and avoiding heartache and see what comes to the forefront of your mind. Remembering cherished memories may trigger even more memories. There are so many buried beneath the busyness of our days and the heaviness of our grief.

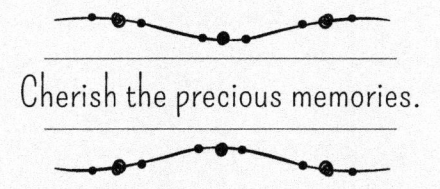

Cherish the precious memories.

Get a big piece of butcher's paper and in the middle write your Loved One's name in big bold letters, maybe surrounded by a love heart. You could also use a big whiteboard. Next you will use the questions below to lovingly brainstorm and mind map all you can possibly remember about them. To do this, you dump all your memories down in any order onto the paper or board (or write them on post-it notes and put them on the paper/board). Do not worry about keeping it neat and tidy or in chronological order; just get it all down for now.

Stop and take three deep breaths. Honour yourself with patience, gentleness and a compassionate spirit. Come from a place of love: your love and the love of your Loved One. The whole point is *love!*

PINK TRIBUTE

Let's get started and see what memories pop up when you think of the following in relation to your Loved One!

1. Where, when and how you first met.
2. Your earliest times together.
3. More recent times together.
4. Best memories.
5. Funniest memories.
6. Saddest occasions.
7. Their support in hard times.
8. Events, tasks, chores and purchases together.
9. Did you live together? Living together.
10. Favourite places.
11. Special events or milestones.
12. Holidays.
13. Did you work together? Working together.
14. Sharing meals together.
15. Musical tastes and concerts or shows.
16. Shared outings.
17. Hobbies and sporting activities.

After you have mind mapped all your answers onto the butcher's paper/board, you can spend some time arranging the thoughts and memories into an order that works for you in your Pink Grief Journal, a notebook or on another piece of paper (or by simply rearranging the post-it notes). You may like to separate the events by years or stages in your life until you have created a timeline of your life together.

> Each step of your tribute you can make as small as a few pages or as big as a book that you may like to publish one day – whatever works for you as their tribute. Keep this exercise close by as you progress through this book and add to it whenever a new memory pops into your head.

My sister volunteered to gather all the information about Dad and his life, and our aim is to publish a family book. We want to preserve his memories and keep his history alive, for us and future generations. We want them to know what a wonderful man our father was and that it is his love and values that filter down through our lineage, helping to make us the people we are today.

Step 2: Family history

Losing your Loved One often brings with it a yearning to learn more about your family history. Grief can bring an almost obsessive memory hunt as we strive to feel connected. This is normal.

This section is about your Loved One's family history, going back to the generations before them. Knowing their history is understanding more about them and helps you to gain an appreciation for their life. I was lucky that we had the time to sit with Dad and find out his history before he passed away. His storytelling brought sharing to a whole new level for us. It came with a lot of fragility and vulnerability, love, amusement and captivation.

Pink Grief Corner – Question Time

Utilise friends, family, libraries, the internet and even long-lost relatives to uncover your family history. These days it is so easy to connect with people through Facebook, even if you don't know them. If you are related introduce yourself, friend them on Facebook and see what you can find out. Maybe even travel the world to connect to the long-lost parts of your family heritage, like I did.

Stop and take three deep breaths. Honour yourself with patience, gentleness and a compassionate spirit. Come from a place of love: your love and the love of your Loved One. The whole point is *love!*

Record your feelings in your Pink Grief Journal:

Let's get started and see what you already know about your Loved One!

1. When were they born?
2. Where were they born: hospital, state and country?
3. Where did they live in their childhood?
4. What siblings do they have?
5. What is their heritage? Do they speak a foreign language?
6. To whom were they born? Include their parents' names and dates of birth.
7. Where were their parents born?
8. If they were born overseas, how did they end up living here?

9. Are their parents still alive? If not, when did they pass away?
10. Where did they go to school?
11. Did they study at university?
12. Did they start a business or work for someone else?
13. What did their parents do for a living?
14. Where do all their relatives live?
15. What do you know about their family tree?
16. Does anyone in the family have a family tree? Can you create a family tree?
17. Do you know anything about their cousins?
18. What did they do as a family when they were younger?
19. How did they survive and afford to live?
20. How far back can you travel with their family history?
21. Did anyone in their family fight for their country? Was anyone awarded any medals or prestigious awards?

Again, utilising these questions as a guide, I am hoping you can put together a family history mind map to add to your timeline and your Pink Tribute. Take a rest when you need; this information can take a long time to unfold.

Since my dad's death I have returned to Italy and feel so connected to my lineage. Knowing more about the miracle that was my dad and his life fascinates me and fills me with love and a sense of connection to him and his family, a place I feel I belong wholeheartedly. All this is so important to me.

Step 3: Your Loved One

This section is the part where you get to remember affectionately and rave enthusiastically about all the parts of your Loved One that you can. From the way they waved their arms when they danced or maybe to the way they combed their hair before an important appointment. Any fun, interesting, different or silly traits and mannerisms should be included.

The remembering and the crying and laughing are all part of the healing process. Don't push yourself though. If you are not ready do it later. If you are ready do it now. Always do whatever feels right to you on your grief journey.

Pink Grief Corner – Question Time

Discover what you know, then see if any other family members can fill in the gaps. Relish in finding out what you can.

Stop and take three deep breaths. Honour yourself with patience, gentleness and a compassionate spirit. Come from a place of love: your love and the love of your Loved One. The whole point is *love!*

Record your feelings in your Pink Grief Journal:

1. What were their major achievements?
2. What did they love the most?
3. What did they fear?
4. What was their one passion in life?
5. What did they believe in passionately?

6. What were their values?
7. What things did they like?
8. What did they dislike?
9. How did they treat others?
10. What were their hobbies over the years?
11. What mannerisms and facial expressions did they have?
12. What made them laugh, and what made them frustrated?
13. Who did they like to spend their time with?
14. Were they a social butterfly or more introverted?
15. What funny things did they do?
16. What music, movies and books did they like?
17. What situations and places did they gravitate to?
18. Is there a smell that reminds you of them?
19. What were their favourite sayings, quotes or words?
20. What three words would you use to describe them?

This is a particularly beautiful section to complete because you get up close and personal with who they were, how they behaved, and all the little traits and mannerisms that made them a unique individual.

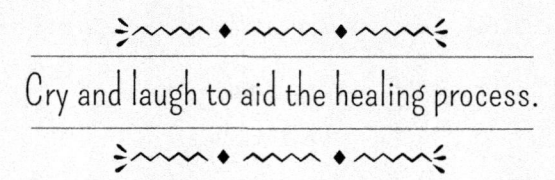

Cry and laugh to aid the healing process.

I often look back on my notes about Dad and giggle quietly to myself about something silly. The next minute I find myself in tears over a warm memory that seemed like yesterday.

Sometimes I think about my grandparents, who passed away long ago, with fondness and poignancy. Quickly I remember that Dad, who was only here what seemed like yesterday, is also now in the category of fond memories and not my everyday reality. Our times together are a distant memory, our conversations just words floating around in my mind, his face only in my dreams. As I realise the magnitude of my loss, the grief washes over me again.

I know that grief diminishes – I've experienced it – but sometimes my grief still has me wondering if I will ever feel the level of love and deep happiness I felt before his diagnosis. I can't fathom what could replace those warm, fuzzy feelings inside to that same level of happiness again. Yet in other moments I do experience profound and abundant joy; it is now just different. It is grief!

Maybe this is just a symptom of getting older and the innocence and naivety of our youth fading, bringing with it a life of memories instead of hugs. I now understand that it is the grief speaking through me that can still lock me in its sadness at a moment's notice. I also know now that this grip will be released if I surrender to it, and it will allow me to continue with the love and happiness I deserve, while keeping Dad close.

Step 4: You and your Loved One

This is a special section as you are gifted the opportunity to think about the relationship you beautifully crafted with your Loved One from the beginning of your relationship to the present moment. It is where you get to show appreciation for their effect on your life and the person you have become.

Grief, Grace and Gratitude

When you are busy and rushing through life, you may not stop long enough to appreciate why you hold certain special traits and values. There are normally specific people in your life that guide and nurture you. I like to think of these special people as your angels who constantly help hold up your butterfly wings, shower beauty like roses on you and sprinkle their adoring love all around you.

It is now time to stop and think about how these people enriched your life, as a dedication to your unique relationship. Know that it was special; they were special and you are special! If there is any doubt, use this section to stand tall in this truth. Your Loved One had a major impact on who you are and how you behave. Reflecting upon the questions below may strongly remind you of their importance and the love you hold so dear. Allow any tears to flow as they likely will.

Each tear is a sign of love and healing. They are a way to remain connected. Move forward with your Loved One tucked up inside your heart, to walk the rest of your magnificent journey with you. They are never far away; in fact, they are with you always!

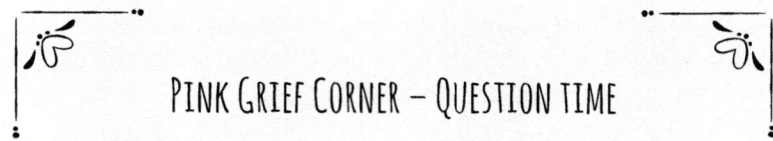

Pink Grief Corner – Question time

Contemplate and celebrate your beautiful relationship.

Stop and take three deep breaths. Honour yourself with patience, gentleness and a compassionate spirit. Come from a place of love: your love and the love of your Loved One. The whole point is *love!*

Record your feelings in your Pink Grief Journal:

1. I thank you for...
2. I learned from you...

PINK TRIBUTE

3. I respect you for...
4. I admire you for...
5. You made me feel...
6. I miss it when...
7. I would love to tell you that...
8. I will in your honour...
9. My favourite words to say to you are...
10. My favourite thing to do with you is...
11. I forgive you for...
12. I ask that you forgive me for...
13. I am grateful for...
14. I wish that you...
15. I hope that you...
16. I love your values of...
17. I appreciate that you...
18. The three words I remember you by are...
19. I accept that you...
20. I love you because...

Stop and feel the love!

Thank them from the bottom of your heart. By compiling this part of your Pink Tribute you are honouring them and their special existence.

Step 5: The letter

You look up from all the pens and paper on the table and focus on your surroundings for a moment. Looking out the window you feel a grounding effect on your soul. Needing a break, you boil the kettle, make a cup of tea and head outside to sit with your garden. You pepper your love and energy through the atmosphere hoping for it to softly float through the air and drizzle gently into the soil. You visualise it attaching to the deep roots of your plants, knowing that love and energy is what will help it grow and blossom.

You have become attached to your garden quickly, considering gardening has never been a passion. The reasons for the garden, and the love that lies under its creation, underlies your drive to create a wonder-filled garden of delight.

Creating the garden is waking you up more to self-love. Loving the garden, loving your Loved One and taking time out is truly loving yourself. You realise that you are starting to understand what self-love is all about, as you go about honouring your Loved One and yourself every step of the way.

The sun and your soul deliver a warm fuzziness throughout your body, telling you that you are exactly where you are meant to be. You let your thoughts float past softly as you bask in the fresh air, the earth and the garden for a moment.

You know it is time to write a letter to your Loved One and that you need time to think about what you will write. So you decide to spend the afternoon in the garden. You ask yourself a question, allow it to sink in, let it go and go about your gardening, allowing your question to slowly sprinkle its wisdom throughout you.

Later, you return to your table to express the ideas and words resting in your heart as you compose your letter. You know exactly what you want to say. You never needed time to think about it as it was always sitting on the cusp of your heart, just waiting to be released and expressed.

You write until you have exhausted all your words. You know you are finished; you feel it. You come to a bittersweet conclusion, knowing you have expressed what you needed to, for today at least. You feel lighter for having articulated your thoughts and feelings.

Writing is truly cathartic. Crafting your words on paper straight from your heart to your Loved One provides a sense of release as you acknowledge the depth of your bond and love. For this stage of the Pink Tribute you will need faith and courage to compose a beautiful letter to your Loved One to say goodbye to them as you knew them, as a physical presence in your life (knowing they are still by your side but in another form). It may be one page or twenty; it doesn't matter. This is an individual exercise, and your heart will inform you when it has fully expressed what it needs to.

PINK GRIEF CORNER – QUESTION TIME

The question: 'What do I wish to say to my Loved One?'

Refer to the sections you have already completed in your Pink Tribute, especially the last section. Think about what you would like to say to your Loved One if they were standing in front of you. What do you want them to know and to take with them forever? Think about your love, your loss, your lessons and what you would like to share.

Close your eyes, find your stillness and visualise them sitting in front of you, their eyes staring into yours. What is resting on your heart that needs to be expressed?

Stop and take three deep breaths. Honour yourself with patience, gentleness and a compassionate spirit. Come from a place of love: your love and the love of your Loved One. The whole point is *love!*

Now, compose your letter.

What you do with the letter is up to you. You may like to place it in your Pink Grief Journal, make it pretty and frame it, bury it in the garden, share it with others or follow any other ritual that will help you find peace.

I wrote and wrote and wrote and shed tears and tears. I had a raw heart needing to self-express. I placed a copy of my letter in Dad's casket with him. I wanted to send him off to his new home with all my words, thoughts and feelings close to his heart.

Feeling tired, loved up and drained, you retire to the kitchen to whip up a quick nourishing dinner. After dinner you hear a warm Epsom salt bath softly calling your name. You know it will melt your muscles, heart and soul and lovingly bequeath the sound sleep your body is craving. Sleep will repair your tired body and helps to bring you to the new day with renewed energy and vigour to face the next part of your grief journey.

Morning comes and brings with it another step in the Pink Tribute. Lighting the fire and boiling the kettle you wander outside to check on your garden and water the plants before settling into the couch, ready to take a walk back in time, your time!

Step 6: Photo album collage

Photos are our visual memory delicacies. They transport us back to a place and time where we had fun times with our loved ones. They remind us of the innocence of afternoon picnics in the sun, long drives to cherished destinations, the simplicity of celebrations, smiles and laughter, and many more times long gone but never forgotten.

Photos help to bring forth the emotions behind the veil we use to suppress our grief. They bathe us in the sweet nostalgia of revisiting our precious times, if only for a moment, to 'see' and feel what we felt once before.

As the photos help us recall those special snaps in time etched on our heart, which we may long for again, we will cry and we will laugh. This is another important part of our healing regime!

Pink Grief Corner – Photo collage

Gather all the photo albums you have access to and have your computer nearby.

1. Take photos from your album that you would like in your photo collage. Number the back of the photo and leave a sticky-note with the same number on it in the empty space in the album, so you can return the original photos later to the right spot.
2. Place these photos in an envelope ready to be copied.
3. Open your computer and create a new folder.
4. Search through all your photos on the computer and any photos you want in your collage. Copy (not cut)

and place the copy of the photo in the newly created folder.
5. When you have finished place this new folder of photos on a USB stick.
6. Take the envelope and the USB stick to a local printing business.
7. Get a copy of each photo reprinted and a copy of each photo from the USB.
8. Buy some nice photo albums.
9. When you get home, replace the original copies in the albums. Use the numbers to ensure they get put back in the correct spot.
10. Sort through the photos that you had printed and put them in the new photo albums in any order you choose (e.g. sort by time, event, year, people).
11. Transfer the photos from the USB stick onto your phone for easy viewing.
12. Finish creating your new albums.
13. Find a nice place they can call home in your house.

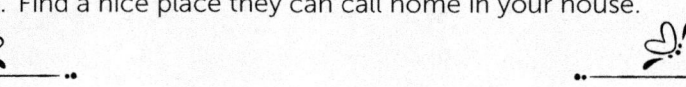

You will now have a special folder on your computer with all the favourite photos of your Loved One plus a copy on your phone to view any time you are feeling sad or just need to see them. You have also created a photo album or two. Holding a photo album in your hands and flicking through the thick pages like we did many years ago is more tender and brings a sounder connection to our memories.

You can bring out your photo album when people visit and sit together and savour the memories. You can put the USB stick into any TV or device and show the photos on a slideshow at family dinners or special occasions.

Photos captured timeless magical moments spent with your Loved One. Treasure and cherish the memories you have and remember to always build more.

Step 7: Other tributes

There may be other tributes you wish to add to your Pink Tribute. Let your imagination and creative style flow. At this point in your grief, your creative style can appear in full force as the deep feelings you tap into draw out an inner passion to honour the one you loved so much.

Pink Grief Corner – Creative time

Some other ideas for tributes may include:

- artwork and drawings
- song writing
- poetry
- building a garden
- planting a tree
- creating a jewellery piece
- hosting a dinner or a gathering
- funding a charity
- rescuing an animal
- making a quilt

- 💘 painting a stone for the garden
- 💘 burning or making candles
- 💘 collecting ornaments
- 💘 making a DVD
- 💘 writing a book
- 💘 cooking
- 💘 arranging flowers
- 💘 practising yearly rituals
- 💘 creating altars.

There are so many ways to celebrate your Loved One's life and remain connected to them, especially in the initial grief stages. Do what feels right for you. Trust your intuition to follow the path it needs to honour them and ease the grief. But be gentle with your broken heart.

Congratulations! Well done on completing this difficult yet loving task. You now hold a Pink Tribute to your Loved One. You can now take a big breath. Inhale into the depths of your tummy, allowing your belly to expand, ribs to open and lungs to fill up with air. Gently and slowly exhale, allowing the belly, ribs and chest to fall while the air fully releases, alongside any grief that you are gripping on to at this moment.

Observe any thoughts floating past while you allow yourself to just be in this moment with your special Pink Tribute, which houses all your love and respect for your Loved One and your time together.

You can now choose to house all this information in your Pink Grief Journal or you may wish to formalise the information into a book that you may give your family or even a book you may

PINK TRIBUTE

wish to publish for the generations to come. What you choose to do from here is very personal and individual, but you have all the information to move forward as you desire or as your heart is guiding you to do.

Your creation with all your individual love and feelings is a special tribute to your Loved One. This tribute can be held close to your heart for an eternity. It is always available to you when you are feeling sad and missing them. It is always accessible when you are happy and have something special you want to share with them. It is a comfort to you for a lifetime.

It is always there just as your Loved One is always there, in a different form.

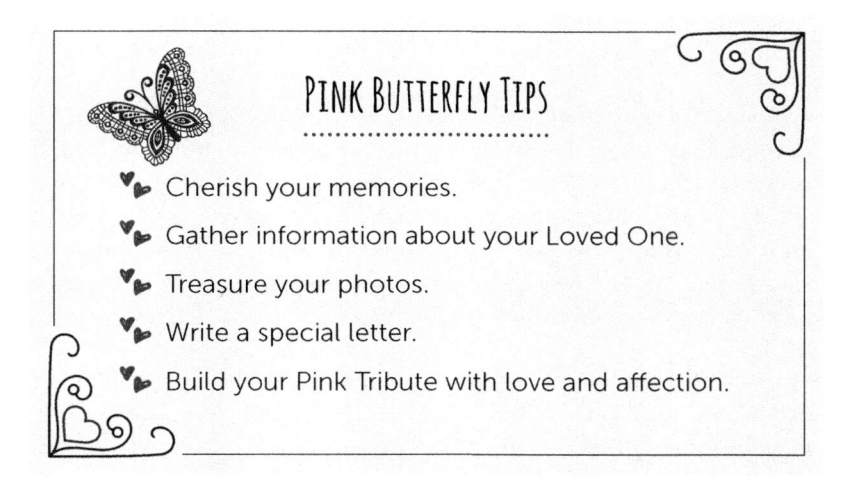

PINK BUTTERFLY TIPS

- Cherish your memories.
- Gather information about your Loved One.
- Treasure your photos.
- Write a special letter.
- Build your Pink Tribute with love and affection.

It is time to stretch your legs. Taking a water bottle and reaching for a jacket, you float out the door feeling a little lighter after completing your Pink Tribute. You decide to take a short walk, hoping not to get lost back in the depths of the Forest of Grief. You only want to keep moving forward. You don't relish the steps backwards that take you by surprise every now and then.

Grief, Grace and Gratitude

You allow your heart to lead the way and follow a path past your newly planted garden. After some twists and turns, a few kilometres away you arrive at a quaint little village buzzing with activity.

A signpost is the first to greet you.

> The Field of Grace welcomes you to its
> heart centre … Population 10,000
> Come and enjoy our hospitality.
> Find your TRUTH. Be YOU!

Why had you never seen this before? Maybe you were not ready. You needed to spend time alone with your introversion and your feelings to sort through the icky clutter of grief inside. Briefly you feel a speckle of joy bubble up as you look at the sign. A little company and distraction from your grief would be welcomed gratefully. The joy expands and showers you with hope that, in time, you can move forward and once again live a rich, full life.

Wandering through the village you notice shops lining the streets like perfect soldiers. They are full of meticulously handmade crafts, freshly-grown produce, aromatic essential oils and candles, and fragrant flowers and greenery – a paradise to heal the soul.

You spend the day here, immersed in the village. When it's time to leave you notice you are smiling. You have enjoyed herbal tea with the friendliest people, shopped amongst beautifully crafted items and patted the silky coats of dogs who endlessly wagged their tails. For today you have been once again immersed in life. A small taste of life has raised a glimmer of hope that when the intensity of your grief journey lessens and you heal a little more, you will dive deeply back into life again.

On the walk home back to the Cabin of Love, you realise that you feel more like yourself than you have in a long time. You are still sorrowful, but in acknowledging the grief and walking the grief path you have accepted who you are and what you need. You are looking after yourself better and being more self-loving. Once again you are connecting to your heart and, despite the grief, it feels sweet.

You are lugging home a few gifts for the cabin to spruce things up a bit: a doormat with a blue butterfly, some new throw rugs in warm, bright colours and a beautiful canvas of pink roses to pretty up the walls. You want to add your touch to the cabin. The friend before you left her touches, which has helped you feel comfortable. So, when you leave, you want to leave a legacy for the next soul who needs to house themselves in the cabin's beauty as they walk through their grief journey.

You pass one of the 'Love' arrow signposts and have an epiphany: Life is about living your truth – being authentic to your heart and soul. It is about taking time out to be with your pain, allowing its truth to surface for healing and giving the new YOU permission to shine out to the world.

> Life is about living your truth.

You turn the corner and the Cabin of Love comes into sight. Home! The planter pots are full of seedlings bursting to grow and show their prettiness to the world. Sitting on the bench at the front door is your critter friend, standing up like a meerkat, waiting patiently for you to return and settle in for the night.

Love, roses and butterflies always surround you, especially when you notice what is going on around you, and inside you, by living delightfully in your truth. The Field of Grace is delivering your truth on a platter and walking you through your grief journey. Hugging this truth quickly brings you to your soul's yearnings, bursting to come forth to be scattered all over your world.

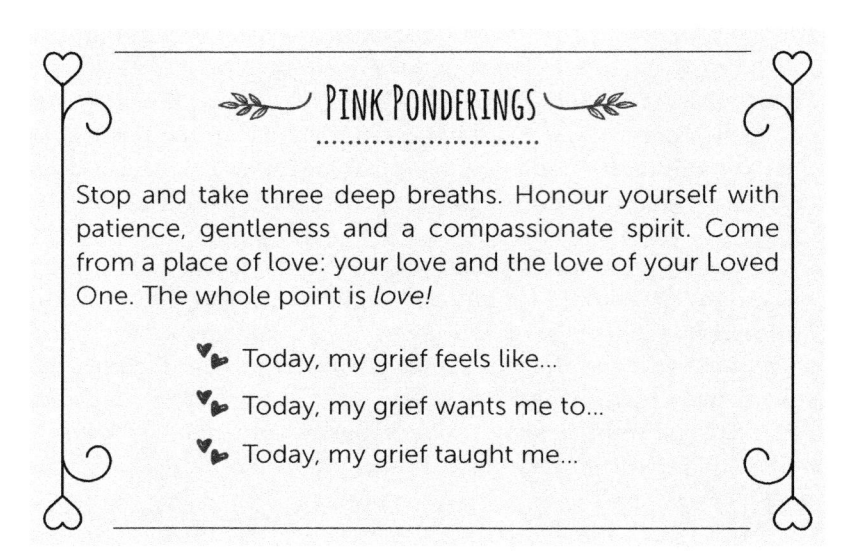

✿ PINK PONDERINGS ✿

Stop and take three deep breaths. Honour yourself with patience, gentleness and a compassionate spirit. Come from a place of love: your love and the love of your Loved One. The whole point is *love!*

- Today, my grief feels like…
- Today, my grief wants me to…
- Today, my grief taught me…

YEARNINGS

"You have the choice to create the life your heart is yearning to live."

–Mahatma Gandhi

Today you wake up and feel a stirring inside, a form of peppy energy that makes it difficult for you to stand still. You feel different – a shimmer of excitement maybe! Breakfast and your cup of herbal tea do not quash the sensations.

Almost on autopilot you dress and step outside to walk your body with its newfound energy back to the village. Something is calling you and you follow its voice. Turning into the main street you are drawn to a shopfront and find you are standing at the local bookstore. Inside you go!

Strolling around inside, with no agenda, you browse through books of all different genres from travel to novels to animals. You immerse yourself in the varied topics and wonder where or what you would like to do next in your life, for a moment taking you out of your grief to daydream.

Suddenly that peppy energy from this morning reappears, making it impossible for you to be still. Something is calling. You feel you are in the right space, coming closer to what you need to do or where you need to be. This seesaws you from excitement to fear to sadness and back again.

You have always loved books from those full of abundant wisdom to glorious fantasy; they take you on a delicious inner journey. Taking your selected books to the counter, the girl hands you a brochure that reads, 'Our local book club is seeking active participants to join them in a passionate journey through the books of our century'.

You hug it close to your heart as you walk to the coffee shop. The brochure has brought a gentle yet giant inner smile and sense of peace. This must be the answer to the strange stirring inside.

Two days later your yearning takes you back through the quaint village to the bookstore. A black Labrador sits on the welcome mat seemingly beckoning you inside. You stop to give her a quick pat and fluff the hair on her head before you go in and sign up for the book club.

The restless energy racing around within calms down with a knowing that this is part of your grief journey. It is joined by a sense of excitement. 'Yay! I'm going to fulfil one of my passions while meeting some new friends!' natters your inner voice.

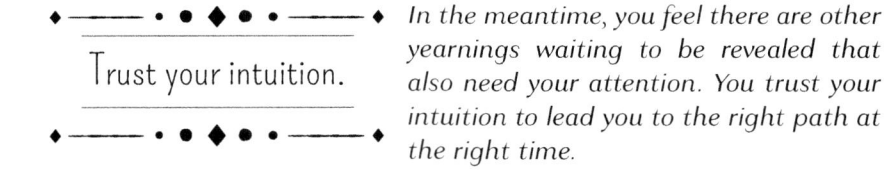

> Trust your intuition.

In the meantime, you feel there are other yearnings waiting to be revealed that also need your attention. You trust your intuition to lead you to the right path at the right time.

Today, as you sit overlooking your garden and sipping tea amongst your colourful throw rugs, you feel an amazing sense of composure and pleasure as you soak up the knowledge of your upcoming new experience. You visualise all the beautiful books you will wrap your heart around and know that many truthful delights will be birthed.

Living your soul's purpose and following its whispered yearnings awakens you in a new vibrant way. It gifts you a sense of aliveness that has been buried for some time, allowing the truth to start shining internally, highlighting its value and significance.

Footsteps of your yearnings

> "Metamorphosis has always been the greatest symbol of change for poets and artists. Imagine that you could be a caterpillar one moment and a butterfly the next."
> —Louie Schwartzberg

In walking with awareness through your grief journey and experiencing the rainbow of grief emotions, you are likely to sense some ground-shaking movement within. This movement can take on its own shape as your soul shifts and transforms, asking you to fulfil its spirited desires. At this stage, it becomes even more crucial to listen to your intuition guiding your footsteps.

Yearnings can be overpowering. They can create desires within you so strong that you may move mountains to attain them. A yearning is like a knowing, an urge or deep longing that is especially persuasive when accompanied by the grief emotions of sadness and tenderness. Its path, when followed, leads you to powerful learnings in your grief journey.

A grief yearning creates excitement inside accompanied by sadness and fear. These intense emotions heighten the desire to fulfil its wishes yet can make it difficult – and frightening – to live up to its requests. You can feel in limbo land as you stand on the precipice and look into the abyss, paralysed by fear and excitement and feeling swamped by indecision. Not a good place to reside! However, your soul knows exactly what it needs and wants, and yearnings are the way it communicates with you. The longer you choose to ignore them the louder they become, creating an urgent energy that can no longer be ignored.

If you do ignore these urges, pressure will continue to build up and create disharmony inside. It will likely take all your energy to suppress the yearning, which will add to your unhappiness and unease.

Find your courage and faith and trust your intuition. Trust yourself. You know what you need to do. You are being directed, and all you need to do is listen and follow your yearning. From there all your learnings will be exposed, bringing about huge transformations in your journey and more healing. Your yearnings know precisely what you need to do next to accelerate the healing and learnings.

Just walk its talk!

Trust your Inner Pink Star

I first coined the term 'Inner Pink Star' in my first book, *Heartbreak, Healing and Happiness*, referring to your inner guidance, intuition, inner wisdom or gut instinct.

She is a part of you that you may have ignored or forgotten. Even so, she is still there quietly in the background, patiently waiting for acknowledgement. You may have neglected to listen to her. You may have overlooked the fact that you always know the answer.

Listen!

Starting to listen to her is where life starts to move you closer to your truth. The three steps forward and one step back starts to become more steps forward. You hear a voice and you know it's your Inner Pink Star. You follow her voice and, voila, healing begins. Life starts to flow with more ease.

She is born from love and holds all your internal creativity and power. She knows, every step of the way, just how lovable and pure you truly are. She knows immediately what is best for you. She doesn't judge nor put you in harm's way. She is the gateway to happiness, serenity, healing and truth. Your sense of confusion, not knowing which way to turn, becomes a calm, evaluated mindset that works perfectly for you.

She is quiet and often gets overshadowed by Lady Chitter Chatter – your ego and inner critic. It's time to let your Inner Pink Star guide you through the darkness into the light and straight into your yearnings to produce valuable learnings.

Calling on your Inner Pink Star

It is difficult to quieten our mind and access our Inner Pink Star. Our mind is usually so busy we can't hear through all the chitchat and the grief. Even when we wish our Inner Pink Star would appear, we still struggle to find her as she can be somewhat elusive. To hear her, you need to slow down and be quiet and still. If you practise this, over time she will appear from behind the noise and chaos. Be gentle and give her a chance. If you have ignored her for a long time, it may take a while for her shyness to fall away.

Follow the steps below to call on and connect with your Inner Pink Star, the beautiful part inside of you that houses your own intuition and wisdom. Practise regularly and celebrate when you finally touch your heart; honour her presence and wisdom. Life will change in profound ways.

Stop and take three deep breaths. Honour yourself with patience, gentleness and a compassionate spirit. Come from a place of love: your love and the love of your Loved One. The whole point is *love!*

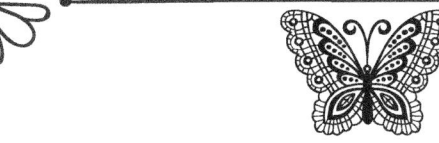

Calling on your Inner Pink Star!

1. Close your eyes and focus on your breath – the inhales and exhales.
2. Be still – Be patient – Be calm – Be silent – Be present.
3. Become the observer; just notice and be aware.
4. Let your thoughts rest and remove any attachment and judgement.
5. Surrender and let go as you go deeper inside.
6. Ask the question that is on your mind.
7. Pay attention and you will find her – the voice of your soul who holds deep your answers.
8. Trust the truth of your Inner Pink Star!

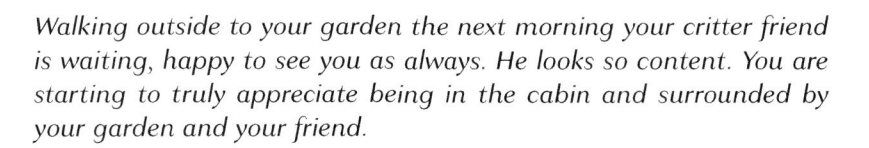

Walking outside to your garden the next morning your critter friend is waiting, happy to see you as always. He looks so content. You are starting to truly appreciate being in the cabin and surrounded by your garden and your friend.

Walking through your garden reveals its magnificence. You are thrilled to see the seedlings have blossomed, showering you with their colourful splendour. You realise that just as you have blossomed and grown, so has your Field of Grace.

You reflect on your yearnings and grief journey while thinking about your first book club last night and the joy and lightness it brought to your soul. Although the grief remains, it is purer and you have cleared out some of the darkness in your soul. You feel more settled and seek a simple yet rich life.

YEARNINGS

The kettle boils and you plop yourself on the couch to enjoy the day with your nose in your book. You ponder your next yearning and your upcoming birthday!

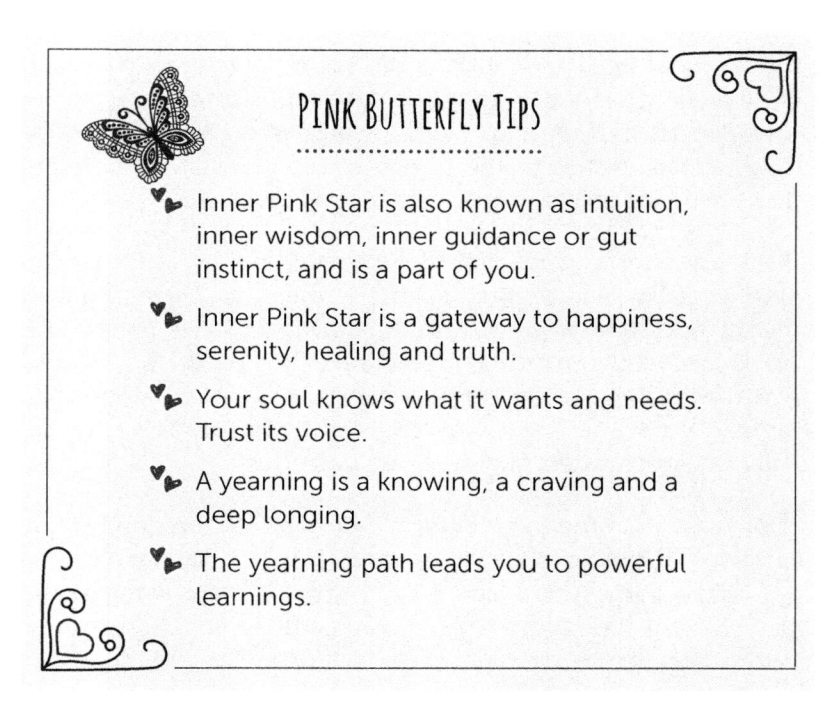

PINK BUTTERFLY TIPS

- Inner Pink Star is also known as intuition, inner wisdom, inner guidance or gut instinct, and is a part of you.
- Inner Pink Star is a gateway to happiness, serenity, healing and truth.
- Your soul knows what it wants and needs. Trust its voice.
- A yearning is a knowing, a craving and a deep longing.
- The yearning path leads you to powerful learnings.

MY YEARNINGS

A yearning may start at any time. At first it may present as a slow, quiet humming within, but it can quickly morph into a loud, intense calling, taking on a potent life force of its own, waiting to burst. This is exactly what happened to me...

With faith and courage, I chose to trust these swirling sensations. Around this time in my grief, I passed an empty block, the ground carved with deep and solid foundations. I stood mesmerised. I suddenly realised that I also had good foundations but needed to rebuild. I needed to find myself, start again, change and grow to reap the gifts of my loss.

So, my Inner Pink Star led the way and on I went!

The first year I had sat tight and delved into the deep, dark grief. The following year my yearnings presented themselves to me and I decided to step up and move towards them and their truths. They had been sitting on the edge of my soul, waiting to be heard. These experiences left me vibrating at my core.

Firstly, I discovered and relished the beauty of a seaside town, the white squeaky sand on the beach, the waves rolling in, the calm and solitude of the yoga studio, the extravagant styles in the shops, the hippie feel of the local markets, the doggy beach full of puppy love, the local music, the fresh air, the lightness of the people, the pampering day spa, the yummy foods, the warm coffees, the long walks, the cool waters and the good books.

I also relished in the inner workings of my soul, the depth of my emotions, the poignancy of my grief, the flow of sadness, the wrap of tenderness, the rawness of my heart, the heartbreak that sat within, the desire for a rich life, the search for my truth, the love for my dad and the sun on my face.

I continued to follow my heart and my next yearning took me to Italy where my family heritage was awaiting me. I disembarked in Rome and instantly felt the healing begin. My heart melted. In a city with millions of people, speaking a language I could only converse in like a school student, I felt I had arrived at my second home.

I nicknamed Rome my 'eternal healing city'. I was drawn into the basilicas by their architecture and charm, leading into an appreciation of the ancient wisdom contained therein. In these magnificent buildings I felt calm yet joyful; it mimicked how I felt about my dad. Peace settled quietly on my soul.

YEARNINGS

Invisible strings connected me to beautiful Italy. It was about the bonds of love between me and Dad. It was about rich and fulfilling adventures on winding roads that led to more beauty and self-discovery. It was about the old nonnas, oozing warmth and affection, serving cannoli or crostoli in small city cafes. It was about the song Volare and artists like Dean Martin trilling their majestic masterpieces over the buildings and waters. It was about the dogs that sat in shops with love in their puppy eyes, waiting for their owners or just going about their business, sniffing and enjoying la dolce vita.

It was about swimming in the Mediterranean and fully appreciating where I was. It was about the men drinking espresso and loudly discussing life. It was about getting lost on cobblestoned roads that led to new and exciting discoveries. It was about walking through the streets marvelling at the lay of the land. It was about sitting and people watching for hours at a time. It was about living life, moving slowly and loving every inch of it. It was about feeling connected to me, my grief, my dad and my healing!

Next, I attended four weeks of immersion in yoga teacher training where I learned not only the yoga asana but also the lifestyle and ancient philosophy of the yogic path. I was lucky to have this wisdom delivered to me by teachers that radiated the yoga charm and had perfected their craft in ashrams around the world. I was truly on a path to my next unfolding of self.

Following this it was time to write this book and invest time in my Life in the Pink business, living my dream and my purpose. It was simple yet complex. I had taken time out to heal my heart and soul. Following my yearnings directly to their source quickly taught me insightful things about my life, my loss and me. I knew I was on the right path to my truth as my swirling energy was subsiding and being satiated.

My yearnings led me to face tremendous sorrow, calm, independence and joy. The whole host of rainbow emotions presented themselves as I walked barefoot through the centre of my soul. My fears were quelled and I awoke to my life amidst my loss. My soul felt immense pleasure. Even though grief was still hovering just under the surface, grief and pleasure were beginning to live side by side and eventually began to unite as one in my heart.

Sometimes it is in the quiet of the night that you find the stillness to access the depth of your feelings, allowing grief to wash over you. You can tell you are on the right path to your yearnings for healing because it feels right, even while dealing with intense grief emotions. The gifts are found in the silence and its beauty. Honouring your feelings allows them to swirl around, moving their energy in circles as they rise up to be expressed.

Yearnings draw you to the middle of your soul to feel, and ultimately heal, all the sadness and poignancy of your loss. Yearnings help you to appreciate the dichotomy of their amazing beauty and grief's devastating sadness and aloneness, all housed together in your heart.

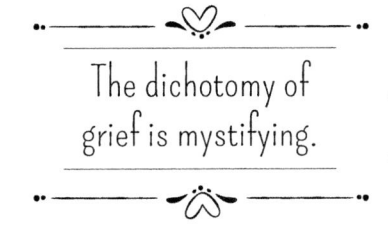

> The dichotomy of grief is mystifying.

This dichotomy is what makes us human; experiencing the full rainbow of emotions including the polar opposites is life. Blocking the not-so-good and trying to see only the good would have us living a half-life or one filled with lifelong angst and disconnection from ourselves. Without the full experience of the not-so-good, you will never experience the full experience of the good.

As you follow your yearnings, the tenderness and poignancy of your grief will surround you while you feel love jump inside your heart. The heart wants to heal and to feel, so it will always take you on the right grief journey adventure.

You may find, like I did, that life becomes more interesting, amazing, magical, poignant and nostalgic. Our inner self can surprise and delight us with every new thought, feeling, experience and part of ourselves that we get to meet. As the connection builds, like

YEARNINGS

bonding with a new friend, the relationship can bestow such exquisite profundity of self that the world around us will seem to illuminate brighter than ever before.

All that matters is that you love and honour yourself. It's how you see yourself, not how others see you. Once you truly love yourself, you can gift this love to others, leaving your own small mark on the world. Believe in your inner truth and yearnings, and you will see this come to fruition.

If you truly follow your yearnings and your heart's footprints to the doors of your dreams, you will be rewarded with love and truth. It can be an emotionally charged time that can lead you to experience the total rainbow of grief emotions. But it leaves you with inner secrets and wisdom that you could only have found from following these yearnings. Your yearnings will most likely escort you to the epicentre of your soul.

Exposing yourself to new adventures allows your soul to blossom. When the quietness and stillness come, the ability to heal presents itself with voraciousness. Learn to live a rich and full life. Experience it all. You get one life, and you are the author and creator of that life. How you choose your life to unfold is up to you. Yes, there will be things you can't control. But you can control and learn to respond with a thought-out calmness instead of reacting quickly or aggressively without thought in the situations and experiences you find yourself in.

Feel your feelings and take the grief journey to the point where the love buried underneath rises to meet you and allows you to follow your truth to your yearnings and authentic life. By following your yearnings, you get to the source that is based on your truth: your authentic you, your true nature. You will find yourself, love yourself and heal yourself, and the transformation begins.

Transformation enables you to live your best life. In this instance, it is to live a rich and full life, blooming and growing into your future, surrounded with love, roses and butterflies.

Grief, Grace and Gratitude

"Happy Birthday" you mouth silently to yourself as you awake with memories of an amusing, vivid dream. It was of a celebration you threw for your birthday where you danced the night away like a princess; everything was perfect.

As you ponder your birthday, you also deliberate your yearnings, which have had you feeling more at ease, making it easier to find some much-needed sleep. You suddenly wonder how long you will be at the Cabin of Love. You had, in a way, forgotten about your journey. Life has just started to be a bit easier of late with a bit less grief. You are taking one moment at a time and finding the good amongst the not-so-good, the acceptance amongst the grief, the delight amongst the sorrow and the beauty amongst the loss.

The dichotomy is better understood and beginning to settle inside. Your birthday creates a deep desire to connect with others, but you know no one except a few from your book club! Sitting at home with your introversion and self-pity will not have potential friends knocking at your door, so you know you must make an effort.

You have an idea! You rise, get changed and walk outside to pick a bunch of flowers, soaking up the colours as you gather pink and white roses. You meticulously create a bouquet and finish it off with a big pink bow.

Carefully balancing the arrangement, you mosey into the village to share your day with others and see how you feel socially now that more time has passed. You step over the black Labrador in the bookstore doorway and, with a quick ruffle to her head, you place the flowers on the counter and ask to speak with Jane, the book club coordinator.

You thank her for organising book club last night. On finding Jane warm and friendly, you fully understand it is time to slowly walk back into your life. You have spent a lot of time looking after yourself,

YEARNINGS

allowing your introversion to reign, and feeling and healing your grief. It remains, and you still have work to do, but your normally extroverted side is peeking out again, looking for friends and a little fun.

You ask Jane if she would like to have coffee with you one day soon. You certainly need a friend and feel you have already connected. "Yes, love to," she replies. "In fact, I am having a dinner tomorrow night. Would you like to join us?" Doing a little inner jump for joy you accept her kind invitation and bid her farewell.

"Lilly!" she yells out as you walk towards the door. "The dog's name is Lilly. Bring some dog treats for her tomorrow night and she will love you forever."

"I will," you say. Cheekily, more words spill out. "By the way, it's my birthday today."

Jane runs up enthusiastically and gives you a big hug. "Dinner tomorrow night will be in your honour. Happy birthday, gorgeous girl! Enjoy your special day."

You blush as you leave the store, leaving the pink and white roses on the counter for others to revel in their splendour.

As you happily leave the village you look high up to the sky. As a big grin bursts upon your face you note two things. First, a lightness and joy has come to visit for a nanosecond that seems clear and fresh like the blue sky above. Secondly, you remember you had noticed a new yoga studio on the main street called 'Baddha Konasana', which is Sanskrit for the butterfly pose. You recognise that love, roses and butterflies continue to follow you wherever you go to bring you closer to your truth and happiness each day.

Home again! Opening the book titled Heartbreak, Healing and Happiness, you feel your mind and heart are a little more settled as you snuggle up for a good, long relaxing read while sipping tea on your birthday.

Grief, Grace and Gratitude

The biggest gift your Loved One would want to give you is to heal. They would not want you to suffer but to heal at all costs and for love and joy to once again blossom in your life. Unfortunately, walking through your grief does hurt a lot but only till you walk past the hot coals into the simmering heat. Then it is more bearable until, one day, the heat cools a bit more and you find yourself smiling and dancing the night away again.

Yes, just below the surface is the grief and, especially in the early stages, this grief is accessible in a single thought. But it is important to keep moving forward. Follow your yearnings, find your truth and allow your journey to unfold as it leads you on the path to your life purpose.

Your journey through your sabbatical will unfold in beautiful and unexpected ways, leading you to feel changed and sprouting beautiful butterfly wings. These wings will lead you forward to reveal new yearnings and discoveries.

Putting the book down for a moment you stare out the window to appreciate the beauty of the garden. Each day it becomes brighter and more impressive. More greenery covers the ground and you feel proud that your hard work is coming to fruition.

Heading outside to the garden shed you notice your critter friend is asleep in his little house, and you drop some seeds for him to eat later. He is quite cute. You are so fond of him now that you have even built him a bigger house. You left the handpainted roses around the entrance and repainted the rest in pink for added warmth and vibrancy.

In the shed you tidy up a bit and ruminate what you will wear tonight at your birthday dinner. You are pleasantly excited to immerse your fragile self into what you hope will be a supportive and friendly group of likeminded women.

YEARNINGS

Hours later, when you have painstakingly yet happily been on your knees in the depths of the garden, hands deep into the earth, you notice you feel grounded and your garden finally is looking tidier. Lastly, you unravel the hose and set up the sprinklers to nourish it with fresh water.

Looking at your meticulous work one last time, you turn to head to the bedroom to decide on your outfit for tonight. As you open the wardrobe, fearing a scarcity of clothes, to your surprise and amusement you find dresses, pants and shirts galore – an entire wardrobe. It's like your nice friend who lived here before never took her clothes with her. Sizing them up you think they will fit you nicely.

You remove your overalls and spend the afternoon trying on pants after dresses after skirts, like a teenager going to her first dance. You have a fun afternoon parading around in wardrobe paradise. Finally, you choose a knee-length little black dress with a boat neck and box pleats from the waist down. A simple yet elegant piece. You team it with black tights, high-heeled, closed-in black shoes and a pink ostrich feather wrap. A Tiffany bangle and an elegant opal necklace finish off your outfit perfectly. Gorgeous!

Standing in front of the mirror you are pleased yet hope you are not overdressed. It's been ages since you have had an opportunity to dress up, but it's your birthday and you want to look like the belle of the ball – or dinner party in this case. Grabbing a pink handbag and filling it with your makeup, keys and doggy treats, out the door you fly.

The cold chills of excitement, nervousness and anticipation produce a quick flash of goosebumps – a tingly delight to savour for a moment. You walk forwards with a skip in your step.

Pink Grief Corner – Your Pink Yearning List
Step 1: Pondering your yearning list

It's healthy to try new things, especially on your grief journey, if you are ready. Your yearnings may lead you to strange places you have never been to or expected to visit before. Mine led me from chanting Sanskrit to sipping espressos in Italy, two different ends of the spectrum. Now it's your turn to create your own 'Pink Yearning List'. You have read all about my yearnings and the profound benefits from following your heart.

Just go with your inner flow and see what eventuates. Not everything you try will stick with you for the long term, or maybe it will. You may surprisingly be delivered your absolute life passion and purpose from your yearnings through grief. I was! The key is to put yourself out there and follow your yearnings. Each experience is there to deliver its own special gift and lesson to your soul.

In this activity you will spend time reflecting on what yearnings mean to you.

While doing this activity, if the 'Who am I?' question raises its head, and it will, just let it be. For now, be your own version of eccentric until you work it out. If the 'What's the point?' question raises its head, just remember love is the point!

Remember, your yearning could be to travel somewhere specific or simply to remove stress from your life. It could be about completing a diploma or loving your body with a healthy diet. It could be about taking a year off work to radiate loving vibrations to everyone you meet or starting a new business. It could be about writing a book or just

YEARNINGS

spending more time with your dog at the dog park or your children at the playground.

A yearning is not necessarily a grand and expensive experience. Sometimes, it's the simple things that our soul is seeking. Find the stillness inside while you let your soul share exactly what that looks like for you. It's your list. Make it individual to you!

Find a safe space, sit still and ask yourself the questions below while you ponder your yearnings, which may lead you in the right direction. I wish you well. Following the yearning path is an amazing journey with gems of wisdom and miracles galore housed in each experience. Enjoy!

Get a big sheet of paper and write 'YEARNINGS' in capitals. Be as creative in your writing as you want.

Stop and take three deep breaths. Honour yourself with patience, gentleness and a compassionate spirit. Come from a place of love: your love and the love of your Loved One. The whole point is *love!*

From there allow yourself to write all the things around the word 'yearnings' that come to mind when you read the questions below. Let the pen flow and see what appears on the page in front of you. Allow the list to have aliveness.

1. What do you get lost in for hours?
2. What do you love doing?
3. What makes you feel excited or alive?
4. If money were no object, what would you do?
5. If you were writing an adult fairy tale, which character would you be, where would you go and what would you do?
6. What are you doing when you feel calm and content?

7. If you won the lottery, what would you do for the next twelve months?
8. What gives you the greatest sense of self? What connects you to you?
9. What boosts your confidence?
10. What does your heart need to express?
11. What do you feel connected to that your Loved One was passionate about?
12. If there were no obstacles, what would you do?
13. What have you always wanted to do but let fear stop you?
14. How can you have the greatest impact in your life?
15. What would you want your eulogy to say? What do you want to be remembered for?
16. What is the greatest gift you could give yourself?
17. What do you daydream about?
18. What will you regret if you don't do it?
19. What three words best describe the values you live your life around?
20. What one thing to bring your yearnings to fruition can you do right now?

Well done in your reflection and your courage to look at your yearnings and how to integrate them into your life to further your healing. I hope this exercise provides the clarity you need to jump on your yearnings path and deliver the miracles that lay deep inside you.

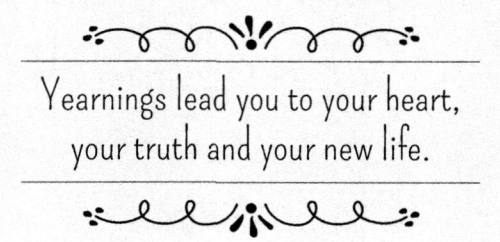

Yearnings lead you to your heart, your truth and your new life.

Step 2: Refining your yearning list

Now that you have a mud map of all your yearnings, let's refine the list and prioritise them into an order so you know what to do next. You can't do everything at once, and you don't want to stress yourself more at this fragile time. You may want to just let it all unfold, which is perfectly fine, or you may want to plan out your next twelve months – what you will do and when. I had a plan. I needed to, so I could fit it all in. It was flexible and things did change along the way. But the list and the time frame gave me something to start with.

Stop and take three deep breaths. Honour yourself with patience, gentleness and a compassionate spirit. Come from a place of love: your love and the love of your Loved One. The whole point is *love!*

Record your feelings in your Pink Grief Journal:

1. Firstly, break down your list into the top ten yearnings.
2. Then try to prioritise the top five.
3. From the top five, pick the one you would like to do first or can realistically do first.
4. Choose the second one.
5. Continue on to the other three in the top five.
6. Write out the months of the year and add your yearnings to the month you feel you can complete them in.
7. Now, get started on organising the first one on your list.
8. Organise any others that need to be arranged ahead of time.

9. Sit back and watch them unfold.

When you are finished you should have a plan for the upcoming year. Again, the plan is flexible but gives you a place to start. Don't forget to tick them off the list as you go; this is so rewarding. And don't forget to write in your Pink Grief Journal about what you are learning as you travel through each experience.

LEARNINGS FROM YEARNINGS

My learnings from my yearnings have come from a sabbatical that took me to the beauty of an overseas trip and deep into yoga teacher training. You do not have to leave home, however, to have the same revelations and epiphanies I had. Some of your biggest revelations may come from sitting in your lounge room looking out your back window. The biggest thing you need to consider is to follow your yearnings wherever possible.

You can connect to yourself anywhere. It's important to follow the soul's footsteps that lead you to your yearning. This will then lead you to your truth and to the connection to self and finally healing. One thing leads to the next. Connect the dots till you have a beautiful map leading you exactly where you need to go.

Your yearnings and truth will be different to mine. Everyone's truth will play out differently and represent your own soul's desires, which you can sprinkle over the world.

Some learnings that may be experienced are:

- Trust your soul implicitly.

YEARNINGS

- Listen to your Inner Pink Star.
- Follow your yearnings as they always know best.
- Live your life amidst your loss.
- Experience the solo adventure to the centre of your soul.
- Live a rich and full life.
- Have patience; the healing will come.
- The more you connect to yourself the more you can feel the connection with others.
- Keep your heart safe and protected.
- Seek a calm and simple existence.
- Find your gift to the world.
- There are things in yourself you will say goodbye to and grieve, and this is okay.
- Change is good.
- Honour your sensitive soul.
- The world is open for you to experience all that you wish for.
- Love yourself, nurture yourself, and be tender, gentle and compassionate with yourself.
- So much love lies below. Give all the love you have and it will be returned tenfold.
- Feel the sadness but don't exacerbate the suffering.
- Walk with fear, sadness and anger straight to healing.
- Seek out the love, truth and purpose.

Grief, Grace and Gratitude

Grief can get you back in touch with your fragile and expressive self. It's this self that is full of aliveness and, although fragile, continues to scream out to be heard and healed. As your healing progresses and you listen to the footsteps of your heart and follow your yearnings, the screaming will slowly abate. Finally, your heart and your fragile self will feel heard. Once heard, it can relax, allowing everything to be just as it is and unfold as it was designed to do.

Standing at the door with a bottle of Moet champagne and adjusting your pink ostrich wrap, you knock softy yet confidently. The door opens, and you are welcomed warmly with a hug from Jane.

Around the room you are stunned to see a big Happy Birthday sign over the fireplace, a beautifully decorated table with silver candelabras, beautifully designed name place cards, and your pink and white roses from yesterday in the centre of the table.

Jane hands you a small gift, and before you can open it Lilly comes over to nudge you with her wet nose. You bend down and feed her some treats.

"I'm just looking after Lilly while her owner is away," explains Jane. "Her owner is the lady who started our book club. She is lovely. Lilly is a beautiful dog, though she always seems to be hungry. Maybe I'm not feeding her enough." You laugh out loud as you explain what Labradors are like. They are master manipulators when it comes to food. Jane joins in your laughter.

Your present turns out to be a ten-class pass voucher to the Baddha Konasana yoga studio. You are thrilled and, maybe a little over-enthusiastically, encase her in a big squishy hug.

YEARNINGS

You try to catch your breath as you continue to be introduced to new and interesting people who you already feel at home with. It's only a small group of twelve, but it takes a while to get around to everyone.

Later in the evening, a cake is served, and your new friends sing happy birthday. Soon the music cranks up and you find yourself following the others to the empty space near the kitchen to take part in your first dance in a long time.

Taking a break to powder your nose, you look at your reflection in the mirror. You feel blessed and realise it's just like your dream. Enchanting!

Looking deep into your eyes, you notice that the sadness you have lived with for what seems like forever is lifting. In its place you sense genuine joy shining out on this special occasion.

You acknowledge your grief, welcome your happiness and bow to your reflection. As you excitedly head back to the group to join the others on the dance floor, you hope one day to meet Lilly's lovely owner.

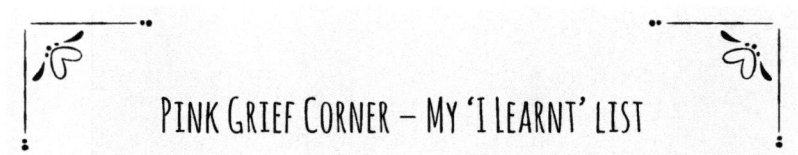

Pink Grief Corner – My 'I Learnt' list

Housed deep in your yearnings are your learnings. It is important and curative to reflect on your experiences and pick out these lessons, which can be anywhere from surprising to mind blowing. Your learnings are the silver lining for all the pain and suffering you have felt. With no appreciation of the lessons it is easy to remain stuck in resentment or ignorance.

At a deep level the learnings allow you to understand yourself: why you think, feel and behave the way you do. Realising the learnings is like problem solving; coming to these epiphanies enables you to begin the transformations you desire. Plus you may find some gratitude for the positives in your grief experience.

In your Pink Grief Journal, list the biggest learning lessons you have received going through this loss so far. Record your thoughts, feelings, reactions and epiphanies.

Stop and take three deep breaths. Honour yourself with patience, gentleness and a compassionate spirit. Come from a place of love: your love and the love of your Loved One. The whole point is *love!*

Record your feelings in your Pink Grief Journal:

My question to you is: What are your learnings from your yearnings?

1. I learnt...
2. I learnt...
3. I learnt...
4. I learnt...
5. I learnt...

And so on, until you exhaust yourself of all your learnings.

Be proud of yourself for completing this. Sit with your feelings for a moment after this self-discovery. Be grateful and compassionate for how you feel. This is an empowering exercise as acceptance of what has been learnt can bring some control and joy back into your life.

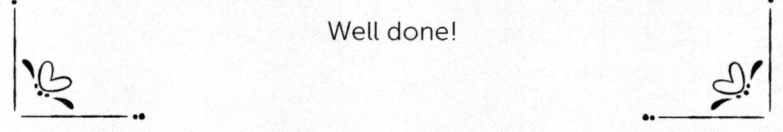

Well done!

YEARNINGS

> ### PINK BUTTERFLY TIPS
>
> ♥ Follow your yearnings to their source.
> ♥ Allow your learnings to connect you to your truth.
> ♥ Bathe in the learnings from your yearnings.
> ♥ Yearnings walk you on a healing path.
> ♥ Bask in the truth at the end of the yearnings rainbow.

The next morning you sleep in and replay again and again the events of the previous night, the wonderful people you met, the interesting and amusing stories you were told, and the scrumptious meal and wet licks you received from Lilly. Your jaw hurts from so much laughter.

Life truly does provide you with what you need when you need it, if you are on alert and listen to your inner knowing and yearnings in your search for your truth. Follow that inner knowing and know that your truth will always arrive as a gift on a silver platter.

You see the voucher for Baddha Konasana yoga studio classes peeking out of your handbag and vow that tomorrow you will visit the studio and book in your classes. You can't wait to get started and allow your body to slow down and open through the much-needed restorative yoga poses awaiting you.

You must remember also to pop in and see Jane with a thank-you card. You are a sentimental and traditional soul, and you feel a note in writing is appropriate to honour the magnificent time you had.

Looking outside your bedroom window you see a butterfly land on your critter friend as he peeks outside his pink house. You wish he could talk, if only a few words, so that he could understand how your affection for him is growing. He looks incredibly content in life, a trait to admire and strive for. And with that thought you give gratitude for your life and doze off back into a peaceful sleep.

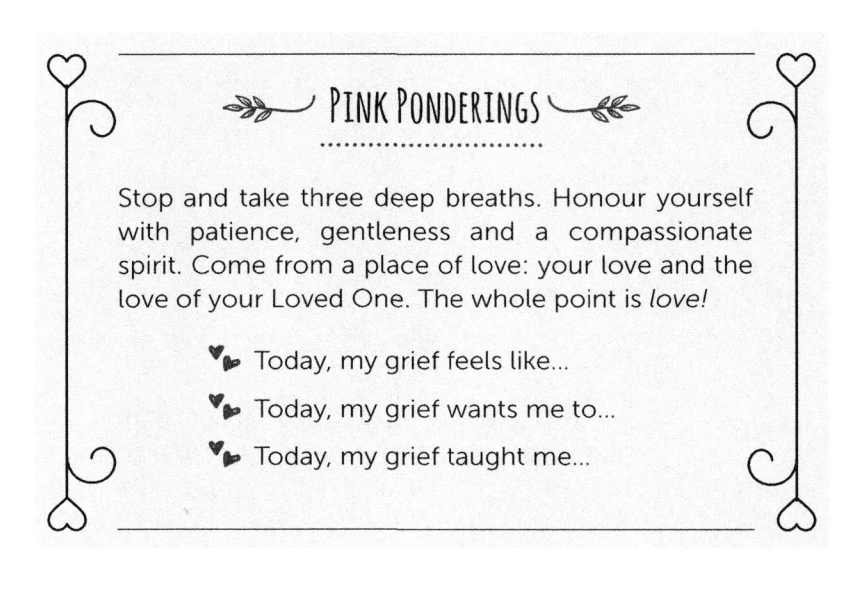

~ Pink Ponderings ~

Stop and take three deep breaths. Honour yourself with patience, gentleness and a compassionate spirit. Come from a place of love: your love and the love of your Loved One. The whole point is *love!*

- ❤ Today, my grief feels like…
- ❤ Today, my grief wants me to…
- ❤ Today, my grief taught me…

SIGNS

"Butterflies hover and feathers appear whenever lost loved ones and angels are near."

—Mary Jac

Yesterday was a day of relaxation and recalling fond memories, basking in the wake of an amazing evening and contemplating life. Today, it's back to reality with things to do, and with that you jump out of bed. Your current energy supersedes that of your last few months.

After a delicious breakfast you head back into town. Entering the stationery shop you look fussily for the perfect card to thank Jane for her overwhelming hospitality and the best party yet. You are not sure she will ever understand how deeply it touched you. It was more than the party; it was the connections that you made, with beautiful people who have already added warmth to your life.

You find a card depicting the love of a beautiful white Golden Retriever and her owner. Unconditional love jumps from the card straight to your heart, which feels wide open, and you think of Lilly and look forward to some pats later. After writing on it with deep thought and love, you leave the shop and feel the sun is shining brighter than before.

The bookstore is shut with a sign on the door: 'Gone to yoga!'

Grief, Grace and Gratitude

A few doors away there is Lilly out the front of the Baddha Konasana yoga studio. A lick and a pat are obligatory as you stop to say hello. The tail wags so deliriously that it's hard to leave her. You open the door to the studio and an instant calm washes over you, bringing you to a halt. It flows like liquid from the crown of your head to the tip of your toes, filling you with a knowing that this is exactly where you need to be. Your body is pulsing with energy, your mind feels quiet and still, and your spirit is familiarising itself with its new warm cloak of joy.

You step inside and see Jane walk out of one of the yoga rooms, looking refreshed and rejuvenated. You think of the 'big fancy Rs' (renew, refresh, restore, replenish, revamp, rejuvenate, redesign and redecorate) as she wears the biggest smile on her face. That is the smile you wish to replicate. You thank her for the night before, and she accepts your card with thanks while gushing over the picture of the dog. She introduces you to Shanti the yoga teacher who explains all about the yoga studio and takes you on a tour.

As you leave, Shanti says, "Goodbye. So lovely to meet you. We will see you tomorrow. Hopefully the owner will be back soon and you can meet her. She is a beautiful person and teacher. Namaste".

You sit on a bench out the front, hoping to feel the vibrations from the studio radiate out the door and flow through you. Lilly is by your side, and with your hand on her head you close your eyes. You feel the sun on your face and allow it to permeate your being. Something feels quite different. You stay seated, soaking it all in.

Rising from the bench you wander home, musing about your brief bench meditation. Was it a dream? Did you fall asleep? It was as if you felt your Loved One with you. But how?

You walk slowly and try to regain the feeling. All you know for now is that you felt filled up with love – a beautiful, strong love that you want to replicate at all costs. You float home and realise your butterfly wings have started to awaken and are beginning to find their form on your grief journey.

SIGNS

Is it a sign?

Beautiful signs may appear all over the place to show you that your Loved One is near. For me they literally appeared as love, roses and butterflies. Some say they find feathers when their loved ones are close. For others it's a rainbow or the scent of their favourite perfume. It is different for all of us. Some may not have any signs; this is normal too.

I'm not sure I believed in signs being sent from heaven, your angel, the 'other side', your Loved One or however you would like to explain it – possibly because I never had a reason to. I hadn't thought about it until my dad passed away and suddenly signs started to appear all over. I knew they were signs because of the way my heart filled up with love when they appeared; there was no other explanation. You too will know when it is a sign. It just is.

Love, roses and butterflies surround me.

Some days your heart can go from feeling heavy and sad to instantaneously feeling lifted and light after a sign appears. Signs often come when you are most connected to your authentic self. They also seem to arrive when you feel sad and are pondering life and death. The more you connect to this the more they tend to appear.

Strange and coincidental things may start to occur the more open you are. Soon after you may realise they are signs, and that is when you will be on the lookout for more and cherish their arrival. You may miss signs if you are disconnected from yourself and your emotions or caught up in distractions.

The signs present themselves in the things you can't explain, as a gift for you to unwrap. Examples of signs are:

- hearing a specific song at a specific time
- body chills or goose bumps
- feelings of being touched
- smells
- feathers
- feeling love
- roses
- butterflies
- vivid dreams
- rainbows
- cloud formations

… and many other things. Some people have even seen the spirit of their Loved One or heard their voice.

I am not an expert on signs and I only speak from my experience, yet I assure you they are real to those of us who experience them. So be open! Dismiss nothing and contemplate everything!

Some ways to become closely connected to your signs are:

- Be open to receiving them.
- Connect to your heart.
- Feel your feelings.
- Allow your sadness to wash over you.
- Ask for a sign.
- Talk to your Loved One.
- Ask them a question.
- Think about your Loved One.
- Visualise them.
- Be in the present moment.
- Be mindful and on the lookout for them.

Practising all of the above will deepen your spiritual connection.

MY SIGNS

On the day of the funeral, I was open and received my first sign.

In my front garden there are thirty standard rose bushes, and when in bloom they look utterly stunning. Walking out to my front garden on the funeral morning, my mind was full of thoughts and my heart heavy with sorrow. To my amazement the rose bushes were nearly bare and my entire driveway was covered by a sheath of beautiful white rose petals. I was speechless!

My heart filled up and tears flowed. I knew this was more than a coincidence; it was a beautiful sign from Dad to help me through his funeral day. Since then, there have been many more coincidences and strange happenings, with roses appearing in many odd places.

Butterflies are another sign that corroborate to me that Dad is nearby. I will think of him and find a glorious white butterfly drifting by gracefully, often almost coming to rest on my nose.

Signs fill your heart.

Random thoughts are another telltale sign. Mine sound like they are being put there by Dad who used to always precede any suggestions to me with my name: "Lara,...", "Lara, go and rest", "Lara, don't work so hard", "Lara, leave it till tomorrow." I hear myself answering the thoughts. They continue to this day and are filled with Dad's personality traits and are his familiar remarks.

One morning, I spotted a black SUV with a big white star with a circle around it on the driver's door. Only moments earlier, I had asked Dad for a sign after putting down a book that spoke of this exact symbol. Coincidence? Not to me.

Grief, Grace and Gratitude

These experiences ignited a desire within to see a psychic medium – something completely out of the ordinary for me. I was open to see where this part of my journey led me. It was an interesting, emotional and, in my opinion, genuine ninety minutes.

I have many other stories of signs with butterflies, playing cards, flowers and other bizarre occurrences. I see them, feel what is inside and write them all down in my Pink Grief Journal so I never forget them. They are important, poignant and loving parts of my grief journey and my awareness that my dad is around.

Learn to honour and follow your Inner Pink Star, no matter which bizarre direction it sends you in during your grief. Allow the experiences to unfold, take the learnings, accept the signs and give permission for the healing to settle your soul.

You may seek things that seem far afield from your current life. This may make you feel uncomfortable or as if you are going crazy, but that is normal. You have been transported to a new realm that you are struggling to manage; things will shift and settle. Your Inner Pink Star will guide you as to what is real and what is not.

Then you will be left with your version of love, roses and butterflies.

Arriving at the yoga studio in your black leggings with your yoga mat under your arm, you notice two dogs waiting patiently outside. Lilly has a friend; how exciting!

You ruffle Lilly's head and quickly move to the white Golden Retriever who has been pushing your arm over to pat her. She is a little pushy, but you don't mind. Who does she belong to?

Walking in you see Shanti. She takes you into the yoga room and helps to set you up with a bolster, some blocks and a strap. She asks you to lie down in Savasana and quietly wait for your teacher.

SIGNS

Your back melts into the mat, your feet fall out to the side, your shoulder blades draw towards each other, you open up through your chest, your eyes close over, you release the tension in your face, and you gently give permission for your thoughts to quieten while you wait for the class to begin.

PINK GRIEF CORNER – QUESTION TIME

Now it is your turn to look back and recollect what may have happened in your life that doesn't have a logical explanation.

Stop and take three deep breaths. Honour yourself with patience, gentleness and a compassionate spirit. Come from a place of love: your love and the love of your Loved One. The whole point is *love!*

Ponder the questions below as you record your feelings in your Pink Grief Journal:

1. Have you experienced strange, unexplainable situations or things that appeared from nowhere?
2. Are you finding roses, butterflies, pennies or other objects lying around?
3. Are there words appearing in your mind that you feel are not yours?
4. Are you sensing someone around you?
5. Do you sometimes feel that you are not alone?
6. Do you sometimes feel filled up with love for no reason?

Maybe you can't recall any. Sometimes it is not till you become more aware, call out to the universe and look

> for signs that they begin to materialise. Stay connected to yourself, feel your feelings, ask for a sign and wait patiently. When the time is right one may appear and then you will know. You will feel it! Breathe in the peace as you wait.

The Curtain

"Butterflies are the heaven-sent kisses from an angel."

—Author unknown

The curtain between life and death is mysterious and puzzling, yet you are only limited by your imagination and thinking. Being on this side of life's curtain, we do not know what is on the other after we pass over. But the phenomenon of many spiritual or unexplainable events worldwide, and even in my small existence, seems to be a desperate call for us to understand – to believe and value the signs from our loved ones in their spiritual realm.

For me, the thought of never seeing Dad again was so horrifying, but I now believe (I *have* to believe) that I will see him again one day. And until that day, our relationship is altered but still full of acceptance, connection, signs and love. This thought gives me hope and the desire to move forward, living my life with passion, enthusiasm and love.

Therefore, I came to accept and believe in signs. These unexplainable events and weird circumstances convince me that he is around still, in some capacity. I call to the universe and to Dad and a sign appears; not every time but most times. I simply have to keep my eyes and spirit wide open, and as Dad hears me he sends his love.

SIGNS

I experience the occasional pure white butterfly gliding past and almost resting on my nose. I find pink and white roses placed subtly in strange places and thoughts popping into my mind that, I believe, are channelling Dad. Other times I just feel filled up with a warm, glowing love. These signs prove to me that Dad and all his love is resting in my heart and always close by.

In these moments, I send my love, reach out for his and continue my day!

Pink Butterfly Tips

- Be open to the signs.
- Ask for a sign.
- Notice the love inside.
- Stay connected to yourself.
- Allow yourself to receive the signs.

Floating back to reception after the best yoga class ever, you meet your teacher at the desk. "How do you feel?" she asks. You find it hard to describe how relaxed and connected you feel, but you do your best.

As you gather your things together, looking up you are stunned to see your friend from the Cabin of Love walking through the reception area wearing a big, soft smile. The gentle soul that welcomed you with opens arms and set you up in the cabin when you felt like everything inside had been lost is standing right in front of you. You don't blink just in case she disappears.

She walks over to you, and as you go to extend your hand she envelops you in one of her squishy hugs. "Welcome to Baddha Konasana, my beautiful yoga space. How are you? Has the Field of Grace nurtured your heart and soul as I expected it would? I knew we would meet again when the time was right."

Trying to get your words out, you eventually manage to splutter something about how you have so much to tell her and it's hard to know where to start. You seem to be doing all the talking yet you can tell she is listening intently and captivated by your stories.

Walking outside together her last words are, "This is Lilly and Miss Maisy, my two dogs, and my name is Erica. I'm so pleased to see you again. I must go, but I can't wait to see you in the Garden of Gratitude and reap its rewards together. Till next time". With that she glides back inside, throwing her scarf over her shoulder and leaving you bursting with words and questions. 'What is the Garden of Gratitude?' you wonder.

You have no option but to wait till you see her again. You remember to let life unfold as it will, with no pressure, no pushing. Just be in the moment and allow the grief journey to unfold as it will. You follow your advice while looking forward to the new moments to unfold. It's been a long time since you felt this childlike excitement, and you stop to realise things are continuing to shift internally.

Your walk home is magical and dreamlike. New friends, new passions and now you have met Erica again, the one person that brought so much joy to you earlier on in your grief. Like the caterpillar, you feel you are nearing the end stages of your growing and ready to emerge from your lonely chrysalis state.

The caterpillar makes a home called a chrysalis or a pupa, which is their resting stage. When they transform into a butterfly, the chrysalis opens and soon after the butterfly comes out, its wings damp, a little soft and folded against its body. It is exhausted and rests some more. Once it is ready to start flying, it will pump blood into its wings, enabling them to start flapping, which is when they learn how to fly. At first, they are not so good at flying and need lots of practice; however, it doesn't take them long to learn.

SIGNS

The butterfly lifecycle resembles your own grief journey, hibernating in a protective space to nurture and rest while you are transforming and preparing your wings to fly you away. Only take one step at a time, though, as patience is paramount!

You continue the walk home, practising floating with your butterfly wings all the way back to the Cabin of Love that is sitting proud, surrounded by roses. You let all the questions, epiphanies and wonderful moments swill around in your mind, while feeling your future is about to change once again for the better.

Your critter friend appears, pauses amongst the roses as if to say hello and drops to the ground, scurrying to his pretty pink house.

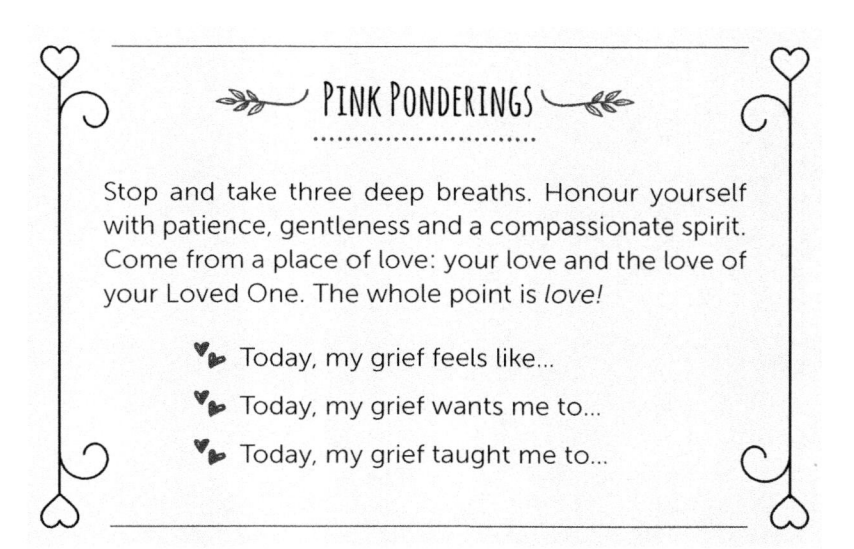

PINK PONDERINGS

Stop and take three deep breaths. Honour yourself with patience, gentleness and a compassionate spirit. Come from a place of love: your love and the love of your Loved One. The whole point is *love!*

- Today, my grief feels like...
- Today, my grief wants me to...
- Today, my grief taught me to...

FINAL CONTEMPLATION

*"Grief knits two hearts in closer bonds
than happiness ever can."*

—Alphonse de Lamartine

Wow. Another great day. Lessons and miracles unfolding around you bring love and light into your life. You have really enjoyed your time at the Field of Grace. What will the Garden of Gratitude be like? Although you look forward to your future you may be sad to move on from this space where life is beginning to shine, externally and internally. You have redecorated and redesigned the Cabin of Love and your life, despite your lingering grief.

Sitting in the garden, you think about your time at the Field of Grace and realise how far you have come. Time has been of no consequence. You have just allowed yourself to be and do what you needed, with no pressure or time constraints. Grief has flowed through you like water through a sieve, washing down all parts of your soul in honour of your Loved One.

When you arrived at the Cabin of Love, you were bereft and full of sorrow. Although you still feel the grief inside, now it does not take up your whole existence. You have allowed space inside to honour your grief while moving on with your life.

Grief, Grace and Gratitude

During your time here, you have savoured the grace. Learning to love yourself and being gentle and compassionate has helped you walk through your grief. Creating a beautiful Pink Tribute to your Loved One has enabled you to honour them. Being aware of your yearnings has taken you on a journey to nurture and honour yourself while learning about yourself and your grief. Understanding and recognising the signs has reminded you of the miracle that your Loved One is still connected to you.

In the Field of Grace you have found your truth, self-love and yearnings, and experienced the signs, which all walk you further along your grief journey. In the Field of Grace you have learnt elegance or beauty of form, manner, motion and action as well as favour, kindness, love and goodwill to self and others. Presence, surrender and mindfulness have become more a part of your life. You have begun to feel grace as a state of being that is earned through commitment to self.

Now it is time to move forward another step and allow the next part of your life to unfold.

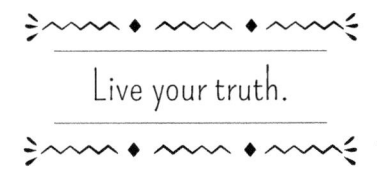

> Live your truth.

It is good to acknowledge and contemplate these times. It helps you to know that you have progressed in your journey even though, at times, your heart has still felt the heaviness of grief.

Looking inside and outside the Cabin of Love, you notice the changes you have made since your stay here. The inside is more colourful and alive, housing pieces of yourself that you have bought specially and placed in apt positions. Outside, the garden is blossoming. Your critter friend's house has had a full upgrade and he wanders freely around the garden, soaking up the sun and filling up on his seeds.

Your love of gardening has grown during your stay here. It has become a healing and cathartic hobby that has allowed many epiphanies to arise. You understand now that in allowing your mind to empty and focus on a creative task, your thoughts reassemble like a jigsaw puzzle and deliver the solutions you seek.

FINAL CONTEMPLATION

You dig a bit deeper and find that your inner world reflects the cabin and you feel a little more colourful and alive. You feel readier to show yourself to the world in all your newfound glory; but you will still go slowly.

Your sense of trust and faith flows more freely. You have come so far even though, occasionally, you still feel you are at day one. That is why it is important to look back to see how far you've come, to give you continued hope that things will carry on improving.

Arriving home you see an envelope sitting on the counter. Inside are five questions. You remember these questions from when you left the Forest of Grief, and you recall feeling so drained back then. Now you feel more alive, and you acknowledge the difference.

Getting out your Pink Grief Journal, you get ready to start writing.

Pink Time Out – Final Contemplation

Stop and take three deep breaths. Honour yourself with patience, gentleness and a compassionate spirit. Come from a place of love: your love and the love of your Loved One. The whole point is *love!*

Refer to your notes from the final contemplation from *Part 1: The Forest of Grief* and notice the differences within you. Record your thoughts and feelings as you answer these questions.

1. What is the most helpful lesson you learnt as you nurtured yourself in the Field of Grace?
2. What would you share with others about the Field of Grace and its lessons?

3. What did you struggle with most in the Field of Grace?
4. Can you acknowledge how far you have come in your journey?
5. Are you ready for the next stage in your journey?

Curling up in bed after finishing your contemplation, you are getting ready to doze off, hoping for the beautiful dreams of your Loved One to arrive with love, roses and butterflies. With that thought you glance through the door to the butterfly on the rug, glimpsing the fresh roses in the vase. You feel the love inside because you know the point is love!

You feel more trust and faith in your heart and you acknowledge your grief journey. You thank it for revealing your true inner self to you.

Now you understand:

In grace lies your truth.

You welcome the Garden of Gratitude and whatever it brings as you say Goodnight!

Love – Truth – Purpose

> "Loss is nothing else but change, and change is Nature's delight."
>
> —Marcus Aurelius

FINAL CONTEMPLATION

<u>When I come to the end</u>

When I come to the end of my journey
and I travel my last weary mile,
just forget, if you can, that I ever frowned
and remember only the smile.
Forget unkind words I have spoken;
remember some good I have done.
Forget that I've stumbled and blundered
and sometimes fell by the way.
Remember I have fought some hard battles
and won, ere the close of the day.
Then forget to grieve for my going;
I would not have you sad for a day,
but in summer just gather some flowers
and remember the place where I lay,
and come in the shade of the evening
when the sun paints the sky in the west.
Stand for a few moments beside me
and remember only my best.

—Author unknown

PART 3

GARDEN OF GRATITUDE

The Rebirth

GREETING GRATITUDE

"When we walk to the edge of all the light we have and take the step into the darkness of the unknown, we must believe that one of two things will happen – there will be something solid for us to stand on, or we will be taught to fly."

—Patrick Overton

You woke up early this morning, eager to discover the Garden of Gratitude. Your mind seems unsettled – a little anxious and a little excited – and you hope that today the next step will be revealed. While you are pondering and making your favourite herbal tea, a knock at the door startles you. You haven't had many visitors here at the Cabin of Love except for Erica all that time ago, so you feel surprised. Eagerly walking to the door, you open it to a beautiful, soft and familiar face and her two furry children, Lilly and Miss Maisy.

"Good morning," says Erica. "We have lots of work to do." And with that she strolls in with a bunch of things under her arm: butcher paper, pens and many other supplies. The furry visitors stride straight over to the couch and proudly hop up to sit in comfort under the rays of sun, just like they own the place.

Helping Erica manoeuvre her bags of goodies she finally settles, lights a jasmine candle and says yes to a cup of tea. Her soothing voice and calming presence bring you to stillness. She presents you with a beautiful note to read!

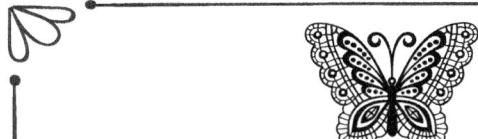

The Garden of Gratitude greets you

Your purpose here is to give permission for the rebirth of self. You will accept the grief a little more and find its place in your life. You will understand that grief does not end; it just changes form. You learn to alter your relationship with your Loved One and to feel the love that still resides with you even though they are no longer here. You begin to welcome delicately the new you to the world and show absolute thanks and gratitude for your Loved One in your life. You will blossom, reap and appreciate all the lessons your Loved One and your grief journey are teaching you. You will move forward holding dear your grief and your Loved One while assimilating fully into your world once again. Finally, holding love and truth alongside gratitude you will feel free to walk towards your life purpose.

You let her written words wash over and through you like a healing liquid, allowing them to rest gently on the cusp of your heart. But before they settle, she starts to speak.

"I thought we could create together special spaces and places around the garden to celebrate your Loved One's life. Through working with what we are grateful for, we can create a heavenly garden of love and gratitude. We will build this in honour of you and your Loved One, me and mine, and all the people that follow us when they come to rest in the Garden of Gratitude to heal their broken hearts."

"Yes." You quickly add, "It feels right. It feels lovely". Working together and building a connection with Erica is what you need. To honour

GREETING GRATITUDE

your Loved One while working in your beautiful garden is the bliss you have been seeking. "When can we get started?"

"How about now? We can create ten expressions of gratitude over ten days," she says as she takes a big piece of butcher's paper out and lays it on the table.

Gratitude is the quality of being thankful and appreciative.

When you walk through the grief journey with conscious awareness, you will appreciate the changes that are taking shape. Once you have moved through the deep, dark grief and further into nurturing yourself, you will notice your transformation and the areas of your life that are wonderful, and you will feel gratitude.

You may not find this gratitude for some time, but when you do you will discover, like me, that grieving with gratitude helps you to find a purpose behind your loss. Despite not being happy about the event, reaching for the gratitude will enable you to move forward a little more. Gratefulness, or gratitude, has been researched extensively and is known to boost wellbeing, induce deep sleep, increase positivity, enhance relationships, enrich the immune system, heighten moods, stimulate energy, promote self-esteem and be contagious in nature.

It is normal to be spiralled back into your grief while basking in your gratitude on grief's winding road. Taking one day at a time and dealing with what arises internally each day is a good strategy.

In the Forest of Grief, you learnt the point is *love!* At the Field of Grace, you learnt that in grace lies your truth.

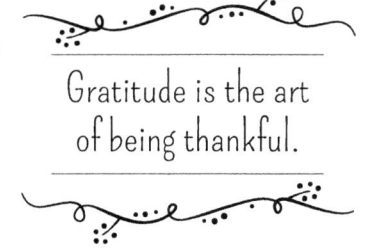

> Gratitude is the art of being thankful.

Grief, Grace and Gratitude

When you come into the Garden of Gratitude, you are still raw from your grief but can rest in the gratitude that surfaces. This gratitude awakens you to a rebirth that is able to reveal a rich and full life, creating the space and desire to walk you to your life purpose.

Certain feelings and situations would never have arisen had you not suffered your loss. If you move through the process, you may eventually come to find appreciation and gratitude in your loss. Gratitude is powerful! You may make big changes in your life externally and/or internally.

It is the good that comes out of the not-so-good. Once you feel the not-so-good you will have access to the good. The deeper you feel the loss, the more you can access the beauty and love.

For some it is a wake-up call, and everything begins to change. For others, it is a rebirth. You awaken to your life the same yet different; your deep values are the same, but you show up to life more connected to them. A deep part of you wants to live your best life, honouring yourself and living your life purpose. The world seems brighter, and the grief and awakening begin to complement each other to bring out a deeper, more connected version of yourself.

You can connect more to your inner true self and your life through feeling both ends of the rainbow of emotions. Your life becomes more expansive as you become more open and ready to engage with the universe. You live less in fear and more in love. When you connect more to yourself, your life broadens, internally and externally. You move out of your comfort zones into new enriching experiences as many opportunities are thrown at your doorstep.

Everyone is different. You just need to allow your journey to take the path indicated to you by your inner self. When you listen, you will know where to go and will be led by your heart with more ease and less effort.

Greeting Gratitude

Working with Erica through the day, enjoying many herbal teas and spending time with the doggy love flowing all around, you finally brainstorm the top ten reasons to be grateful in the wake of your loss.

You acknowledge that there are many more. But ten is the perfect number for creating memorial spaces for each Gratitude in special spots in the garden. You will birth your Garden of Gratitude in all its glory while rebirthing a part of yourself.

You have worked hard today, and after sharing memories of your Loved One with Erica, you prepare for bed thinking of your ten Gratitudes.

Love Gratitude

"Love makes your soul crawl out from its hiding place."

—Zora Neale Hurston

You know the point is love! You lived through this as you trekked through the Forest of Grief.

Sitting under the oak tree the next day – a magnificent gift from Mother Nature – you think about its roots and longevity. An oak tree can live for more than 1000 years, like the 1500-year-old Seven Sisters Oak in Louisiana, which has a trunk that measures 11.9 metres – strong and hardy in its roots and its structure.

You reflect that the beauty of the oak tree is something to be grateful for, as is the love that springs from your heart as you bask in the energy the tree radiates. It is only a baby tree now, but it is on its way to transformation, living through the trials and tribulations nature *sends it way. Regardless, it will stand grounded in its roots, swaying in the breeze as needed and resting still when the wind subsides.*

Like the oak tree you are young and aiming to blossom into your new existence, to change. You dig deep to find the love in your heart and learn to honour and live in the love, even in the dark hours of your grief.

Rolling out a piece of your butcher's paper underneath the tree, you write 'Love' in the middle and start to brainstorm all that love means to you in relation to your Loved One and your Gratitudes.

Walking through the grief journey with awareness and consciousness, you will uncover the love you seek. This love, hidden beneath the rainbow of grief emotions, is deeper and purer than any you have known before. You will unearth so much love that you can walk through life emanating an inner glow. You are able to give love to others instead of just striving to receive love, and you will realise things are different. You are different.

When you only look to receive love, you may be simply trying to fill an empty void inside. When you walk instead to give love unconditionally, you become so fulfilled that all you want to do is give more love. Naturally, you will be rewarded with receiving it back from others in a myriad of beautiful ways.

> Give love unconditionally.

Suffering a loss and walking the grief journey can transform you so massively that everything seems to spin on an axis. When you find the love, you can feel it swilling inside. You will feel the love on the days when the clouds don't clear and the skies are grey. Your moods won't waver according to the weather; you will feel solid in your inner love and grounded on the earth like the magnificent oak tree.

GREETING GRATITUDE

Then one day you may turn around and realise that, even though you would reverse your loss in an instant if you could, you acknowledge the changes that are transpiring internally. The changes that drizzle love throughout your life are like raindrops on roses, and you thank your grief for being the catalyst for massive inner change and all the love raining down upon you.

Because the point is *love!*

I would often walk around the streets of my neighbourhood simply loving life, just for a small part of the day. Since my loss this has amped up. I realise how precious life is. I now face my losses and mortality honestly and with a gentle, loving appreciation for the fragility of life.

I have learnt to love with a vengeance, for that is all that matters. Some days my heart fills with so much I can hardly sit still. I feel it rising from inside and sense a strong urge to share it with others. Other days I struggle to find the love and am covered in unpleasant emotions that blanket the love. Unfortunately, this is life; this is the human existence. But the more you find the love and bask in it, the more you know what is available and the more you will seek it. The more you seek it, the more you find it and the more you will live it, for it is love that matters.

So, keep seeking and remember to stop and be grateful for the love that warms your heart, especially as you think fondly of your Loved One.

Be grateful for *love!*

Pink Grief Corner

Stop and take three deep breaths. Honour yourself with patience, gentleness and a compassionate spirit. Come from a place of love: your love and the love of your Loved One. The whole point is *love!*

Take out a big piece of paper and write 'Love' in the centre. Brainstorm all the things you love and are grateful for and write them around your central word.

Now ponder the following questions and record your feelings in your Pink Grief Journal:

1. Am I grateful for love?
2. What do I love? What warms my heart?
3. What is it about love that my Loved One instils in me?
4. Can I find the love buried inside?
5. What impedes me from feeling the love?
6. When it comes to love, what am I grateful for?

Bask in your gratefulness of love. Enjoy each moment that shines love within, for those are the moments we look for. When you bask in the love, live in its moment for often it passes too quickly.

Before you finish this first day of gratitude, you erect a beautiful wooden artefact close enough to the tree but not where it will encumber its

GREETING GRATITUDE

roots. Etching carefully with a special wooden implement you draw a butterfly and write the words:

> 'Here lies the love we are grateful for.'

Standing silently for a moment you are taken back to the times when your Loved One was by your side and their energy was soaring into your energetic radius, surrounding you like a halo. You wish you could magically touch this energy and once again be immersed in its beauty.

As you connect back to the present moment, you feel their love flow over and through you and are immensely grateful for the wake they left behind. It is in their presence and the loss that the love is found, and Love Gratitude settles on your soul.

Kissing the wooden artefact, a butterfly gracefully floats by and you follow its path as you both slowly head back to the Cabin of Love. In honour of today's achievements, after you say goodbye to Erica, your mind conjures up a delicious dinner that will warm your stomach and mimic your heart's newfound love.

Truth Gratitude

"Hard times arouse an instinctive desire for authenticity."

—Coco Chanel

You know in grace lies your truth! You learned this as you nurtured yourself at the Field of Grace.

Waking up refreshed, you float with Erica past the oak tree and the loving Gratitude from yesterday. With a big grin you sit beside the array of potted perennials you meticulously planted, taking in the *beauty of all their pinks, purples, whites, yellows and oranges sitting proudly in planter boxes. An exquisite display smiling to the world and spruiking "Look at me!"*

Proud as punch of the gorgeous creation of colour, you lay out your things for today's expression of gratitude and write 'Truth' in the centre of the butcher's paper. Erica pours a cup of herbal tea from the thermos.

The brainstorm begins.

Today you return to your learnings from the Field of Grace and appreciate them, offering gratitude for truth. Living in accordance to your heart and your inner world's truth your unique beauty and originality shines. In your truth, you can give permission for your individuality and eccentricity to glow. In your truth and authenticity, life flows with the ease of leaves floating with the breeze. Knowing yourself and being truthful to the deep inner self sees you walking the path that is meant for you and you only.

> In your truth your beauty shines.

Admiring the perennials shining in their glory, not masked by an ego, you ponder how your truth is so easily concealed by people pleasing, perfectionism, expectations, doing instead of being, drama, fixing and rescuing, worrying, overachieving, comparison, pressure, judgement, overwork, playing victim and a lack of self-love. You realise that burying yourself under all these dysfunctional pressures creates suffering upon suffering and gives energetic life to your ego, shadowing your beautiful inner truth. You recall that removing the veil of all the ego traits reveals a beautiful, pure soul eager and awaiting to live by its truth. This is where the calm and the peace reside. In being truthful to yourself you are beginning to find a freedom that radiates serenity and pure joy.

GREETING GRATITUDE

In living your truth everything feels right. You are living an authentic life and following your heart and soul's path. You do not need to feel unworthy or seek external validation. You can choose to sit still in any situation and feel grounded and peaceful, filled with your own internal validation. Situations will come and go, but you can remain strong and happy with the person you are and respond more and react less. You remove yourself from drama, stop apologising for who you are and instead choose alignment with your authentic self. You can give and receive respect and gently walk your path being kind to all you meet.

It's difficult to live like this all the time. But once your inner truth has been exposed to you, that is the only place your heart wishes to reside. Every time you mosey off that path, an inner knowing will communicate that you are not living your truth by making life uncomfortable for you. You will begin to recognise you are off track and know to stop and listen to your Inner Pink Star. She will then guide you forward to a healthy and happy authentic space.

Truth is a beautiful thing; it is raw, exposed and vulnerable. It is showing a side of yourself that has previously lived in regret, guilt or shame. It is dropping any false bravado concealing your beautiful heart. It is removing any arrogance that you may use to protect yourself. Once you live in your truth, you don't need to project the ego to protect yourself. Regardless of external happenings, you feel a tender, silent humming of inner protection.

It is saying yes to your vulnerability and knowing it is not to be feared. Embrace it alongside the gentle heart that sits quietly underneath. Your heart will shine and dazzle the world when you grant it permission. When you live your truth and love and honour yourself, you are proud to be who you are. You accept your human imperfections and love them. Any negative or judgemental thoughts of others are of no consequence. You protect yourself naturally and habitually without projecting the dark shadow side of self.

The knowledge that no one can hurt you unless you give them permission will walk you to self-protection. In truth, you accept that all situations and decisions are your own and that you are the author of your life. You know you can make different choices at any time to walk a different path to follow your own truth.

Each significant experience in your life will come to highlight a little more of your truth. The bigger the experience, the bigger the realisations and epiphanies.

The truth is often revealed just by sitting in the stillness and silence. By allowing the chitter-chatter of your mind to quieten for a moment and detach from its often-absurd thought patterns, the truth can make itself known. The truth speaks quietly and sincerely; it is the ego that screams the opposite and holds you hostage to its elements and false promises.

Trust in the quiet truth to live your life authentically with integrity, shining out your beautiful true self, talents and kindness to the world, so others will benefit from its beauty and wisdom. Each small difference you make in the world becomes respected by those who are on their own journey to seek their truth. One truth leads to another's truth until you are surrounded by a tribe of truthful likeminded people all striving to shine out their authenticity. When you find your truth you begin to focus on the bigger things.

Once you take responsibility for your world, you finally understand that the only person you can change is yourself. You learn not to expect others to change just to make your world better, and you begin to focus solely on yourself. As you do so, you may start not only making changes internally but also making changes outside yourself to the world. You look at how you can give back. The world opens up with endless possibilities. Then, like the perennials you planted, your beauty shines its colour outwards and drops your sparkles all over the world.

Be grateful for truth!

Greeting Gratitude

Pink Grief Corner

Stop and take three deep breaths. Honour yourself with patience, gentleness and a compassionate spirit. Come from a place of love: your love and the love of your Loved One. The whole point is *love!*

Take out a big piece of paper, write 'Truth' in the centre and brainstorm all the things that emanate your truth that you are grateful for. Write these around your central word.

Now ponder the following questions and record your feelings in your Pink Grief Journal:

1. Am I grateful for the truth within me?
2. Do I know and live my truth?
3. Am I shrouded by my ego instead of my truth?
4. What is stopping me from living my truth?
5. What is one small step I can take to live more in my truth?
6. When it comes to truth, what am I grateful for?

Bask in your gratefulness of truth. Present on a platter to the world the true, pure version of yourself that lives her truth. In doing so, not only will you be more alive, so will your world. The universe will thank you, and you can live more in accordance with your plan and your life purpose.

Lilly and Miss Maisy wake up after sleeping for hours and wander over to drop and roll in the grass at your feet. You are envious of the simplicity of a dog's life. They live in their truth, not shrouded by human dysfunction. You reflect that in observing a dog's life we can appreciate a simple, loving existence.

Setting up a small birdbath with a fountain amidst the perennials, you attach a small plaque on the side with the following words on it:

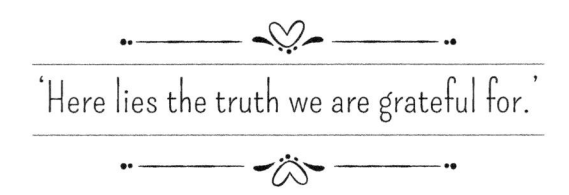

> 'Here lies the truth we are grateful for.'

You step away to see birds quickly flying in to take a bath. They flitter in and out, spraying the perennials with water as they play. In this moment, the world feels right – calm and peaceful with all creatures coexisting in truth. This simplicity of life has brought beauty deep to warm your heart. In finding your truth you can now appreciate these small things with sincere appreciation.

Walking back to the cabin that day, sharing more stories with Erica, you feel lighter on your feet. Living in your truth means you are not weighed down by unnecessary internal dysfunction. Erica turns to you and says, more like a statement than a question, "Isn't authenticity beautiful?"

Looking her in the eyes, you respond, "Here's to truth".

Later that day, looking out the window, you can see the oak tree and perennials and feel pleased with your accomplishments. Erica and the dogs leave for the day and you sit in stillness and gratitude for your blossoming friendships. As you look forward to your next Gratitude you think of your Loved One and laugh gently at a fond memory.

You are a little startled; it's the first time the memory of your Loved One has brought laughter instead of tears. Tears follow the laughter but, surprisingly, not because you are saddened – just because it feels so beautiful.

Closing your eyes softly, you allow yourself to feel the rainbow of emotions that arise as you savour the trip down memory lane.

Purpose Gratitude

"The purpose of life is to live it, to taste experience to the utmost, to reach out eagerly and without fear for newer and richer experience."

—Eleanor Roosevelt

"Another day, another Gratitude," *you say to Erica as you wander in your garden and decide where you will dedicate today's symbol of gratitude. You find yourself amongst the peonies flaunting their voluptuous blooms that have become more striking every day. This is the perfect place, so you sit, roll out your butcher's paper and write* 'Purpose' *in the centre.*

Everyone has a purpose, a reason for being; something that only they can give back to the world to make themselves and their world a better place. Finding that elusive purpose is the tricky part! Our yearnings, however, point us in the right direction.

While you are first caught in a grief cycle and not being loving to yourself, you go around in a chaotic spin cycle, just surviving. There is no time to ask the bigger questions of life. When you pass this stage, however, you can begin to delve deeper to find what adds the fireworks to your life. You will be ready to walk through the grief journey with conscious awareness and allow healing to take place. Slowly you can move back to the place where love and truth coexist. When you find the love and truth, your purpose has space to be birthed. The three combined make up the Life in the Pink equation: Love + Truth + Purpose.

Allowing your soul to speak and following the map she lays on your heart will walk you headlong into your purpose. However, you may not know you are heading this way till you arrive. One day you may suddenly reach the destination that houses the cherry on top of the pie and proudly shout, "I am here. My purpose is fulfilled!"

Allow your soul to speak.

Then you will know! Everything feels in the flow, life becomes easy, and a depth of fulfilment and joy is added to each moment and each day. You are absorbed in the task at hand and time passes by. You are not looking to fill empty voids with distractions because you are so present in the moment, living life with joy, calmness and contentment.

Finding your purpose is sometimes a process of elimination. You may have to try a few paths before you find the right one for you. Try everything your heart suggests and don't question. Allow the path to take you to the next opportunity. One day you will arrive at your purpose and understand why all the previous paths were imperative to travel.

You will know when you are off track as your inner disquiet will heighten, telling you that you have stopped listening. When this happens, be gentle with yourself. You are only human after all. Gently steer yourself back to the soft humming of knowing inside and drop anxiety in its wake.

Know and believe that every moment is an accumulation of necessary lessons and learnings. Have faith in your ability to know your next footstep and take it. Tune in and listen if anxiety speaks or stillness prevails. Watch for the subtle clues. Appreciate all the opportunities, the good and the not-so-good, as they will take you to your purpose.

You deserve to live a life filled with passion and purpose. Loss and grief transform us and we often seek to make a difference, asking the bigger questions in life like, "Why am I here?", "What is the point?", "What can I contribute?", "How can I grow?" and "What have I been brought here to achieve?" Take the time to sit back and deliberate the questions and find the path to your purpose.

Living your purpose sees you going to sleep invigorated and, like an excited child, you can't wait for tomorrow. You jump out of bed in the morning, eager to continue your passions. Trudging through life is replaced by a heightened aliveness propelling you forward. You carry an energetic aura that draws in likeminded individuals. You meet your spiritual tribe and have a sense of finally arriving home.

I didn't always know my passion was writing. I had to take the journey that had many pitfalls before it announced, "I have arrived". After I left school I worked my way up to management in the business world, but one day it started to become brutally obvious I was in a soulless corporate role. Each day that I sat in my big office I shut down my heart a little more.

I knew I was seeking something more. I had a love of studying and self-development, so I eventually took a different fork in my road. I emerged in the holistic world and completed qualifications in business management, counselling, life coaching, remedial massage, Pilates instruction and, finally, yoga teacher training.

Still, I had a niggling feeling that all the pieces of the jigsaw had not yet come together. One more piece had yet to be placed to reveal the exquisite masterpiece. It was not till I suffered intense heartbreak that my heart woke me up and led me to writing and later yoga (my other purpose). In my grief's wake, I stand delighted and proud that my purpose has fully revealed itself.

Grief, Grace and Gratitude

In following my passions and expressing my story I am fulfilling my purpose. I know this because when I am writing, I am channelling something bigger than myself. The words come with no effort and spring to life on the pages in front of me. Sometimes words pop into my head that I don't recognise. My fingers translate the thoughts floating around in my mind to a presence on the page.

When teaching a yoga class I have a similar experience. I close my eyes and sink into the asanas (poses) and words rise from within about life, love, truth and purpose, alongside the technical instructions for the pose, all of which I share with my class. My teaching is seated deeply and expressed from my heart space, which is always a strong clue that you are on your purpose path.

I am filled with love, energy and joy when I express my story or am immersed in a yoga asana. Hours pass by, and I realise I have been captured in the flow of my purpose. I arise from my writing desk or yoga mat invigorated, rewarded and joyful.

Living your purpose is fulfilling and beyond amazing; the entire world opens up. It's akin to prying open an oyster and a beautiful pearl is exposed for all to see. It's tough to get open; it takes strength and commitment. But once it springs open, its magnificence shines through and captivates you.

Be kind to yourself and seek your purpose in life. Sit still and see what is sluicing around through your grief journey. Your vulnerable heart is wide open right now and speaking to you. It's up to you to actively listen, trust and follow her lead to bring the beauty to fruition.

You are capable of so much more than you may think. Allow your life and your purpose to unfold and watch with awe what is revealed.

Be grateful for purpose!

GREETING GRATITUDE

PINK GRIEF CORNER

Stop and take three deep breaths. Honour yourself with patience, gentleness and a compassionate spirit. Come from a place of love: your love and the love of your Loved One. The whole point is *love!*

Take out a big piece of paper, write 'Purpose' in the centre and brainstorm all the things that come to mind when you think about your life purpose. Write these around your central word.

Now ponder the following questions and record your feelings in your Pink Grief Journal:

1. Am I grateful for feeling a sense of purpose?
2. What am I good at, and where do I find life flows and time goes unnoticed?
3. If I had one year to live, what would I do?
4. What is stopping this from coming to fruition?
5. What impact would I want to make on the world if I could change anything?
6. When it comes to purpose, what am I grateful for?

Bask in your gratefulness of purpose. Grant yourself the biggest wish, pave your path and go live your life purpose. Make your life so worthwhile. Help yourself and give back by helping others. By helping others you help yourself. Life becomes full of your desired love, roses and butterflies.

Grief, Grace and Gratitude

Erica turns to you. "It was the day I opened my yoga studio. I knew I had found my purpose. I now feel like I am floating through life as the authentic version of myself. I love every moment of my days even if I am in a moment of grief. The people that come to my studio share a part of themselves with me, and I feel so rewarded. I move my body and it thanks me in so many ways. I am so grateful for finding my purpose despite the fact I only found the last piece of the puzzle through grief."

You acknowledge, understand and feel her joy. Your own purpose is still unravelling, but you know you are on the right path. You just have a few pieces of the puzzle to lay before the picture is completed.

"I can feel your purpose radiating from you. I am so attracted to your joyful energy and hope to be in the same place soon," you reply.

Together you carry a small wishing well to the garden of pink peonies and place it nearby. The round wooden base is covered with a pitched roof, which seems the fitting feature for the peony garden. The pretty flowers seem to wish you all the way to your purpose. On the side of the well is a carving that reads:

'Here lies the purpose we are grateful for.'

Both of you throw a coin into the wishing well and make a wish. You breathe your wish deep to your heart, hoping to always live your purpose with passion. You hope your wish comes true very soon and you find yourself helping others and transforming even further.

GREETING GRATITUDE

Surrender Gratitude

> "The moment of surrender is not when life is over, it's when it begins."
>
> —Marianne Williamson

On day four of your Garden of Gratitude, Erica suggests you pack a picnic to take with you. You assemble delicacies in your picnic basket: hummus dip, Thai olives, mortadella, salami, cheeses, anchovies, crackers, carrot and celery sticks, and a thermos of warm herbal tea. Yum!

You decide to add a few doggy treats, call for Lilly and Miss Maisy and walk together out into the garden to find the perfect spot for today's gratitude.

Wandering past your earlier efforts, you feel the warmth of the Garden of Gratitude as it slowly comes to life. You can't wait to see what the final product will look like. For today you decide to enjoy your picnic amongst your striking succulents while you contemplate surrender.

You roll out your butcher's paper and write in the centre 'Surrender'.

It is in the surrender, the letting go that we begin to walk our grief journey with less resistance and allow it to take us where we need to go. At first, we kick and scream and want to do things our way. This can go on for some time until we step sideways to rest, possibly feeling drained and overwhelmed.

At this stage, when you almost feel like giving up, you let go a little bit, ready to re-evaluate. In doing so, your grief and life journey will become a little easier and a gift is delivered called 'surrender'.

Many of us try to control everything and everyone. We shower expectations over ourselves and others. This only serves to rain down disappointment and unhappiness when we can't live up to our unrealistic standards, and it destroys relationships when others cannot live up to our expectations.

Underlying the desire to control is fear of what will happen if things don't turn out the way we expect or if someone doesn't do what we expect. It can also be a fear of how you will cope with that, fear of rejection, fear of losing love, fear of so many things and, lastly, maybe a fear of life itself.

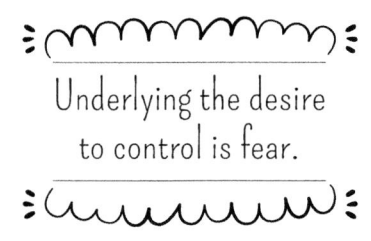

> Underlying the desire to control is fear.

Trying to control others assumes you know what is best for them when, in fact, that's only your perspective. They will be living from a totally different perspective and need to be allowed to make their own choices and mistakes. Be the author of your life, no one else's.

Surrender means you trust in something bigger than you. You trust in yourself and that you can cope. You trust that the universe will provide wholeheartedly for your wellbeing. It means having faith in your journey — listening to and following your heart, knowing it will always take you where you need to go. This allows you to release the high expectations and judgements you place on others and allows them to live their own lives.

It is about seeing what is causing reactions within yourself, watching out for what others are projecting onto you and what you are projecting onto them. These projections generally highlight where you need some further healing and guide you to follow that path.

Surrender and allow the ego to fade away, and instead allow your beautiful, broken heart to lead the way. Give permission for the entire rainbow of emotions to be felt. Repression and avoidance will cause even more pain and sorrow in your life, while expression will free you. In walking towards the pain, surrendering to it and feeling what it has to say, you are able to grow and will emerge stronger and wiser.

Listen deeply to your heart and embrace its wisdom. Its messages are pure and full of emotional and spiritual insights with all the knowledge needed for surrender.

Choosing to accept surrender and let go signifies your trust and faith. Embracing the belief that you will be okay, no matter what, will empower you to transform your life. You will begin to move out of the thinking, logical mind and into the sphere of Spirit.

Living from a spiritual perspective summons you to see and feel beyond form, trusting the unknown and unseen. Your heart and Inner Pink Star can then shine the path forward and allow you to let go of the ego and instead live in your truth.

A major relationship breakup in my twenties saw me resisting every message my heart was throwing at me to wake up and heal. My aversion marathon left me in inner turmoil and severely disconnected from myself. Upon hitting rock bottom, I eventually had to turn around and have the hard conversations with my heart and ego. Then I began the road to healing.

In the wake of my father's passing, however, I chose to sit in the emotions from day one. There was no avoidance. I had a gentle and honest face-to-face meeting with myself and surrendered to my heart. She knew exactly what was needed for us to manoeuvre through the twisting turns of grief and find our way home.

This was the start of a beautiful, compassionate grief journey that firstly shattered my heart, then pieced it back together and finally blew it wide open with the capacity to love more deeply. It walked me to the happy place I live today, carrying the scars but loving more than before, living my truth and following my purpose.

Surrender teaches you how to manoeuvre through the grief journey and to let go a little in everyday life. Let go to feel the love, smell the roses and watch the butterflies. It is a gift you can carry forward and incorporate into every beautiful day.

Be grateful for surrender!

Pink Grief Corner

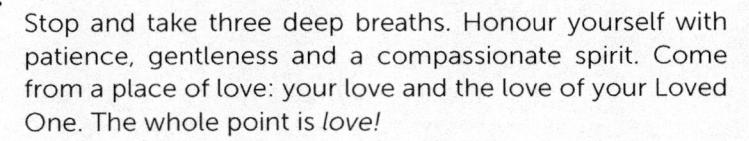

Stop and take three deep breaths. Honour yourself with patience, gentleness and a compassionate spirit. Come from a place of love: your love and the love of your Loved One. The whole point is *love*!

Take out a big piece of paper and write 'Surrender' in the centre. Brainstorm all the things that come to mind when you think about surrendering to your grief journey and to life. Write these around your central word.

Now ponder the following questions and record your feelings in your Pink Grief Journal:

1. Am I grateful for surrender?
2. Am I able to surrender, and do I have trust and faith in my journey?
3. Am I willing to look to my heart for the path?
4. What core beliefs or fears are stopping me from surrendering?
5. If I could surrender to my journey, what would be different?
6. When it comes to surrender, what am I grateful for?

GREETING GRATITUDE

Bask in your gratefulness of surrender. Let go – surrender – and feel resistance float away. Choosing to live with surrender is wiser than living in the moment racked with fear. Fear after all is False Evidence Appearing Real. Choose surrender over fear and walk a new path, receiving all life's gifts and sprinkling them over your beautiful heart.

You and Erica both acknowledge this was a hard Gratitude to learn. And yet it delivered a rewarding outcome once you grasped the concept and trusted your journey. The succulents don't exhibit the pretty colours of the peonies or perennials or stand strong like the oak tree, but they are green, luscious and healthy, multiplying playfully in many shapes and sizes.

Their green leaves and stems complement the array of colour in the nearby spots and add to the beauty of the garden. They bring a unique element just as each of our expressions of gratitude are beautiful in their own distinct way.

Carrying over a golden-stained wooden bench, you place it near the succulents, facing the colourful display nearby. The carving on the bench reads:

'Here lies the surrender we are grateful for.'

Erica and yourself sit silently side by side on the bench, enjoying the energy radiating between you. The connection you have with your new likeminded friend is so gratifying. When nothing is being said and you still feel fulfilled in the silence, you know you are in the company of your tribe.

Having been isolated on the trek through the Forest of Grief and having limited contact while nurturing yourself at the Field of Grace, you are finally delving into building deep relationships. It feels like the right time, and you notice you are beginning to reap the rewards of the Garden of Gratitude.

You finally speak. "What will the next Gratitude be for tomorrow?"

Erica softly replies, "Let's send it out to the universe, surrender, and just see what tomorrow brings. We will know". With surrender, trust and faith gently resting in your hearts you head back to the cabin to arrange dinner, with the doggies following obediently behind.

Moment Gratitude

"What day is it?" asked Winnie-the-Pooh
"It's today," squeaked Piglet.
"My favourite day," said Pooh.

—A.A. Milne

Opening the door after a loud knock, you find no one is there. 'That's strange.' Looking down you see a box with a big multicoloured bow. You are ready to open it, but Erica says, "No, not now. Later". Respecting her knowledge on this journey, you put the box (and your excitement) on the table and hope to find out what is hidden inside soon.

Erica asks you to join her on the bench with the succulents for a brief meditation to see which Gratitude the universe will send you to work on today.

Opening your eyes ten minutes later, you look at each other and say, "The moment". It's all about the moment. Today's Gratitude begins. You roll out your butcher's paper and write 'The moment' in the centre.

GREETING GRATITUDE

Next to the succulents a lattice fence stands up against the garden shed. The smell of the jasmine running through it is delightful. It heightens your senses and brings you right into the moment. You allow the smell to gracefully circle you. As you luxuriate in it, you feel that in this moment, right now everything is how it should be: Perfect!

Each moment is a beautiful gift wrapped up in a big colourful bow. It is all we have. We have memories of the past and we have plans for tomorrow. But it is only in this present moment that we live our life. Life happens in the moment – this moment!

Many of us fantasise about a better place, dwell on past events, fret over unnecessary things and allow our monkey minds (as Zen Buddhists call them) to leap from thought to thought like monkeys swinging in the trees. We allow the thoughts to control us and detach us from this precious moment where life is to be lived.

The busyness of the world we live in with its distractions contributes to this feeling of detachment and fragmentation and makes it an even more difficult task to find the peace inside.

We will always want to bask in memories, and we will always want to plan. Doing this with conscious awareness is important as our minds are not meant to be constantly hijacked, removing us from life in the moment. Gently taking control through conscious awareness and techniques such as mindfulness gives us back an appreciation and enjoyment of life.

Most of us know this in theory, but practical application can seem elusive. The calm and peace therefore continue to elude us as we swing from tree to tree with anxiety and disconnection on our backs. Instead of squandering your moments, however, you can seize the day and be alive in the moment just by taking responsibility. Learn all you can about being present and mindful to bring wonderful changes to your world.

Mindfulness practices have become popular in the Western world in the past decade, but their roots, originating in Hinduism and Buddhism, reach back years. Mindfulness is the psychological process of focusing your attention on the experience that is taking place right now. To practise mindfulness, sit quietly and observe your thoughts, without judgement or attachment, and then let them go, gently bringing your focus back to your breath.

In Buddhist teachings, mindfulness is applied to acquire self-knowledge and wisdom that gradually leads to enlightenment or freedom from suffering. Fully attending to what is happening in the moment, and not being dragged to the past or hauled to the future, sees you engaging fully in your life. This makes it possible to function more in the flow and connect to yourself and others at a deeper, more authentic level.

With mindfulness comes many benefits: deeper sleep, improved immune system, decreased stress, increased self-esteem, and a more joyous and content life. Sitting in meditation and contemplation of thought, in both my yoga and meditation practices, has bestowed upon me the rainbow of emotions on my grief journey. Feeling the emotions as they arise, being non-judgemental and releasing them when they are done has been my model to allow grief to lead the way. This cycle has been repeated as needed to promote my healing.

I am grateful in the wake of my grief to be more in touch with the moment, and I thus feel more connected to my dad, myself and life in general. To heal your grief consciously and healthily sees living in the moment become automatic and obligatory. You move with the flow and the flow takes you straight to the moment.

Striving to live in the moment is a journey, and the human experience always gives you moments of perfection and moments of desperation. You are eternally on a learning path. Always hope

GREETING GRATITUDE

to do better in the next moment but stay in this moment, instead of getting yanked out of your serenity.

Emotions, when given a chance to be expressed, come and go like the wind on a stormy day. You don't always know when an emotion will hit, but when it does you buckle down, face it head on, feel it and live through it. Don't judge it. Just allow it to pass. And it will. The storm of emotion will halt, and serenity will come where you can sit in the quiet and savour the stillness.

When you practise mindfulness, your mind feels free and light, which allows a sense of warmth and contentment to flow freely. Serenity is deep, and it slows down your thinking and movements to allow you to experience the moment. You will notice the bird flying past and think his wings are beautiful. You will notice the butterfly and think it is another sign from your Loved One. You will see your dog rolling at the park and grin because you feel its joy. You will see a child playing and it will warm your heart. You will be attuned to the beautifulness in each moment. And the more you tap in, the more beauty you see.

The moment is a gift.

When you are disconnected from the moment, you may find yourself living in drama, feeling anxious, dark and gloomy from depressive thoughts. In such times, pause and tune in to see where you are, take responsibility and make a different choice. The moment is there zealously waiting for you, and when you arrive your smile will widen. You will feel love and overwhelming joy as you smell the roses and sense the butterflies all around. You will then know you found the moment!

Be grateful for the moment!

Pink Grief Corner

Stop and take three deep breaths. Honour yourself with patience, gentleness and a compassionate spirit. Come from a place of love: your love and the love of your Loved One. The whole point is *love!*

Take out a big piece of paper, write 'The moment' in the centre and brainstorm all the things you are grateful for that come to mind when you think about living in the moment. Write these around your central word.

Now ponder the following questions and record your feelings in your Pink Grief Journal:

1. Am I grateful for the moment?
2. Am I living in the moment?
3. How do I feel when I live in the moment?
4. What benefits do I receive from living in the moment?
5. How busy is my monkey mind? Would I like a more serene existence?
6. When it comes to the moment, what am I grateful for?

Bask in your gratefulness for the moment. Enjoy every moment and watch for the serenity and joy to arrive quietly.

GREETING GRATITUDE

Walking back to the jasmine, you carry the box with the colourful bow that Erica asked you to retrieve from the cabin. You are excited! What is inside? It's big and reasonably heavy. "Can I open it now?" you ask.

"Of course," she whispers with a cheeky smile

Discarding the bow, you open the box and inside sits a dark grey statue and a bronze plaque. The statue is of a serene and calm lady. She sits peacefully in Sukhasana, a cross-legged meditation position, with her hands gently resting in her lap. You love it!

Finding the perfect place for your new lady friend near the jasmine, you sit, cross-legged like her, while you attach the plaque:

'Here lies the moment we are grateful for.'

Erica joins you. Feeling grounded and sensing the mindfulness, you join her in closing your eyes and focus on your breath flowing through your body. You enjoy the sun on your skin and the serenity running through your being.

Opening your eyes a while later, you name the statue 'Dhyana', meaning 'meditation' in Sanskrit. When you feel lost and disconnected, she will be your reminder to sit quietly, cross-legged, close your eyes, breathe, let go of your thoughts, observe, just be and wait for the stillness to arrive, placing you tenderly in the moment.

Lessons Gratitude

"If you truly want to grow as a person and learn, realise that the universe has enrolled you in the graduate program of life, called loss."

—Elisabeth Kübler-Ross

An early morning yoga class leaves you energised and full of ideas for today's Gratitude. You have learnt that in the stillness, questions are invited and answers revealed. Your mind quietens to allow your heart to speak and divulge the gifts and lessons from your grief.

Arriving back at the house you walk over to your magnolia bush. Magnolias are named after the French botanist, Pierre Magnol, and bequeath an aura of elegance, style and uniqueness. They bear beautiful white flowers, a piece of sophistication in your garden. Sitting next to the chic magnolia you take out your piece of butcher's paper and write 'Lessons' in the centre.

While you are deep in your grief, you may feel like you are just surviving, not transforming. The lessons are happening unconsciously, not yet assimilated internally. But be reassured they are transpiring under the surface. They will arise to be grasped later, when you contemplate the gratitude and the trauma of the grief journey has faded a little. Then, when your heart speaks she will deliver honesty, authenticity and beauty in the gentlest ways. It is she that bestows gifts and lessons galore as you travel through your grief journey.

The gifts are in the lessons.

GREETING GRATITUDE

Sometimes the lessons appear as epiphanies, shocking us out of reality. Sometimes they appear more slowly. Sometimes you feel different but can't put your finger on what has changed. At other times things change and there is no awareness; it just becomes integrated and you move on.

It is in the awareness, the stillness and your curious introspective nature that you can pinpoint your lessons and be thankful for the gifts. You can then contemplate how they have transformed you and how you will move forward with them.

It is in these lessons that your transformation can take shape in many ways. You become a little or a lot different inside because of your experience. You behave a little or a lot differently and make wiser and healthier choices. You may love yourself a little more and follow your yearnings all the way to your rich and full life because of the gifts and lessons.

Being aware of the lessons allow you to bask in gratitude. Living in ignorance of any transformation sees you carrying on in life without the beautiful realisations. Being consciously aware of the lessons embeds your transformation, benefiting you at a much deeper level.

You will be gifted many lessons in the wake of your loss, and every day more realisations may come to the surface, giving you a chance to stop and be thankful. Some of the biggest learnings I experienced were:

- The point is *love!*
- Live in your truth.
- Find your purpose.

These learnings have walked me through my grief to a calm and content place inside. It's in the learnings and the gifts that the healing and transformation takes place. Lessons are your gifts from grief. Honour your Loved One by dedicating your learning to them.

Be grateful for the lessons!

Pink Grief Corner

Stop and take three deep breaths. Honour yourself with patience, gentleness and a compassionate spirit. Come from a place of love: your love and the love of your Loved One. The whole point is *love!*

Take out a big piece of paper, write 'Lessons' in the centre and brainstorm all the things you have learnt and are grateful for on your grief journey.

Understanding the lessons do not minimise the grief. Give yourself permission to live in the lessons despite the grief.

Now ponder the following questions and record your feelings in your Pink Grief Journal:

1. Am I grateful for the lessons?
2. Am I able to realise the lessons while still feeling the grief?
3. What are my three most important lessons and any other lessons?
4. Do I see the lessons as gifts?
5. When it comes to the lessons, what am I grateful for?

Write your answers around your central word.

Now take some time out to see if any of the lessons below relate to your personal experience:

GREETING GRATITUDE

- Slow down and smell the roses.
- Watch the butterflies flitter past.
- Loss is inevitable.
- Lessen the stress in your life.
- Quieten your thoughts.
- Nurture your body with sleep, food and exercise.
- Soothe your soul.
- Integrate body, mind and soul.
- Find the stillness.
- Spend time with your loved ones.
- Put the to-do list down and connect.
- Have faith and trust in your journey.
- Surrender to the grief journey.
- Practise patience.
- Be self-loving.
- Follow your yearnings.
- Live the richest and fullest life.
- Honour yourself.
- Honour your Loved One.
- Live engaged in the moment.
- Give back to the universe.
- Always believe you can make a difference.
- Be surrounded by likeminded people.
- Remove the drama.
- Feel your feelings.
- Smile every day.

- Allow the tears to flow.
- Feel the anger and let it go.
- Anxiety can be your teacher.
- Understand that feelings pass.
- It's not the material things that are important.
- Running around being busy doesn't make you important.
- Don't run away from grief; face it head on.
- Live the good and live the not-so-good together.
- It's possible to live with the pain and the joy at the same time.
- The more you feel the pain, the deeper the joy.
- You can become an empty shell with the ability to start again.
- Your heart can be cracked wide open and heal better than before.
- You seek calm, peace and fulfilment.
- Practise yoga and meditation for a calm life.
- There are so many lessons in loss.
- Be grateful.
- Be one with the universe.
- Walk with your feet firmly planted on the earth.
- People pleasing is not necessary; please yourself.
- Grief never passes; it just assimilates within you.
- There is beauty in the small things.
- Say "I love you" all the time.
- Live in the love.

GREETING GRATITUDE

- 💕 Be thankful for all the good things in your life, especially your loved ones.
- 💕 Carry a piece of your Loved One with you always.

Bask in your gratefulness for the lessons. Be proud of what you have learnt on this gruelling journey of grief. Dedicate the lessons to your Loved One and apply them to live a more engaged and enriched life as you move forward.

Standing up to stretch your legs, you look down and see your critter friend lounging in the shade of the magnolia on this warm day. As you lean in to pick a beautiful flower, you take in the fragrance. Surprisingly, the critter doesn't scuttle away and looks you straight in the eye; you see deep into his heart. You immediately experience a knowing, a feeling of oneness with this little creature. A moment of love under the magnolia bush fills your heart with warmth.

Erica comes over and hands you a tin of paint, a paint brush and a terracotta animal that looks almost exactly like your critter friend. He has been on your journey from the start and has become a part of your little family at the Cabin of Love.

Love comes in all shapes and sizes and should never be understated. So, under the beautiful magnolia bush you put your terracotta critter right next to the real thing. Finally, you decide both should have a name. You turn to Erica and all she says is, "Wally. Please call him Wally in honour of a dog since passed that I loved with all my heart".

So, Wally it is, and the terracotta ornament sits under the magnolia tree in the shade. A wooden plaque honours him and his memory, providing a space to recall fond memories:

GRIEF, GRACE AND GRATITUDE

> 'Here lie the lessons we are grateful for.'

You go to the critter's house, lay some seeds on the pink house and paint 'Wally's home' above the handpainted roses. As you head back to the house with love in your heart, Erica tells you all about the memories of her beautiful dog Wally. It's the end to a beautiful day.

LIFE GRATITUDE

> "Although the world is full of suffering, it is full also of the overcoming of it."
>
> —Helen Keller

The next day the gratitude continues. Sitting under the crepe myrtle tree, you admire its pretty pink flowers and contemplate life. You roll out your piece of butcher's paper and write 'Life' in the middle.

Sitting cross-legged on the ground and looking over to Dhyana, your meditation statue, you close your eyes and allow the big questions to echo around in your mind.

Life! Such a big, wonderful, complex, mysterious, astounding, magical, perplexing and phenomenal place we are born into and have the privilege of experiencing. How did we get here? What is our purpose? What came before us? What happens at the end? Why? A philosopher's chocolate cake of delights. When you stop the asking you realise you are here, right now, in the middle of this big miracle. You are living it and it's all up to you how you choose to do it. Pretty simple, really!

Yet on the grief journey questions swill around in a labyrinth of thoughts through the darkness and light of our minds as we ponder our new peculiar world. Perhaps we hope to jump off the emotional rollercoaster by making sense of the loss. It's common to sit in the sorrow and ask the bigger questions. However, they may only take us further down the rabbit hole, with an answer never arising. Sometimes we just need to stop persisting and instead surrender and let go, looking to trust and have faith instead.

> Life is a mysterious, marvellous experience.

We may find answers to some questions that differ to the next person's. This has the potential to create minor dinner table discussions through to world scale wars. War and peace, opposite ends of the scale, each lie at our doorstep to trip over every morning while we strive to live our lives and hope to be the best person we can be.

Loss transforms the way we look at life. What we feel about life. What we take for granted. It agitates us at the core and throws us off balance, and we stumble around looking to feel grounded again. In an instant our world, with less one person, is upturned and unequivocally different. And there is nothing we can do about it.

One day though, a speck of hope and lightness will shine through the dark. It is the beginning of crawling your way out. This is what life and grief is like. Life teaches you to hold on and to let go, and it is in seeking the symmetry that you are often thrown off balance and fall off the seesaw.

Moving further through the grief journey, at some point you sit back with your grief still hugging you tight yet you also begin to marvel at the beauty and magic of life. It really is that special! And when you can remove yourself from your monkey mind and step outside your grief, this realisation starts to cover you like a warm, cosy coat on a cold winter's day.

Yes, you still need to feel your grief, but consciously walking through the grief journey with an appreciation for finding the gratitude will likely see you being gently placed at the other end saying "Thank you" with humility. It is a transformative experience, despite your Loved One no longer standing by your side.

The dichotomy of loving life and hating life during loss can befuddle you for some time. Yet, accessing the gratitude is a step closer to finding the much sought-after liberation and respite.

Be grateful for life!

Pink Grief Corner

Stop and take three deep breaths. Honour yourself with patience, gentleness and a compassionate spirit. Come from a place of love: your love and the love of your Loved One. The whole point is *love!*

Take out a big piece of paper, write 'Life' in the centre and brainstorm all the things you are grateful for on your grief journey. Write these around your central word.

Think about the bigger picture and life in its entirety.

Now ponder the following questions and record your feelings in your Pink Grief Journal:

1. Am I grateful for my life?
2. Am I battling with any questions about life?
3. Are there any questions I need to let go?

GREETING GRATITUDE

> 4. What are the marvellous things about my life?
> 5. When it comes to life, what am I grateful for?

Bask in your gratefulness of life. Realise how special and intricate it is that you are here in a body experiencing life. Accept you are the author of this life, and as the author you can construct any masterpiece you desire on your blank canvas of life. If you don't like what you created, get another canvas and start again. Make it big, bright, colourful and fabulous.

Both Erica and you are a little overwhelmed and drained after finishing this Gratitude. It is such a big area to cover, yet you are both grateful for your life and understand that painting your canvas with a new spectacular picture is a good place to start.

To finish your Gratitude, you hang a beautiful heart-shaped crystal suncatcher over one of the branches. You place it in the perfect spot to capture and reflect the light and throw it out over all the branches of the tree. Your tree of life.

As you sit to treasure the dazzling display of light you find yourself cherishing your life and light up inside like the fractal light around you. Before you leave, you place a plaque on the tree that reads:

> 'Here lies the life we are grateful for.'

Heading back to the house, you are delighted with your efforts and note you are close to finishing your ten Gratitudes. You wonder, 'What happens next?' But for the rest of today you will relax as tomorrow is another big day.

Connection Gratitude

"You may say I'm a dreamer, but I'm not the only one. I hope someday you'll join us. And the world will live as one."

—John Lennon

Looking out the window you see Erica arriving with Lilly and Miss Maisy, five other people from your yoga class and your beautiful friend Jane. They all are chatting happily and carrying their yoga mats and colourful meditation cushions under their arms. It's the first time you have had a group of visitors here and you are a little excited. You quickly gather some cups and different herbal teas and place them on a tray for later.

Grabbing your yoga mat you skip outside to join them with your happiness in tow. Together you lay your mats on the ground facing the garden and lie down for Savasana pose to relax and prepare. Erica winks at you; you know that she can almost read your mind. You love connecting with others and it has been a little lacking in your grief journey.

Erica takes everyone through a beautiful flowing yoga class, which you find embeds your gratitude for life from yesterday. Afterwards, sipping on a liquorice tea, your conversation is centred around connection.

You invite your new friends to stay for today's Gratitude and roll out the butcher's paper on the newly laid luscious green grass. In the centre you write 'Connection' and ask your friends to take part in this exercise.

GREETING GRATITUDE

Connection stems straight back to our childhood. Even as a little baby, love and emotional connection are profoundly important for us to feel worthy and lovable. Sadly, some of us are not fortunate to have a loving upbringing and the consequences can reach deep into adulthood and lace our relationships. This can see people striving to fill their empty voids with unhealthy patterns or people. Adding a grief journey on top of this already fragile soul can create even more trauma.

Others are blessed to have a healthy childhood yet still struggle during grief to find connections that can help move them through their grief journey. In disconnecting from ourselves we find it harder to connect with others. Social isolation through grief can result in loneliness and depression.

We all aspire to move away from pain towards pleasure. How we deal with our journey through the pain from loss will impact our healing and future wellbeing and happiness.

The secret is to move through pain to the centre instead of trying to skip around the edges. The most essential form of connection is the one you have with yourself. Walking through the middle of your grief will have you strongly connected to yourself and your journey. Listening to your heart and feeling all your emotions will solidify this connection. It can be so easily lost when you try to run away, avoid or ignore your inner self. By staying connected to yourself and your grief, you will make progress.

Once you have solidified the connection with yourself, you are able to give more fully and connect to others. You may stop reaching out to people who are unhealthy for you just to connect with someone, anyone, to fill a void. You will know to save your precious energy, value yourself and connect to those who will draw out the best in you and provide love and emotional support.

Build deep connections.

At times on your journey, you may want to be more introverted and sit at home pondering life and shedding tears. This may surprise you if you have always been a social butterfly. That is a normal part of grief for some people. They need to assimilate and make sense of their world before they return to their social lives. At these times it could benefit you to check if you need more interaction with helpful support people to process your loss.

You may be tempted to ramp up your social interactions, possibly in an unhealthy fashion to avoid facing the pain at all costs. It is at these times you could benefit from checking if you need more time alone to process your loss.

Everyone is different; there is no set schedule. But the healthy grief journey coerces you to know yourself intricately. Choosing to resist this only creates more pain. Surrendering to the journey, although painful at first, will alleviate the pain over time. Once you have mastered this you will know what you need, when you need it and how you need it, and you can walk to fulfil it at all costs.

I stepped back from life and allowed my introversion to lead the way and my heart to ask for what it wanted. I had no real desire to socialise except for immediate family and a small group of friends. I needed to stay within the safe circles I knew as I needed to process everything while feeling like I was spinning around. I needed to sort out my new reality and put the pieces of my life back together, and it was enormously hard to hold my focus when I was in the company of others.

One day, much later, I followed a niggling sensation to be more social and was thrilled at the thought of being with others. I felt more balanced and connected to myself again, and because of this I was ready to share it. Slowly I balanced my introversion with my extroversion; my time alone with my time with friends. Eventually, I realised I was in the flow again and wasn't actively analysing what was happening; it was just occurring around me. The spinning had abated, and I had grounded both feet and began to live with joy and contentment.

GREETING GRATITUDE

I built and strengthened a more loving, stable connection with myself. I understood more the nooks and crannies of my complex existence. Accepting and appreciating the imperfections and the beautifulness within, I found gratitude for both.

I faced head on my weaknesses and learnt how to live with them along with my strengths. To have both sides living harmoniously together, creating the masterpiece of the whole me, is very fulfilling. I have learnt to accept the parts of myself I was ashamed of and wanted to disown and know that without them I wouldn't have had my life experiences and be who I am today.

Learning to own and welcome all parts of yourself is to love yourself. While you are still hating aspects, you will not access self-love in its entirety. Digging deep and finding the parts you are not proud of, and forgiving them, will aid in loving yourself at a deeper level. The quickest way to find the parts you are trying to disown is to notice the parts that you dislike or are annoyed by in others. These are generally the parts you have not accepted or forgiven and dislike in yourself. This is called projection.

Ultimately, with awareness, your existing relationships can become deeper and more beautiful because of the loss. They can move you to a more profound relational existence, allowing you to delight in the wisdom, intensity, playfulness and genuineness they provide.

This allows you to align with your spiritual tribe: the people who get you, understand you and support you. You may start to spend more time with people who like what you like and ask the same questions about life that you do. They will exist at the same depth of spirit as you do, which serves to enhance all your daily experiences and connections. In your connections you can find beauty, warmth, fun and joy. You will learn about yourself and others, giving you the opportunity to grow every day if you choose to.

Be grateful for connection!

Pink Grief Corner

Stop and take three deep breaths. Honour yourself with patience, gentleness and a compassionate spirit. Come from a place of love: your love and the love of your Loved One. The whole point is *love!*

Take out a big piece of paper, write 'Connection' in the centre and brainstorm all the things you are grateful for on your grief journey. Write these around your central word.

Think about the connections that exist in your world.

Now ponder the following questions and record your feelings in your Pink Grief Journal:

1. Am I grateful for connections?
2. Do I have a solid connection with myself or do I need more time alone to build my connection to myself?
3. Do I have a solid connection with others or do I need to spend more time with others to build these connections?
4. Have I found my spiritual tribe?
5. When it comes to connections, what am I grateful for?

Bask in your gratefulness for your connections. Be kind to yourself and build a strong, deep connection to yourself. Then shine this connection out to others who live a kindred life and want to share in your love and authenticity. Mastering this will heighten your existence, deepen your connections to self and others, and brighten your world.

GREETING GRATITUDE

Finishing for the day, having deepened the connections with your new yoga friends, you smile with delight as a truck pulls up in the driveway beeping its horn.

Everyone's eyes are wide with surprise as a big stone fountain is hoisted from the truck. The delivery men carefully place its pieces on top of each other in the middle of the lawn. The result is a gorgeous memorial in the form of a lady standing tall with a pitcher on her back, pouring water into a round basin. The humming of flowing water soothes your soul and adds to the serenity of the Garden of Gratitude.

While the others are chatting away sitting cross-legged on the meditation cushions, you sit quietly on the bench near the succulents. Taking in the sights and sounds you look around at your garden and are extremely proud of what you have created so far. A heavenly delight!

You think of your Loved One and hope they know that this picturesque space only exists because of the love you have for them, and it is now reaching out and touching people they never met.

To finish this grassy space of your garden you erect a plaque that says:

'Here lie the connections we are grateful for.'

Saying goodbye to your friends, your thoughts reverberate to remind you that the small things you do in the wake of your loss have long-reaching ramifications. Living your purpose and fulfilling your passions sees you travelling the path intended for you, touching others' lives and beautifying them as you move through yours.

Me Gratitude

"It is never too late to be who you might have been"

— George Eliot

Sitting amongst your little field of pink poppies you think about your Connection Gratitude from yesterday and how important it is to connect. Erica arrives with all the supplies for today and sitting beside you she writes 'Me' in the centre of the butcher's paper.

Sometimes it is hard to be kind and appreciate your strengths, honour yourself and be grateful for who you are. Our body is a miracle. A marvellous machine that starts off in a pure form. Yet many of us sabotage and vandalise it over the years with bad decisions and impulsive urges without considering it needs to carry us through to old age.

Sometimes you are lucky though to get a wake-up call, like a tragic loss or health concern, that gives you a second chance to re-evaluate how you care for yourself. At this turning point you can make a big difference.

Feeling gratitude and loving your body leads you to treating yourself better. When you lose someone you love, it stops you in your tracks. Suddenly you may realise you are not indestructible. You may contemplate your older age and decide to value your body to ensure you arrive there in one healthy piece.

The same applies with your mind and heart. Feed your mind healthy thoughts and it will live a healthier life. If you nurture your soul, tune in, sit quietly, follow its wise voice and breathe, it will nurture you right back. If you care for your body, mind and soul, they will

GREETING GRATITUDE

be in a better position to carry you through to a healthy older age. Cultivating and uniting mind, body, heart and soul will see you thrive in your own magnificent way.

Perhaps you may find this an ideal time to commit to live a healthier life. A healthier life has you jumping out of bed looking forward to every day with a body radiating energy, a mind circulating creativity and a soul breathing contentment, peace and joy. Striving to live to old age with no pain or disease and free of medications.

> Unite body, mind and soul.

This traumatic loss may instigate a deeper understanding that what you do now is what you will deal with in the years to come. Mistreating yourself now will likely catch up with you at some stage. Reality may hit you hard. However, releasing any ignorance and implementing the changes now may increase the chances that you see a healthy older age. Walking headlong into responsibility for your health, your mind, body and soul, sees you rejoicing in its benefits.

My philosophy is the 80/20 rule. If you can live a healthy life 80 percent of the time and the other 20 percent loosen the reins a little and treat yourself, there is a good chance you will find a balance. My experience has seen me wanting to eat better, with more vegies and less chocolate and chips. I go to yoga and move my body in a gentle, restorative way. I practise meditation and go deeper into the stillness, promoting a calmer existence, believing meditation is the food for our emotions. I slow down and listen to my inner self, then follow its direction; spend less time doing, and more time being; seek out what nourishes my body and act accordingly; problem solve illnesses until I arrive at the root cause and eliminate it; and strive to spend time with my loved ones often. In essence, I practise more self-love.

What works for you may be different. The important thing is to do whatever engenders wellness and happiness for you. Try slowing down your busy ways and reducing your to-do list. Go to bed earlier and sleep well. Hydrate a lot and minimise your coffee intake. Where possible, decrease alcohol, unnecessary medications or bad foods that you put into your body.

Look at your cellulite and wrinkles and celebrate them. Spot a grey hair and value being alive long enough to get them. Appreciate the ageing process and bask in the knowledge that as you get older, you get wiser. As you get wiser and go deeper, you love yourself more, which allows you to wake up every day showing gratitude for your unique personality.

So with self-love and strong gratitude for yourself, you will be doing the best you can to live to a ripe and healthy old age where you can enjoy your loved ones and your life for longer.

Be grateful for you!

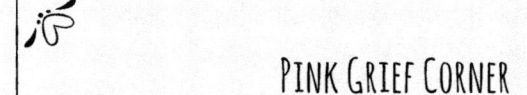

PINK GRIEF CORNER

Stop and take three deep breaths. Honour yourself with patience, gentleness and a compassionate spirit. Come from a place of love: your love and the love of your Loved One. The whole point is *love!*

Take out a big piece of paper, write 'Me' in the centre and brainstorm all the things you are grateful for on your grief journey. Write these around your central word.

Now ponder the following questions and record your feelings in your Pink Grief Journal:

1. Am I grateful for me?
2. Do I treat myself with kindness and care? If not, what can I do to treat myself better?

GREETING GRATITUDE

3. If I make no changes now, what will my life look like in 10, 20 or 30 years?
4. If I do make changes now, what can my life look like in 10, 20 or 30 years?
5. When it comes to me, what am I grateful for?

Bask in your gratefulness of you. You are a special, unique and extraordinary individual. You can choose today or any day to make better decisions, care for yourself better and operate from a deeper, more fulfilled space. It just takes you to decide. Honour, love and respect yourself and watch how your life profoundly alters for the better.

In the mess of poppies you place a rusted metal heart-shaped ornament to remind you to always sit and soak up this field of beauty and honour a deeper connection. A reminder to always take care of your body, mind, heart and soul.

Written around the love heart it says:

'Here lies the me that we are grateful for.'

Moving to the grassed area, you lie down on a pretty turquoise pillow, allowing the rays from the sun to touch your bare skin. You listen to the soothing water flowing from the fountain and it dawns on you that tomorrow is your last day of creating the Garden of Gratitude. One last Gratitude to go – the most special one.

My Loved One Gratitude

"To live in hearts we leave behind is not to die."

—Thomas Campbell

Your last gratitude is dedicated to your Loved One. The most special Gratitude of all!

Gathering your supplies, the doggies and Erica you walk to the area of the garden where ten resplendent white standard rose bushes queue. Your last piece of butcher's paper is laid down, and you look to Erica with a tear in your eye. You write 'My Loved One' in the centre.

Just the mention of your Loved One can fill your eyes with tears representing the sadness of the loss and the beauty of the love. You find harmony bathing in both as each brings you closer to your Loved One – a feeling always welcomed. Without one there is no other. And living in the contradiction bears the delicious fruit of our lives. It's these feelings that heighten the gratitude you have for them, which you are able to access at any moment.

You have wandered through this grief journey from day one because of the strong love you have for your Loved One. The gifted piece of love they left with you radiates its love, lighting up your heart. Never underestimate the power of this love, and always distinguish between the grief and the love. The love that is an extension of your grief outweighs any love you have felt before. It illuminates your path forward.

GREETING GRATITUDE

You can walk the rest of your life with two feet securely on the ground, moving forwards at your own pace while occasionally resting briefly to gently tiptoe through the beautiful and poignant meadow of shared memories. The memories will often arise with tears as their bedfellow. At other times it is laughter. Both will take you in and out of the special space in your heart where these memories dwell. They are attainable forever to soothe you when needed.

Your Loved One has been the person you look to for comfort and love. This need not change; you are learning to assimilate their love, which is now more spiritual in nature. You call and they are there, if you believe them to be.

This is the ultimate Gratitude because not only are you profoundly grateful for your Loved One and their presence in your life, you realise that because of your loss the other Gratitudes have become more known. The Gratitudes have become entrenched in your soul, enabling you to live a richer and fuller life, engaged in each moment.

Be incredibly grateful for your Loved One!

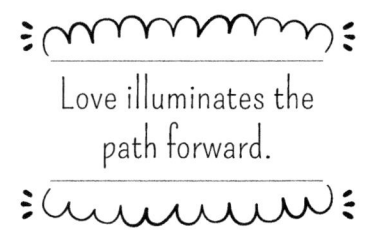

Love illuminates the path forward.

Pink Grief Corner

Stop and take three deep breaths. Honour yourself with patience, gentleness and a compassionate spirit. Come from a place of love: your love and the love of your Loved One. The whole point is *love!*

Take out a big piece of paper, write 'My Loved One' in the centre and brainstorm all the things you are grateful for on your grief journey. Write these around your central word.

Now ponder the following questions and record your feelings in your Pink Grief Journal:

1. How am I grateful for my Loved One?
2. What am I most grateful for because of my Loved One?
3. What brings tears and laughter of gratitude to my heart because of my Loved One?
4. How has being grateful to my Loved One changed my life?
5. When it comes to my Loved One, what will I always be grateful for?

Bask in your gratefulness of your Loved One. Do something in honour of your Loved One: for example, create a foundation or run a charity. Live your purpose with enthusiasm despite your loss and because of it. Live your life in honour and gratitude of them and, through the loss, strive to make a difference to yourself and others. Live your purpose, whether it is a grand gesture or just fulfilling your daily responsibilities with joy – however your purpose looks to you.

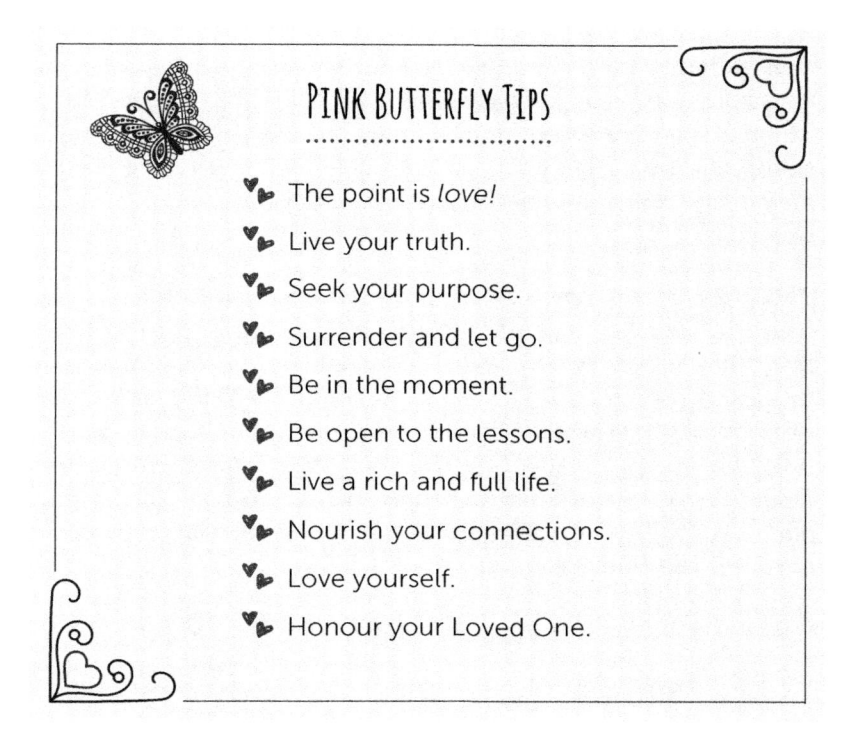

> ### PINK BUTTERFLY TIPS
>
> - The point is *love!*
> - Live your truth.
> - Seek your purpose.
> - Surrender and let go.
> - Be in the moment.
> - Be open to the lessons.
> - Live a rich and full life.
> - Nourish your connections.
> - Love yourself.
> - Honour your Loved One.

You pack up all your supplies and sit on the bench at the front door of the Cabin of Love with Erica. The blue butterfly on the doormat is brought to your attention as three white butterflies float mid-air nearby just a little longer than normal.

A sign! You feel your Loved One at the front door of your heart, thanking you for your beautiful Gratitude, wishing you onwards, sending you signs indicating they are only a call away.

Lilly and Miss Maisy have a drink and then curl up at your feet. Wally pops his head around the corner before scuttling off to sit in his favourite spot near his terracotta friend under the magnolia tree.

There is one last detail you need to finalise before you can finish your Gratitudes. The finale needs to be revealed by placing a special dedication near the rose bushes.

You have been waiting patiently all day for Erica to reveal what you are to place there, as she has sneakily hidden it from you. As you are waiting, you hear voices from around the corner getting closer. A beautiful hand-carved wooden bridge emerges, carried by a group of men. Its startling size and beauty are an apt representation of this Gratitude.

They walk directly past you, balancing it precariously. It looks quite heavy, but finally it is gently lowered and placed over the creek right near the rose bushes. This is the creek that you crossed by foot when you first arrived from the Forest of Grief and the Cabin of Love was revealed to you. The bridge symbolises your entire journey, crossing over from your life to the Forest of Grief, the arrival at the Cabin of Love, your time at the Field of Grace and the Garden of Gratitude and now finally your walk home. It also represents the crossing over of your Loved One. Beautiful!

Next to the bridge they place a bronze plaque that reads:

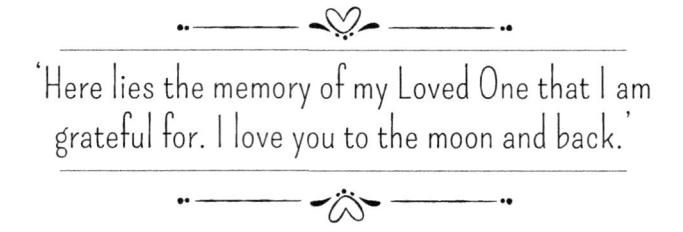

> 'Here lies the memory of my Loved One that I am grateful for. I love you to the moon and back.'

It is perfect! You walk over the bridge and sit on the water's edge to reflect on your long journey, full of twists and turns. The song Edelweiss is gently humming a tune in your head, diffusing love to the centre of your heart.

You smile, shed a small tear and reflect. Life feels good. Despite your Loved One not being by your side you can feel all the Gratitude

GREETING GRATITUDE

shining its beauty through you. You know in this space of gratitude, with the love, roses and butterflies surrounding you and your heart, moving forward without your Loved One is now possible more than ever. With that thought, leaving to head back to the cabin, you feel a new buoyancy in your step.

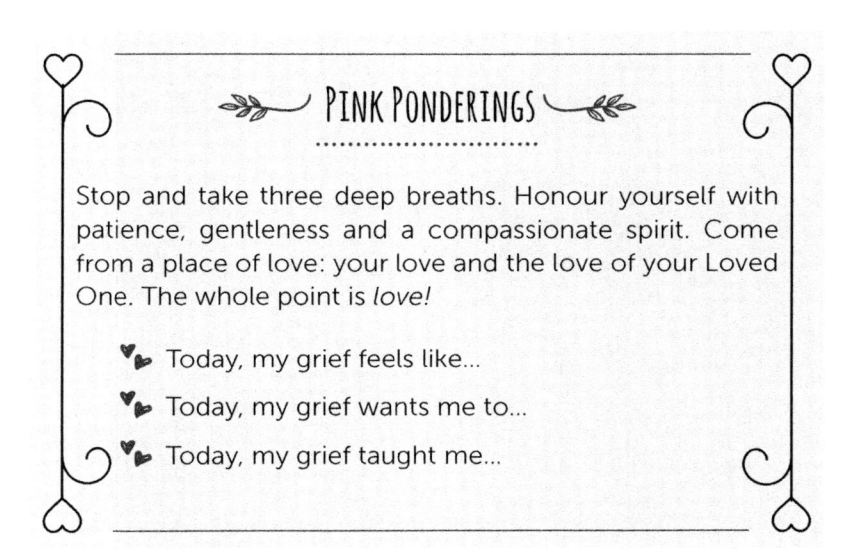

PINK PONDERINGS

Stop and take three deep breaths. Honour yourself with patience, gentleness and a compassionate spirit. Come from a place of love: your love and the love of your Loved One. The whole point is *love!*

- Today, my grief feels like...
- Today, my grief wants me to...
- Today, my grief taught me...

FINAL CONTEMPLATION

"The pain passes, but the beauty remains."

—Pierre-Auguste Renoir

Here at the Garden of Gratitude you have created ten dedications of gratitude in ten days, bringing to life your blossoming garden and reaping the rewards deep inside your heart. You have looked to find your yearnings and to integrate them as you seek to live your life purpose. You feel elated, overwhelmed, content and sad; the rainbow of emotions has appeared at the conclusion of your Gratitudes.

You have accepted the grief and its place in your life a little more and understand that grief does not end; it just changes form. You are learning to alter your relationship with your Loved One and to feel the love that still resides within you even though they are no longer here.

You begin to delicately welcome the new you to the world and show absolute thanks and gratitude for having your Loved One in your life. You have started to blossom and appreciate all the lessons your Loved One and your grief journey have taught you. You briefly float the pictures of the ten Gratitudes through your mind.

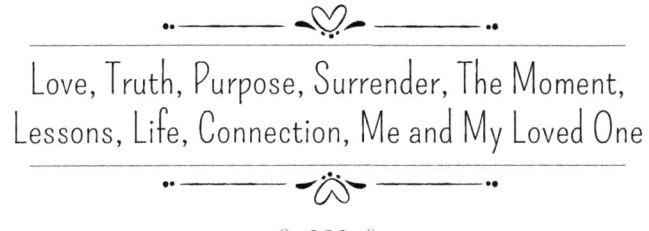

Love, Truth, Purpose, Surrender, The Moment, Lessons, Life, Connection, Me and My Loved One

Grief, Grace and Gratitude

You think of the first day you stood at the entrance of the Forest of Grief and how far you have come to be standing, in this moment, with gifts in your heart and good friends by your side at the Garden of Gratitude.

You think about your journey:

In the Forest of Grief you learnt that the point is love!

In the Field of Grace you learnt that in grace lies your truth.

Now you understand that in the Garden of Gratitude once you combine the love and truth with your Gratitudes, you are free to walk forward to your life purpose.

It is not a journey you would ever choose to take, but you walked the challenging path with courage and strength. For that be proud. The rewards and the experience have changed you deep inside and the time has come to move forward another step. The next step takes you back into your life.

It's time to leave the Garden of Gratitude and reassimilate!

Realising it's time to say goodbye strikes a poignant and saddening chord. Although you are ready to return home, you don't want to leave behind your journey, your garden, your critter friend, Wally, the cabin and your new friends Erica, Jane, Lilly and Miss Maisy.

You realise, though, that saying goodbye is a part of life, and sometimes you need to say goodbye when you don't really want to. Sometimes it comes from nowhere and other times you get time to prepare.

Our human experience sends us situations over and over where we need to say goodbye. Holding on is detrimental yet saying goodbye causes heartache and grief. Staying in limbo and not doing anything is most unhealthy and not an option.

FINAL CONTEMPLATION

With emotional maturity, and by listening to your inner self, you will know when it's time for goodbye and will be able to say it with grace. While knowing it will cause angst and sadness, you will also know you can cope with whatever life brings and that your heart will always lead you on the right path. Remember, you need to walk through the middle of the pain to find the love.

Now is the time. Walking to the Cabin of Love, you notice the colour, the love, the beauty, the warm, homely atmosphere and the healing aura that echoes through the entire space. You are proud to notice how your fingerprint of style and elegance is there for the next soul that needs a space to heal and realise their gratitude.

As you gather your things and close the door behind you one last time, you feel like you are closing the door to a piece of your heart and a chapter in your journey. Trust and faith step up to remind you that when one door closes, another opens, and your heart helps you put your next foot forward.

You head out to Wally's house. He is sitting there looking at you like he knows now is the time. You sense he has experienced this goodbye before. You place some seeds and are surprised he lets you stroke him on the head. His silky fur touches your hand and through the tears you say, "Thanks, Wally, I will always remember you. I love you and I'll miss you".

You sit down on the new bridge to wait. Will Erica, Jane and the doggies come before you leave? You must cross over soon.

Listening to the water flow, with your feet resting in its coolness, you get out your Pink Grief Journal to answer the final five questions that were left at the cabin for you. You get ready to write.

Pink Time Out – Final Contemplation

Stop and take three deep breaths. Honour yourself with patience, gentleness and a compassionate spirit. Come from a place of love: your love and the love of your Loved One. The whole point is *love!*

Record your thoughts and feelings. Refer to your notes from the final contemplation from *Part 1: Forest of Grief* and *Part 2: Field of Grace*. Notice the differences within you.

1. What is the most helpful lesson you learnt in the Garden of Gratitude?
2. What would you share with others about the Garden of Gratitude and its lessons?
3. What did you struggle with most in the Garden of Gratitude?
4. Can you acknowledge how far you have come in your journey?
5. How do you feel about moving forward with Love + Truth + Purpose?

Finishing your five questions, you see Erica running towards you. She opens her arms to take you in one of her big warm hugs. Lilly and Miss Maisy, only moments behind, start licking your legs, always overexcited to see you.

The last goodbye. So many words to say and none that can truly express your gratitude. Without her as your support person and butterfly wings, you feel you may never have come this far. So you

FINAL CONTEMPLATION

look deep into her eyes, feeling her heart, and say gently, "Thank you". Erica smiles so big and bright. She appreciates the depth of its sincerity.

Bending down, you hug the doggies and look deep into their souls. You know they understand your soul-to-soul thank you. They relax to a well-mannered sit. Their sad eyes understand.

Then Jane comes from nowhere just in time for a final hug and farewell. So, it's time. As you walk away you only turn back briefly to send another big smile to your friends and take one last look at your beautiful Garden of Gratitude.

Everything is perfect. Dhyana, the meditation lady, is observing you through the jasmine, the terracotta Wally is resting under the magnolia tree next to the real Wally, the oak tree is larger than life, the birds are flitting in and out of the birdbath near the perennials, the wishing well is standing proud amidst the peonies, the bench is nestled amidst the succulents, the suncatcher is radiating light under the crepe myrtle, the rusted love heart is diffusing love out through the pink poppies, the fountain is flowing on the grass and the bridge you are standing on adjacent to the rose bushes is your gateway home.

It's a picture-perfect space to heal and you realise that the Gratitudes are there because of you, your grief, your love and your Loved One. Looking at the garden in its entirety takes your breath away as you acknowledge its magnitude and exquisiteness.

Crossing over the bridge, holding one big white rose and carrying a heavy backpack, you are ready to retrace your steps through the Forest of Grief. On the way home you place all the required items back in the necessary places just as Erica had done for you: the trekking boots, the food, blankets and the myriad of other supplies you used on your trek. You wander past the 'Love' signposts, the butterfly chimes and the picnic table, and lastly you place the luscious white rose at the entrance to the Forest of Grief.

Looking down, you notice Wally has followed you and your heart swells. You instruct him to wait with the rose and to walk the next grieving soul through the Forest of Grief safely and carefully, seeing them arrive safely at the Cabin of Love, just like he had for you. "Stay out of their way for a while. You don't want to crowd them as they will be very fragile," you say as he scuttles obediently to a nearby tree to wait inconspicuously.

Exiting the Forest of Grief, you think about the welcome note and the pink and white roses you left on the counter for the next person arriving at the Cabin of Love. You wonder how they will live their experience and add to the Cabin of Love and the Garden of Gratitude to illustrate their uniqueness and their journey.

Carrying in your heart the love, roses and butterflies, you finally spread your own beautifully healed butterfly wings and allow them to carry you all the way home, transformed and ready to live in love, truth and purpose.

LOVE – TRUTH – PURPOSE

"I wish heaven had visiting hours."

—Author unknown

FINAL CONTEMPLATION

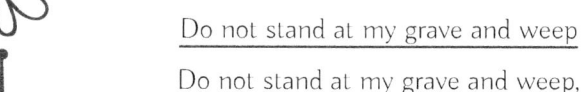

<u>Do not stand at my grave and weep</u>

Do not stand at my grave and weep,
I am not there; I do not sleep.
I am a thousand winds that blow,
I am the diamond glints on snow,
I am the sun on ripened grain,
I am the gentle autumn rain.
When you awaken in the morning's hush
I am the swift uplifting rush
Of quiet birds in circling flight.
I am the soft star-shine at night.
Do not stand at my grave and cry,
I am not there; I did not die.

—Mary Frye (1932)

EPILOGUE

> "If there ever comes a day when we can't be together,
> keep me in your heart. I'll stay there forever."
>
> —A.A. Milne

I have walked through the middle of my grief straight to the epicentre of the pain, authentically and lovingly. My life has transformed because of it, leaving me feeling lighter, awakened, enriched, more loving and with a strong connection to self.

My butterfly wings were lying flat on the floor at the start of my grief journey and I looked to Dad to help me rise. Now that I am further along in my journey, I once again feel the wind beneath me, picking my wings up, giving me strength and carrying me along to my future.

Dad gifted me the ability to listen to my heart and follow its path, unearthing the yearnings that enrich my life and facilitate my healing even further. I appreciate and acknowledge that because of him and the wake of his death, I am committed to live a richer and fuller life. I choose to fill it with more love than before, to keep my eyes open for all the signs sent in the form of love, roses and butterflies. I know I am perpetually blessed for my human experience.

Grief, Grace and Gratitude

There is always an end to a story, but the end can also be just a beginning. Maybe it's the end of a beautiful era, but also the beginning of a transformed relationship with your Loved One where infinite love, trust and respect continues to be shared between you.

Your Loved One is in your successes and in the wind flowing through your hair. They are in the sunrise and the sunset, in the sand as you walk along the beach and all the flowers you see. They are in the quiet yoga poses and silent meditations. They are in everything because they are love.

When you find the love they gifted you in your heart and you find your own self-love and gratitude in your grief, you will understand that the point simply is *love!* You will feel your Loved One everywhere because you will feel the love. You are love.

See a sign, believe it to be true and look out for more. When a white rose appears out of nowhere and you look for a logical answer, give your heart to the unknown. Observe how two worlds meet to continue the love between you in the form of this beautiful sign.

Follow the yearnings and continue uncovering the signs. Looking behind, you will see that they are trailing your footsteps. When you flail, look in front and they are leading the way. When you fall, look beside you and they are holding out their hand to lift you up and walk alongside you.

To live in the wake of grief and still be shrouded by the colourful rainbow of grief's emotions at times is normal. Live in the dichotomy of love and grief and live both to their fullest. To understand that without the grief there is no love is to understand life and be open to living it.

Basking in the beauty of your scars, you can still feel your Loved One. Even though your heart may be in a million pieces, it will slowly piece itself back together. The body, mind, heart and soul

EPILOGUE

are incredibly proficient in healing themselves if given the space they need to do their thing.

We love our loved ones from day one, to their deathbed and eternally beyond. Your love hasn't changed; only your human experience has. I visualise Dad's mannerisms and hear him say, "Hello, darling" as he answers the phone, and I say out loud, "I love you, Dad, to the moon and back". You likewise can visualise your own special Loved One.

Then you can sit and allow this love to flow through you as the answer becomes clear.

Through Grief, Grace and Gratitude you can transform your grief and realise that love is the point; in grace lies your truth and gratitude walks you to your purpose. As this sinks in and you ponder your life, you will feel the love once again, seek the roses and watch the glorious white butterflies flitter past.

Rest in peace, my beautiful dad. I thank you for everything. I love you to the moon and back forever.

I am because of you!

LIFE IN THE PINK

Through my work at In the Pink I aim to radiate healthy vibrations into the world through positive writings, powerful consultations, yoga teachings and heartfelt services for those aiming to walk to a rich life full of love, truth and purpose.

Life in the Pink helps you learn how to travel and transform through your difficult journeys in life, facing your fears, heartbreaks and grief, bringing you home to a Life in the Pink. I hope to help you unearth your true self and inner wisdom that leads you to know, understand, nurture and love yourself. I wish to help you to travel on your journey in life feeling alive, rich and full, choosing to live authentically following your soul's desire and life purpose.

I genuinely know it is possible to dig deep to find the love that is buried below the pain. It's there; trust me! Sometimes it just takes a while to find it and allow it to flourish. When you find it, and you will, it grants you the ability to feel strong, joyful and happy. Accessing all your love buried deep below and bringing it to the surface will allow you to become one with it and shine it out to your loved ones and everyone you meet.

Using your traumatic experiences as a learning tool and a gift can help to springboard you to a new life full of deep richness and joy. Acknowledge you need patience, allow heartbreak and grief to pave your path, don't repress or suppress, be open to everything, remain strong and brave, keep your Loved One alive in your heart and just *be!*

Services

Positive writings

Heartbreak, Healing and Happiness – Flourishing after a heartbreak. 2015

Allow me to accompany you on the journey through Heartbreak via Healing and arriving home flourishing in Happiness. Share in a comforting array of self-loving insights and tools, plus my very own raw personal experiences. Use the practical activities and exercises to help move you through the pain and suffering.

Redesign and redecorate your life and heal any old lingering hurts forever. Emerge feeling healed and happy with oodles of energy, and eager to embark on your new, fun and exciting life adventure.

Heartbreak – Learn how to pick yourself up, transform through the grieving process, benefit from the lessons and create self-love.

Healing – Unearth your true self and inner wisdom. Befriend your inner critic and learn how to live a truly authentic life.

Happiness – Expose, design and chase your passions, create your vision, map your goals and start living your soul's desire and life purpose.

Flourish and live your individual version of happily ever after.

Life in the Pink

Heartbreak, Healing and Happiness is my first book and is available at local bookstores and most online stores. You can find more details on the Life in the Pink website.

Be inspired and informed through my Pink Stories blog on the Life in the Pink website.

Ecourses

Continue to walk through your healing via my Ecourses on the Life in the Pink website.

Yoga teachings

Join me in a Hatha flow yoga class to nurture, nourish and heal your body, mind and spirit. Class timetable and special events' details are listed on the Life in the Pink website.

Powerful one-on-one consultations

I am available by appointment for consultations. Email me through the Life in the Pink website.

Join my community

Subscribe to my blog/newsletter at the Life in the Pink website and receive a free Ebook *The 13 Life Lessons to Healing*. I will keep you updated monthly with the happenings at Life in the Pink.

Like my Facebook page and access daily inspirational, meaningful and fun reminders on how to live a Life in the Pink.

Join me on Instagram for more colourful inspiration.

Thank you so much for allowing Life in the Pink into your heart. I wish you always a beautiful Life in the Pink. I would love you to stay in touch and share your stories.

Live in the love, truth and purpose.

Lara x

Web: www.lifeinthepink.com.au

Email: lara@lifeinthepink.com.au

Facebook: www.facebook.com/InthePINKxx/

Instagram: www.instagram.com/lifeinthepinkxx

LIFE IN THE PINK

Thank you for reading my book!

I so appreciate all of your feedback, and I love hearing what you have to say.

I would really love your input to help make my future books better.

Please leave me a helpful review on Amazon letting me know what you thought of the book.

A big PINK Thank you!

Lara Casanova

THANK YOU

> "Hold dear to your parents for it is a scary and confusing world without them."
>
> —Emily Dickinson

To Dad. Thank you for allowing me to be me. You gave me a life full of love. The experience of your passing has awakened me internally, giving me the opportunity to discover more about myself and who I want to become. I will respect, honour and love you wholeheartedly as I live my life out. It's all because of you. Dad, it's not goodbye as you are always with me. I treasure the piece of love you embedded in my heart when you left, and I sent a piece of my heart with you. Until we meet again. I love you to the moon and back forever. I thank you for everything. Rest in peace my beautiful dad.

To Mum. It's the parental love that cannot be replaced. Thank you, Mum, for being the only other one who shares in this mutual love. You are my other 'I am because of you'. It's an honour to live my life as your daughter.

To my sisters, three love miracles birthed by Mum and Dad to share in the beauty and love I hold in my wonderful life. I am forever grateful and feel enormously fortunate to have this endearing and magical sisterly love as part of my life.

Grief, Grace and Gratitude

To Pat. You are a beautiful source of family, friendship and love that I carry deep in my heart. Your support is amazing, and our time together is treasured beyond belief. You were to Dad his other half and what an amazing whole you both made. Thank you for being so devoted.

To my nieces. You are the next generation of love blossoming and growing from babies to young teens and into adulthood. I am blessed to have your presence, energy and love in my life, which shines so much more brightly because of you.

To my extended family, my aunts, uncles, cousins and beyond. It's family and love that makes life so very special, and I am reminded of that each joyful moment we spend in each other's company.

To my late family, the distant generations and loved ones who preceded me, leaving behind beautiful memories and eternal wisdom. You are forever loved, housed deep in my heart, never forgotten and a special part of me.

To Suzy and Chelsea, my two fur children. You live every moment on my heels displaying your love and joy, allowing me to stop and live in the moment. You make every day more special by just being there.

To Gemma and Anna. My constant and reliable butterfly wings when mine fail and my best friends forever. I love your ability to be serious conversationalists and hilarious characters in the same breath.

To all my friends. You bring love and brightness to my life, enabling it to shine a little more in each moment shared together, be it with tears, conversation or joyful laughter.

To Alex, Wendy and Natasha, my incredible editors, and Sylvie, my extraordinary designer. Without you there would be no book. An amazing debt of gratitude goes your way for bringing it to fruition with me.

THANK YOU

To Sona at Real Moments Photography. Thank you for the beautiful photos and your professionalism and friendship. Much appreciated.

To my mentors. Thank you for sharing the knowledge that precedes me, adding growth and understanding to my grief and life experience.

EXTRA RESOURCES

My theories and ideas are collated from my journey of many years of study, reading and personal experience. I have been privileged to find many mentors, as well as resources from others in my field. Here are publications from some of the most influential mentors and authors I have come across to date. They will provide additional inspirational and soul-provoking reads to expand your spiritual healing and journey to amazing heights.

Ahlers, A. (2011). *Big Fat Lies Women Tell Themselves: Ditch your inner critic and wake up your inner superstar*. New World Library.

Ahlers, A., & Arylo, C. (2015). *Reform Your Inner Mean Girl: 7 steps to stop bullying yourself and start loving yourself*. Atria Books/Beyond Words.

Arylo, C. (2012). *Madly in Love with ME: The daring adventure of becoming your own best friend*. New World Library.

Arylo, C. (2009). *Choosing ME Before WE: Every woman's guide to life and love*. New World Library.

Beak, S. (2013). *Red Hot and Holy: A heretic's love story*. 1st edition. Sounds True.

Behrendt, G. (2006). *It's Called a Break-Up Because It's Broken: The smart girl's breakup buddy*. Harper Element.

Bernstein, G. (2012). *Spirit Junkie: A radical road to self-love and miracles*. Harmony.

Bernstein, G. (2014). *Miracles Now: 108 life-changing tools for less stress, more flow, and finding your true purpose*. New York Times bestseller edition. Hay House, Inc.

Bernstein, G. (2011). *Add More ~Ing to Your Life: A hip guide to happiness*. Harmony.

Brathen, R. (2015). *Yoga Girl*. Touchstone.

Casanova, L. (2016). *Heartbreak, Healing and Happiness. Flourishing after a heartbreak*. Lara Casanova

Chase, M.J. (2013). *The Radical Practice of Loving Everyone: A four-legged approach to enlightenment*. Hay House, Inc.

Chase, M.J. (2011). *Am I Being Kind: How asking one simple question can change your life…and your world*. Hay House.

Chopra, D. (2010). *The Shadow Effect: Illuminating the hidden power of your true self*. HarperCollins Ebooks.

Coombes. M. (2016). *Sensing spirit*. Xou Pty Ltd.

Dalai Lama, Tutu, D., & Abrams, D. (2016). *The book of JOY. Lasting happiness in a changing world*. Hutchinson.

Dass, R. (2013). *Polishing the Mirror: How to live from your spiritual heart*. 1st edition. Sounds True.

De Angelis, B. (2015). *Soul Shifts: Transformative wisdom for creating a life of authentic awakening, emotional freedom and practical spirituality*. Hay House, Inc.

De Angelis, B. (2009). *Are You the One for Me?: Knowing who's right and avoiding who's wrong*. Dell.

Desai, P. (2014). *Discovering your Soul Signature: A 33-day path to purpose passion and joy*. Yellow Kite.

EXTRA RESOURCES

Dooley, M. (2014). *The Top Ten Things Dead People Want to Tell YOU*. 1st edition. Hay House, Inc.

Dowrick, S. (2012). *The Universal Heart: A practical guide to love*. Allen and Unwin.

Dyer, W.W. (2015). *I Can See Clearly Now*. Hay House, Inc.

Elliott, S.J. (2009). *Getting Past Your Breakup: How to turn a devastating loss into the best thing that ever happened to you*. Da Capo Press.

Fox, B. (2001). *Working Through Panic: Your step by step guide to overcoming panic/anxiety related disorders*. Prentice Hall.

Gilbert, E. (2007). *Eat, Pray, Love: One woman's search for everything across Italy, India and Indonesia*. 25th printing edition. Penguin (Non-Classics).

Hale, M. (2013). *The Single Woman: Life, love, and a dash of sass*. Thomas Nelson.

Hassler, C. (2014). *Expectation Hangover: Overcoming disappointment in work, love, and life*. New World Library.

Hay, L., & Holden, R. (2015). *Life Loves You: 7 spiritual practices to heal your life*. Hay House.

Hay, L.L. (1984). *You Can Heal Your Life*. 2nd edition. Hay House.

Hay, L.L. (2014). *You Can Heal Your Heart: Finding peace after a breakup, divorce, or death*. Hay House, Inc.

Hickman, M.W. (1994). *Healing After Loss: Daily meditations for working through grief*. 1st edition. William Morrow Paperbacks.

Holden, R. (2011). *Shift Happens!: How to live an inspired life... starting right now!* Revised edition. Hay House.

Jackson. L.L. (2015). *The light between us. Stories from heaven. Lessons for the living.* Century.

Jeffers, S. (2006). *Feel the Fear and Do It Anyway.* 20th anniversary edition. Ballantine Books.

Kipp, M. (2014). *Daily Love: Growing into grace.* Hay House.

Kirshenbaum, M. (1997). *Too Good to Leave, Too Bad to Stay: A step-by-step guide to help you decide whether to stay in or get out of your relationship.* Reprint Edition. Plume.

Kübler-Ross, E., & Kessler, D. (2014). *On grief & grieving: Finding the meaning of Grief through the Five Stages of Loss.* Scribner.

Nichols, L. (2009). *No Matter What!: 9 steps to living the life you love.* 1st edition. Grand Central Life and Style.

Romeo, E. (2015). *Meet Your Soul: A powerful guide to connect with your most sacred self.* Hay House.

Rosen, R. (2011). *Spirited: Unlock your psychic self and change your life.* Reprint edition. Harper Perennial.

Silver, T. (2014). *Outrageous Openness: Letting the divine take the lead.* Atria Books.

Spencer, K. (2013). *Twelve Lessons.* The Lightworkers Academy.

Stosny, S. (2013). *Living and Loving after Betrayal: How to heal from emotional abuse, deceit, infidelity, and chronic resentment.* 1st edition. New Harbinger Publications.

Thomas, K.W. (2007). *Calling in "The One": 7 weeks to attract the love of your life.* Harmony.

Tolle, E. (2004). *The Power of Now: A guide to spiritual enlightenment.* Namaste Publishing.

EXTRA RESOURCES

Tracy, B. (1995). *Maximum Achievement: Strategies and skills that will unlock your hidden powers to succeed.* 1st fireside edition. Simon and Schuster.

Vanzant, I. (2002). *Living Through the Meantime: Learning to break the patterns of the past and begin the healing process.* Touchstone.

Virtue, D. (2013). *Assertiveness for Earth Angels: How to be loving instead of "Too Nice".* Hay House.

Virtue, D. (2015). *Don't Let Anything Dull Your Sparkle: How to break free of negativity and drama.* Hay House.

Virtue, D., & Van Praagh, J. (2013). *How to heal a grieving heart.* Hay House.

Williamson, M. (1996). *A Return to Love: Reflections on the principles of "A Course in Miracles".* Reissue Edition. HarperOne.

THE END

Printed in Great Britain
by Amazon